# President Trump and the News Media

# Lexington Studies in Political Communication

**Series Editor:** Robert E. Denton, Jr., Virginia Tech University

This series encourages focused work examining the role and function of communication in the realm of politics including campaigns and elections, media, and political institutions.

## Recent Titles in This Series

*President Trump and the News Media: Moral Foundations, Framing, and the Nature of Press Bias in America*
By Jim A. Kuypers

*Media Relations and the Modern First Lady: From Jacqueline Kennedy to Melania Trump*
Edited by Lisa M. Burns

*Alternative Media Meets Mainstream Politics: Activist Nation Rising*
Edited by Joshua D. Atkinson and Linda Kenix

*Political Humor in a Changing Media Landscape: A New Generation of Research*
Edited by Jody C Baumgartner and Amy Becker

*The Influence of Polls on Television News Coverage of Presidential Campaigns*
By Vincent M. Fitzgerald

*Political Conversion: Personal Transformation as Strategic Public Communication*
By Don Waisanen

*The 2016 American Presidential Campaign and the News: Implications for the American Republic and Democracy*
Edited by Jim A. Kuypers

# President Trump and the News Media

## Moral Foundations, Framing, and the Nature of Press Bias in America

Jim A. Kuypers

LEXINGTON BOOKS
*Lanham • Boulder • New York • London*

Published by Lexington Books
An imprint of The Rowman & Littlefield Publishing Group, Inc.
4501 Forbes Boulevard, Suite 200, Lanham, Maryland 20706
www.rowman.com

6 Tinworth Street, London SE11 5AL, United Kingdom

Copyright © 2020 The Rowman & Littlefield Publishing Group, Inc.

*All rights reserved.* No part of this book may be reproduced in any form or by any electronic or mechanical means, including information storage and retrieval systems, without written permission from the publisher, except by a reviewer who may quote passages in a review.

British Library Cataloguing in Publication Information Available

**Library of Congress Cataloging-in-Publication Data**

ISBN 978-1-7936-2604-2 (cloth)
ISBN 978-1-7936-2606-6 (pbk)
ISBN 978-1-7936-2605-9 (electronic)

*For*
*Joan K. Floyd*

# Contents

Acknowledgments ix

1 Examining Moral Foundations and Framing in
   News Media Coverage of President Trump       1
2 News Media Biases and the Framing of Issues and Events   5
3 Moral Foundations and Journalistic Bias       25
4 National Security                            39
5 The Economy                                  69
6 The 2019 State of the Union                  91
7 Immigration Reform                           127
8 Concluding Thoughts on Framing, Moral Foundations,
   the Press, and the American Republic         149

Index                                          197
About the Author                               209

# Acknowledgments

I thank my family for their unreserved and continual support of my writing. It is with gratitude that I mention Virginia Tech, which paid my salary and also funded library services such as interlibrary loan, Ebscohost, and other databases all absolutely necessary to the completion of this project. The value Virginia Tech places on research allows projects such as this book to be undertaken and completed. I extend a special thank you to Dr. Michael Horning, who provided feedback concerning the theoretical implications of the findings. Thank you also to Margaret O'Meara, and Jordi Shelton, who helped with data collection for this book, to the anonymous reviewers who provided feedback, and to my Lexington editor, Nicolette Amstutz.

*Chapter 1*

# Examining Moral Foundations and Framing in News Media Coverage of President Trump

When I began writing this book, I was interested in exploring the contentious relationship between the mainstream news media and President Trump; by the time I had completed the project, I was forced to conclude that political reporting by the mainstream news media today had devolved, certainly with regard to President Trump, into a partisan endeavor. I realize that such a conclusion is itself not without a degree of controversy. I have, however, always believed that a good argument takes the form of "state your case, then prove it," and you will certainly find assertions in this book. You will also find evidence taken from a wide variety of sources: academic books and articles, mainstream press sources, internet sources, alternate press sources, liberal, conservative, alternate political sources, and, importantly, the case studies presented herein. At its heart, this book is a comparison between what President Trump actually said about an issue and what the mainstream news media subsequently reported he said. While writing I relied on previous research using comparative framing analysis, but also extended this work into important new areas; for each analysis chapter, I use both framing and Moral Foundations Theory to examine Trump and the main stream news media. Through this analysis, then, two important questions are asked and answered.

First, how do Trump and the news media "frame" issues and events? I answer this question using a rhetorical understanding of framing analysis.[1] A frame is a central organizing idea for making sense of relevant events and suggesting what is at issue. Facts are neutral until framed, and frames can reside in ourselves—we impose a frame or storyline on the facts we receive—or they can be imposed by others and presented to us. By examining how issues and events are framed by the press, we can gain a better understanding of any changes to original meaning the press adds to its reporting. After all, journalists are supposed to frame facts neutrally outside of specifically labeled opinion pieces or editorials. Because frames act to make some facts more obvious, or more salient and easier to apprehend than others, they can act to help or hinder a particular politician or policy. We can discover frames by looking for key words, metaphors, images, labels, and so on that act to push or pull our attention one way or another. And a particularly effective way of doing this is by comparing the original source of news reports with the news reports themselves.

Second, what are the moral aspects embedded in both Trump and news media discourse? I answer this question using a rhetorical understanding of Moral Foundation Theory that links embedded values to ideological leanings. This is new territory in relation to the press and presidents. Frames provide clues about problem definitions, causes of those problems, and solutions to those problems. It is also asserted, but little examined, that frames convey moral dimensions associated with the situations and persons involved. News stories, since they contain frames, should also convey some aspect of this moral dimension. What remains unexamined, however, are the means through which news reports convey the moral qualities of the reporters writing the reports, and also explanation of how these moral dimensions can reveal the underlying political ideologies of the reporters (and, in our case, of President Trump). In this sense this project is unique in that it uses moral foundations to assess the reportorial practices of the mainstream news media. Although there have been a handful of published studies looking at how press stories contain elements of our moral foundations, they do not link this to reporters themselves, or to larger concerns about reportorial practices, or to the role frames play in moral foundations. At its heart, Moral Foundations Theory posits that our morality is both innate and learned. We have five distinct moral foundations, expressed as dichotomies: Care/Harm, Fairness/Cheating, Loyalty(ingroup)/Betrayal, Authority/Subversion, and Sanctity/Degradation. Research into these foundations distinctly show that those possessing different political ideologies prioritize them differently.

In exploring these issues, I looked at four key concerns addressed by President Trump: national security, the economy, the state of the American union, and immigration. The idea was to compare the frames and moral foundations found in Trump's speeches with those found in the mainstream news media's coverage of those speeches. In each area I examined, using the method of rhetorical criticism,[2] a major speech given by President Trump using critically applied concepts of framing and moral foundations. I then examined the news products of seven outlets representative of the mainstream news media coverage of each speech, using the same concepts, and then compared the results. I used *The Washington Post*, *The New York Times*, ABC News, CBS News, NBC News, Fox News, and CNN as the news sources, and looked at all hard news or labeled news analysis articles focused on the speeches. By examining the frames and moral foundations in each speech and subsequent press coverage, we can understand how the reporting on these speeches provides evidence of the core political values of the press, and how this may or may not impact news coverage.

Chapters 2 and 3 introduce framing and moral foundations theory drawing upon a wide range of literature from the disciplines of communication, history, journalism, political science, and moral psychology. Subsequent chapters, 4 through 7, are case studies that detail the president/press interaction in four key areas mentioned above. As noted by Stephen J. Farnsworth, such "close textual analyses of . . . speeches and the reports on them allow for the richness of detail found via the case study method" and that such studies can complement traditional social scientific content analyses.[3] In the last chapter, I present the conclusions of the four case studies that collectively examine the relationship among moral foundations, frames, and the ideological biases of the news media, in the end demonstrating that the political ideologies of reporters are revealed in their reporting.

Some of the major findings of this study include:

That the news media framing acted to treat President Trump not as a source of news, but as a political opponent, while at the same time helping the political opposition of the president.
That frames do not give rise to moral foundations but rather the presence of moral foundations provide moral substance to frames as they are developed and found throughout news coverage.
That the moral foundations of journalists privilege liberal concerns and enervate conservative concerns.
That journalists inject bias consciously and unconsciously into hard news stories.

These findings are discussed in the conclusion, along with the implications and solutions for the American Republic.

## NOTES

1. For a discussion of the difference between a rhetorical and social scientific understanding of framing studies, see: Jim A. Kuypers, "Framing Analysis from a Rhetorical Perspective," in *Doing News Framing Analysis*. Paul D'Angelo and Jim A. Kuypers, eds. (New York: Routeledge, 2010), 286–311.

2. For those unfamiliar with this method see: Jim A. Kuypers, "Rhetorical Criticism as Art," in *Rhetorical Criticism: Perspectives in Action*, 2nd ed. Jim A. Kuypers, ed. (Lanham, MD: Rowman and Littlefield, 2016): 21–39. See also note 1 above.

3. Stephen J. Farnsworth, review of *Bush's War: Media Bias and Justifications for War in a Terrorist Age*, by Jim A. Kuypers, *Presidential Studies Quarterly*, December 2007, 783.

*Chapter 2*

# News Media Biases and the Framing of Issues and Events

President Donald J. Trump and the mainstream American news media share a contentious relationship. Although generally receiving positive press prior to his announcement in 2015 that he would run for president, following that moment Trump increasingly received negative press culminating with highs of up to 93 percent negative coverage by the end of 2017. The negative coverage remains at those levels even as this book is being written.[1] Yet all presidents have received some degree of negative coverage, just as they have received positive coverage, and certainly not all coverage should be positive or approving in tone, just as it should not be negative; neither should journalists be presidential stenographers. However, journalists who strive for objectivity in hard news stories and news analyses should write in such a way that their personal views remain outside the story; in short, they ought to remove themselves from the story, allowing instead the context, factual details, praise or blame, to emerge organically from the event/situation upon which they report. Consistently, however, Democrat presidents receive more positive and fewer negative stories than their Republican counterparts,[2] a trend extending even into late night news comedy shows,[3] signaling that something other than journalistic objectivity is operating. This disparity in reporting has only increased since Trump took office. For example, The Pew Center, looking comparatively at the first sixty days of the Obama and Trump presidencies, found that Obama received 42 percent positive news coverage with only 20 percent negative; Trump, on the other hand, received only 5 percent positive news coverage with 62 percent of the coverage being negative. No other president since this type of tracking began, Democrat or Republican, has received such negative press. The striking nature of these numbers are all the stronger if one keeps in mind that hard news coverage should strive toward neutrality.

This book investigates the relationship between the mainstream news media and President Trump, looking into the nature of this overwhelmingly negative coverage. Building upon past studies of the relationship between presidents and the press, I seek to uncover any biases operating. One proven method of detecting any news media bias in coverage involves using framing analysis. By looking for frames in both the discourse of the president and the following press coverage, one can detect bias. Moving beyond framing, one can also look for the moral foundations in the discourse of both the president and the following press coverage and, in so doing, shed light on the underlying political ideologies of the president and the mainstream news media, and how that contributes to any bias detected. In order to better understand the nature of the mainstream media (MSM) coverage of President Trump and its potential effects on the American Republic, I examine in detail four important speeches of the president representing different policy areas—national security, economics, the State of the Union, and immigration. For each area, I looked for both frames and moral foundations in both presidential and press discourse. Specifically, I answered the following questions:

1. How did President Trump frame the issues in his speeches?
2. Which moral foundations are in his speeches?
3. What do the moral foundations in President Trump's discourse suggest about his political ideology?
4. How did the mainstream news media frame the president's speeches?
5. Which moral foundations are in the news coverage of the president's speeches?
6. What do the moral foundations in the press coverage discourse suggest about the political ideology of the press?

Answering these questions allows us to determine the nature of any bias operating in coverage of Trump. So, to answer these questions, in the remainder of this chapter I look at major types of news media bias; briefly review the concept of framing and how one can detect them in news stories. This is followed in chapter 3 by a discussion of Moral Foundation Theory, then four chapters, each consisting of a case study in the areas mentioned above. Finally, the book concludes with a summation of framing, moral foundations, press bias, and how it works to help or hinder the functioning of the American Republic.

## BIASES OF THE NEWS MEDIA

The phrase "press bias," or "news media bias," usually conjures thoughts of overt ideological biases, or partisanship in a news story, for instance a reporter injecting political bias into the news with the effect of helping one side in a political struggle. Although such bias certainly exists, there are also other biases operating that potentially influence what gets reported and how it gets reported. Researchers in political communication and political science have noted many of these biases that exist in addition to political bias, and what follows are ten of the most common of these biases.[4]

*Coverage Bias* refers to what journalists decide to publish, when they decide to publish it, and how much they decide to publish about it. The press functions of *gate-keeping* and *agenda-setting* operate here. Gate-keeping "is about story selection; who decides what stories shall pass through the media gate. Agenda-setting goes a step beyond this; it shows that the amount of emphasis given to a particular event or issue raises awareness about that event or issue in the mind of the public."[5] So, for instance, when we speak of news stories about President Trump being around 90 percent negative, we can ask which stories. Between June 1 and September 30, 2018, about two-thirds of all mainstream news stories about Trump were on only five stories: the Russia investigation, immigration, the Brett Kavanaugh nomination, North Korea, and US-Russia relations. Senior editors made a conscious decision to run these stories to the exclusion of others. Not only did they decide to run these stories, they also decided how much emphasis to place on them in terms of total time devoted to them. As another example, during the eight years of the Obama administration minimal reporting was seen in the MSM about the separation of illegal immigrant family members at the Mexican-US border, or the use of tear gas there by American law enforcement. But the policies became big news under the Trump administration immediately following the release of an Obama administration-generated inspector general/FBI report in June of 2018 critical of the Trump administration, and as the Central American immigration caravan of Fall 2018 began its march toward the southern US border. News coverage spiked and stayed on it, with only the Mueller investigation receiving more air time.[6]

*Theoretical Bias* refers to the sociopolitical role that the MSM have assumed for themselves. By the end of World War II, the press saw itself as a professional organization undergirded by principles of objectivity. By the time of the Hutchins Commission (1956), however, we begin to see a movement away from objectivity and a more libertarian-style press to one that has elements of social responsibility built in. This idea is summed by the authors of the report: "Freedom carries concomitant obligations; and the press, which enjoys a privileged position under our government, is obliged to be responsible to society for carrying out certain essential functions of mass communication in contemporary society."[7] These principles, which in some senses blended both objective and an emerging activist voice, are:

1. The press must provide "a truthful, comprehensive, and intelligent account of the day's events in a context which gives them meaning."
2. The press must serve as a "forum for the exchange of comment and criticism."
3. The press must project "a representative picture of the constituent groups in society."
4. The press must assume responsibility for "the presentation and clarification of the goals and values of the society" in which it operates.
5. The press must provide "full access to the day's intelligence."[8]

At the time of the report, both reporters and editors continued to adhere to the principle of objectivity, but the advent of the Johnson administration witnessed a slowly growing activistic and progressive, social responsibility-inspired turn in reporting.

In the 1970s, the growth of the activistic impulse shifted into the press assuming a "watchdog" role, also known as "accountability journalism": holding American leaders and government agencies accountable to the citizens. Objectivity was still stressed, but increasingly was giving way to social responsibility and activistic impulses. Since the turn of the new century, we increasingly see the press moving further beyond this by assuming an advocacy role, speaking on behalf of its favored political outcomes. This removes advocacy from the citizenry and objectivity from the press. Reporters might not engage in outright propaganda, but by engaging in advocacy, the facts they select, and the framing of those facts, often support their political end goals.[9]

*Perceptual Bias* refers to the concept that those who produce the news do so in a neutral manner regardless of their personal politics, and thus the news is actually unbiased. Instead, any perception of bias is supposedly a function of the audience consuming the news; in other words, the audience "imagines" bias operating. Veteran PBS NewsHour anchor Jim Lehrer sums this concept up well: "I do not have a liberal bias. . . . I don't have a conservative bias, either. I don't have any bias. I am bias-free. . . . Bias is what people who hear or read the news bring to the story, not what the journalist brings to the reporting. . . . [My newscast] is a flavor of neutrality."[10] As this concept goes, if a person is liberal, they see conservative bias; if a person is conservative, they see liberal bias. This "selective bias" has some merit, in that humans do tend to look for that which supports their point of view, and notice that which might contradict it. However, this conception of bias is flawed as applied to news production since it presupposes both an audience incapable of objectivity or ignorant of facts and a reporter class actively holding its political biases in check. As such, it demeans the intelligence and perceptual abilities of news audiences, which tend to be among the more highly educated of Americans[11];

additionally, according to Pew, 76 percent of Americans feel very or somewhat confident that they can check the accuracy of the news.[12] Beyond this, survey after survey shows that independents and moderates generally see the same bias as conservatives and Republicans, thus suggesting strongly that something other than perception is the cause of bias; on the other hand, the same surveys show that liberals and Democrats tend not to see conservative bias, but bias toward the status quo, bias toward one Democrat position over another (e.g., Bernie Sanders and Elizabeth Warren), or no political bias operating at all. Pew found in 2019 that 89 percent of Republicans felt that the mainstream news favored one side over another; 72 percent of moderates felt the mainstream news favored one side over another; and even 57 percent of Democrats felt some form of bias operating.[13]

*Money Bias* refers to the simple notion that in America the news is a business and that the press is in the business of making money. So, it goes without saying that the press will cover stories that it thinks will attract audiences and make money. This can lead to a trivialization of what constitutes news, and it can also lead to the imposition of a conflict or negative frame on news stories since that attracts more attention than other forms of news. Simply put, conflict, controversy, and also sex sells. For instance, as I write this section I took a quick look at CNN's website. The top story, center of the page, is, "A mother and kid were attacked by a coyote. Then police shot the animal dead."[14] Other news swirls around alleged misdoings of President Trump, different murders, an alligator that keeps swimming with a knife stuck in its head, and so on. Looking at the website of Fox News, one finds "LA accuses rich neighbors of 'dumping' homeless as street population explodes to crisis level."[15] Other news stories talk about a defector from North Korea, an embattled Mark Zuckerberg, an ex-reality star busted on larceny, and a moonlighting teacher being given a $100 tip. Just a little below all that is a section titled, Features and Faces. Here we find pop culture references galore, including a picture of rather large breasts poking out of a bra captioned, "Breast Implant Regrets," a story on Meghan Markle forcing her nanny to sign a nondisclosure agreement, graphic pics of botched plastic surgery, again showing torso skin, Christie Brinkley and her daughters in bikinis, and so on. All these stories sell to someone; they attract audiences.

*Visual Bias* refers primarily to broadcast news (and increasingly news conveyed via the Internet). Since humans are dominated by our sense of sight and attention to motion, that which is action oriented often is promoted as news over less action-oriented news. Think if you were watching an evening broadcast show and suddenly the local news service broke in with this announcement: "Good evening, we interrupt this program to let you know of a high-speed pursuit by State Police on Interstate 81. With speeds reaching in excess of 120 miles per hour, it is the most dangerous chase in our area's history." Immediately, you would be interested, and fully expecting a live video of the chase. And you would see one, because the news service would never interrupt your regularly scheduled programming without it, because without the action, the story simply belongs on the news channel's website as a short story, or in the next day's local paper, probably buried in the back.

Images also convey a particular meaning and help audiences interpret the preferred storyline. For instance, in its July 2, 2018 issue, *Time* used as its cover an image of President Trump looking down at a small illegal immigrant child in an attempt to highlight what the magazine felt was an inhumane policy of separating children from their parents during their criminal proceedings. Of note here, though, is that the child was not actually separated from her parents at all, and *Time* was caught pushing an emotional yet inaccurate image for the sake of either advocacy or sales.[16] Images are important for stories; think of the stories mentioned above in the section about money bias. The coyote story showed the officer holding up the bloody corpse of the coyote; and the plastic surgery stories hinted at nudity, although never really crossing that line; and the Brinkleys were shown in their bikinis.

*Recency Bias* refers to the preference for news organizations to publish what is most currently happening; after all, it is called *news* for a reason. Although some stories stick around longer than others, with emphasis on the latest development or speculation—consider daily injections about the Mueller investigation for almost two years as an example—in general, what is "new" is news. We have an appetite for this, easily seen in the popularity of twenty-four-hour news (Fox News, CNN, for example), as well as news websites which are constantly changing their leading news articles. And the news plays into this contemporary American desire, which also plays into their profit motive. The more often you think you will see "new" news, the more often you might return to the site, and the more often ad revenue is generated. Recall the CNN and Fox News examples in the section on money bias. A mere fifteen minutes after writing about those examples, I checked the websites again looking for the top story. The CNN center story had changed to "Authorities: Toronto Raptors president struck officer after team won NBA title," and the Fox News main story had changed to, "She Died Defenseless: Virginia Beach victim feared killer, wanted to carry gun but was barred by city law: attorney." A problem with this "new is better" approach, especially with cable and broadcast news, is that complex issues and events must be nestled in historical context in order for audiences to understand them, and the quick news cycle diminishes the ability of the press to provide such information well. The focus in on "now" and into the future, and thus providing historical context receives little, if any, attention. Additionally, this focus on the present is so extreme in some ways that news is increasingly moving from what is happening to reporting on what will happen, or reporting its own speculations, especially with regard to political news.

*Status Quo Bias*, sometimes misleadingly called "conservative bias," refers more to an inherent function of news produced in the United States than an actual bias. In a sense, since America operates within an ideology of Democratic Capitalism,[17] the news, by its very nature as a business and a nongovernment controlled news gathering organization, upholds Democratic Capitalism. When the news reports on government functions, it of necessity seeks government sources, anonymous or not, and using government officials actually acts to keep the present system of government in place. Additionally, since the news routinely reports on the spectacles of government (inaugurals, conventions, celebratory addresses, Congressional hearings, etc.), it actually reaffirms the structure of our government if it does not actively critique the nature of the government (regardless of which party is ascendant). The press is to help maintain our Constitutionally based government, not seek to radically alter it. As political communication researcher Robert E. Denton wrote, "It is virtually impossible to distinguish between our political system and the media as separate entities."[18] Those who call this conservative bias, usually coming from a Marxist perspective, do so because they feel the press ought to be actively seeking to change our governing ideology, not keeping it in place.

*Fairness and Balance Bias* seems a bias for which one would wish. Yet, in an extreme form, it can have negative effects, and used by unscrupulous journalists it can outright mislead the public. Today, fairness means presenting "both sides" and balance means giving relatively equal space or time for points to be made. The difficulty in this is that there are often more than two sides, and very often a side is weaker than the "other" side, or not as well supported. By being "fair and balanced," news organizations can make the weaker case look stronger or the reverse, or not even mention a "side" on a complex issue. For instance, during the debate on the Partial-Birth Abortion Ban Act,[19] between 70 and 95 percent of Americans (depending on how the poll question was phrased) supported banning the procedure. News stories on this issue, however, made it seem as if it was hotly contested, with strong support on "both sides," even as an overwhelming majority of Americans wanted it banned.

*Bad News Bias* simply refers to what most Americans already feel is the case: the news media overwhelmingly focuses on negative news. The old adage applies here: "if it bleeds, it leads." Bad news also refers to unusual news, though, so "dog bites woman" would not make national news; "woman bites dog" just might. For instance, Fox News recently reported that a woman had gone down a slide holding her infant child. The child broke its leg, and the network showed a photo of the event; yes, you could see the child's broken ankle in the picture (visual bias).[20] The story was used to push the idea that sliding down a standard child's playground slide with a toddler in one's lap is dangerous. And it is, to a limited degree; but the story did not contextualize, only terrorize.[21] Of note, however, is that tens-of-millions go down just such slides yearly, multiple times, and without incident. And this points to one of the dangers of this type of bias. Evidence suggest that when there is a focus on negative news, news consumers tend to adopt an overly negative view of the issue being reported upon. This seems especially true in national news coverage. For instance, national news presents a constant stream of negativity concerning race relations. Most Americans think race relations are at an almost all-time low nationwide; yet these same Americans, black through white, think that race relations in their own neighborhoods are good.

*Liberal Ideological and Partisanship Bias* is typically what most Americans think of when hearing about "bias in the news." Here we essentially have the political positions and beliefs of reporters influencing their reporting on issues and events to varying degrees. Although an overwhelming majority of Americans see liberal political bias operating in the mainstream news media reporting on political issues, it is the very type of bias so often denied by both journalists and academics.[22] The evidence of this bias is simply overwhelming, however. First, we have the actual political makeup of the press; that it is overwhelmingly liberal/progressive in its composition is uncontested.[23] Study after study, poll after poll, all point to the same general results. Second, in terms of political and social actions, in every way, from church attendance to voting habits, to personal support for specific progressive policies, to political affiliation and political donations, journalists are far to the left of the average American. For instance, as of July 2019, Gallup found that 29 percent of Americans were Republican; 38 percent were independent; and 27 percent Democrat.[24] Yet only 7 percent of all journalists identified as Republican.[25] And in the most recent presidential campaign, journalists donated to Democrat candidate Hillary Clinton at a rate of 27 to 1 over Donald Trump, with even more donating to the campaign of Democrat Bernie Sanders than to Clinton.[26] Voting habits show an inarguable leftist and Democratic party tilt as well, with journalists voting overwhelmingly for the Democrat party nominee for president going all the way back to Reagan versus Carter when such studies began.

But the real question is: Does this overwhelming leftist political identity influence journalists' production of news? Through my own research and a thorough review of relevant literature, I have concluded that it does.[27] Most journalists,[28] and many academics,[29] say emphatically no, however. As *Slate* founding editor Michael Kinsley pointed out when the magazine began the practice of revealing how its journalists voted in the presidential elections, "an opinion is not a bias!"[30] Of note, though, is the overwhelmingly lopsided voting at that magazine. Since it began, only Democrats have won; which is not dissimilar to MSM publications such as *The New York Times* and *The Washington Post*, which have endorsed only Democrat presidential candidates since 1960 and 1980, respectively.[31] In the last presidential election, not a single *Slate* writer voted for Trump, and only two did not vote for Clinton. Although *Slate* is to be congratulated on openly sharing the political dispositions of its writers, and has acknowledged it liberal slant,[32] one has to wonder why it does not have writers who support Republicans or conservatives. Moreover, given such lopsided political composition and predispositions, how do journalists at that magazine, or in any mainstream news office, keep from engaging in groupthink in what certainly is simply a comfortable echo chamber for liberal/progressive thought?

Simply put, they cannot, and instead exist in a cozy pool of confirmation bias. With no others to challenge their thinking or to present different ideas, reporters and editors simply confirm what they already know to be true. Facts that confirm are more easily seen than those that contradict the inherent newsroom point of view. This notion of groupthink helps explain how both individual news rooms and the mainstream news industry espouses such a narrow and consistent political point of view:

> Group think describes a situation in which groups, in our case, news organizations, exhibit a high level of cohesiveness with members reluctant to deviate from the preferred group consensus. Because of this consensus, there is little, if any, argumentation or conflict of ideas among group members. Members tend to be isolated, possess biased leaders, and be exposed to stress. In our case, journalists are isolated socially and politically from the public they purport to represent; they possess politically biased leaders; and they are under constant deadline stress. The decision-making process is made inside the organization, and journalists listen to fellow journalists and editors over and above those outside the organization.[33]

The pressure and inducements to conform when within a groupthink environment are quite strong, and are pressures of which one may be aware or unaware. The effects of groupthink are well known, and have been studied for decades, as evidenced in this summary from communication researchers in 1993: "the pressure of cohesiveness results in faulty, inadequate analysis. . . . Not enough possible solutions are examined because there is an early preference for a particular solution. Groupthink fosters an inadequate approach to information. When groupthink operates, there is typically inadequate research and thus a shortage of necessary information."[34] Moreover, since "there is an early preference for a particular solution, the information is processed in a biased fashion."[35] This, of course, has serious ramifications for the production of "objective" news.

In 2015 *The New York Times* published an opinion piece entitled, "Liberal News Media Bias Has a Serious Effect," in which the author made the point that the overwhelming numbers of leftist journalists could not help but produce left of center news: "Clustering of left-of-center viewpoints in the newsroom leads to a cloistering, and thus reporters end up *unfamiliar* with conservative viewpoints. This shows up in the tone of daily coverage (for instance, 'property rights' gets put in scare quotes, while 'abortion rights' does not)."[36] Still, it is true that opinions are not bias. But in the case of the press, there is an exceptionally strong correlation. As I and others have demonstrated, the political leanings of the press find their way into its coverage of political issues, and these insertions of bias, intentional or not, almost always benefit liberal/progressive candidates and policies.[37] It is well known that opinions flow from our worldviews (or our mental schemas, to use another way of describing how we organize our thoughts). As humans we find it easier to see that which supports our points of view than that which does not, and it is easier to believe that which comports with our version of the truth or of reality than that which does not. Some degree of this confirmation bias is inherent in us all: "Once we have formed a view, we embrace information that confirms that view while ignoring, or rejecting, information that casts doubt on it. Confirmation bias suggests that we don't perceive circumstances objectively. We pick out those bits of data that make us feel good because they confirm our prejudices. Thus, we may become prisoners of our assumptions."[38] This is a common cognitive process, one that all human beings possess to a greater or lesser degree. In its simplest form, confirmation bias is someone essentially seeing or looking for only that evidence which supports what one already believes. This is not dissimilar to the theory of Identity-Protective Cognition, which is simply the notion that as a means "of avoiding dissonance and estrangement from valued groups, individuals subconsciously resist factual information that threatens their defining values."[39]

Given all the above, how easy is it, then, for reporters and editors, almost exclusively liberal/progressive, with liberal friends and coworkers, working in liberal-dominated newsrooms, donating to liberal politicians and causes, voting for liberal candidates—in other words, saturated with liberal culture—to only see what agrees with their version of reality, and to report the "facts" *as they see them*? Confirmation bias is rampant in the news industry, just as it has been shown to exist in other industries, including higher education, dominated by a single type of political orientation.[40] And the effects from the lack of different points of view are noteworthy. As a representative example consider psychology, where a "lack of political diversity . . . is said to lead to a number of pernicious outcomes, including biased research and active discrimination against conservatives. In decisions ranging from paper reviews to hiring, many social and personality psychologists said that they would discriminate against openly conservative colleagues. *The more liberal respondents were, the more they said they would discriminate.*"[41] Given the very real lack of viewpoint diversity in the MSM, it is unsurprising that its bias, which does not appear as bias at all to them, injects itself into "objective" news reporting.

## FRAMING THE NEWS

How does this bias manifest itself in news coverage, and how might it work to influence Americans? More to the point, how do we go about detecting it? Even with hundreds of billions of dollars spent in the United States each year on advertising (both merchandise and political), media effects researchers still find it difficult to discover the degree and manner in which media exposure affects our behaviors and beliefs. One concept involving media effects that is almost universally accepted, though, is the MSM function of agenda-setting. In its basic form, agenda-setting asserts that the news media do not tell its audiences *how* to think, but do tell audiences *what* to think about. We know from literally thousands of studies in this area that the greater the concentration of stories on a particular topic/issue, the greater is the importance the public places on that topic/issue.

Looking at the news through this agenda-setting lens, "the press is an independent force whose dialogue with other elements of society produces the agenda of issues considered by political elites and voters. Witness the major role of the elite press as a source of information among major decision makers. Through its winnowing of the day's happenings to find the major events, concerns, and issues, the press . . . plays an agenda-setting influence role."[42] The press does, however, move past simple agenda-setting to actually influencing *how* the public thinks about an issue or event. This "agenda-extension" function of the press is the process through which the media not only focus attention on particular attributes of an issue or event, bringing public attention to some aspects while ignoring others, but doing so in such a manner that a particular point of view or even political agenda is advanced.

One way to see how this function operates, to actually begin to see how political bias is introduced into what should be neutral new reporting, is to look at how issues and events in news stories are "framed." For our purposes, a frame is "a central organizing idea for making sense of relevant events and suggesting what is at issue."[43] At its core, framing "is the process whereby communicators act--consciously or not--to construct a particular point of view that encourages the facts of a given situation to be viewed in a particular manner, with some facts made more or less noticeable (even ignored) than others."[44] Frames have been demonstrated to make some facts more salient to an audience than others, and act to define problems, diagnose causes, and suggest remedies; of note, they "are located in the communicator, the text, the receiver, and the culture at large. Frames are central organizing ideas within a narrative account of an issue or event; they provide the interpretive cues for otherwise neutral facts."[45] Importantly, they also provide consistent meanings through time, since once established they help to guide the interpretive process.

Framing occurs through "the presence or absence of certain keywords, stock phrases, stereotyped images, sources of information, and sentences that provide thematically reinforcing clusters of fact or judgments."[46] We can add other items to this list including, metaphors, concepts, images, labels, and symbols. All work to highlight some features of reality over others. The MSM frames issues, then, through both the conscious and unconscious language choices made by its journalists. For instance, how often are words such as "budget cuts" versus "controlling costs" used across time by journalists when describing Republican efforts to construct a balanced budget? Or using "undocumented migrant" or "undocumented citizen" instead of "illegal alien" or "illegal immigrant"? Or writing "anti-abortion" instead of "pro-life"?[47] Or writing "single payer healthcare" instead of "tax-payer funded healthcare"? Such "an inherent bias—which springs from the 'conspiracy of shared values'—requires no memos, no e-mails, no FAXes, no phone calls. It operates purely by the collective worldview of reporters."[48]

Facts are neutral until framed, and frames can reside in ourselves—we impose a frame or storyline on the facts we receive—or they can be imposed by others and presented to us. We do this all the time as a normal process of thinking. This takes place also with what we read or view in the news about an issue or event since reporters are in the business of arranging facts for our consideration. In short, facts are given meaning, a particular understanding. Some facts are made more important, or salient, than others once an issue has been framed. And to the degree that confirmation bias operates in journalistic circles we can assume that the way journalists frame facts will be influenced by the political opinions, values, and beliefs they hold dear.

As an example of how this works, consider the 1972 Watergate break in coverage by the MSM. Initially, news about the break in was framed as part of the 1972 election campaign between Republican Richard Nixon and Democrat George McGovern; the public replied with a shrug of indifference. However, after the news media switched frames, moving from a campaign frame to a frame stressing continual Washington corruption, Americans took note, became obsessed, and President Nixon eventually resigned.[49] Another powerful example of framing involves a study using a fictitious Ku Klux Klan march as its controlled frame. Researchers separated study participants into two group, with each group being presented with a mock news story that was framed in one of two ways. One group viewed a news story that framed the Klan march as a disruption of public order. The audience was presented with "facts" stressing the tension reporters felt between marchers and crowds; images of police protecting Klansmen from an aggressive crowd; and interviews with participants stressing violence and disruption of public order. The other group viewed a news story that framed the Klan march as an issue of free speech, and the audience was presented with "facts" stressing how both protesters and Klansmen wanted to share their respective messages; interviews were presented with Klan supporters saying they wanted to hear the Klansmen's message; images were shown of protesters and Klan leaders with bullhorns speaking to their crowds. The findings of this study are stark reminders of the power of frames: "Participants who viewed the free speech story expressed more tolerance for the Klan than those participants who watched the public order story."[50] There are legions of such studies showing the power of frames in news stories. Given this, if news stories frame a certain way, does it not seem highly probable that our thinking will be impacted in ways similar to those shown in these studies? The answer is yes.

Frames are powerful because they are necessary for us to make sense of the world; we all have them and use them. It is clear that the power of frames is great, and that by examining how issues and events are framed by the press, we can gain a better understanding of any bias the press adds to its reporting. After all, journalists are *supposed* to frame facts neutrally outside of specifically labeled opinion pieces or editorials. Because frames act to make some facts more obvious, or more salient and easier to apprehend than others, they can act to help or hinder a particular political party, politician, or policy. For example, a reporter whose personal worldview frames Antifa members as heroic civil rights activists bravely confronting "fascism" will find it easy to frame, intentionally or not, a story about their activities in such a manner that privileges his or her worldview (recall confirmation bias), so a "free speech" or similarly positive frame will probably dominate. The converse of this is that the violent, anti-Democratic actions of Antifa members will be minimized, justified,[51] or ignored—they do not fit the "frame" the reporter has. Now, it is possible that a well-trained reporter, just like a well-trained researcher, can minimize the imposition of his or her own frames. But evidence shows that, with reporters, such is not the case, as we will see in our investigation of President Trump.

We can discover frames by looking for key words, metaphors, images, labels, and so on that act to direct our attention one way or another. A particularly effective way of doing this is by comparing the original source of the news report with the reporting that follows. An example of how this works is seen in a study comparatively examining the frames used by the MSM and four nontraditional news sources, two self-described as liberal and two self-described as conservative, during coverage of the Jena 6 incident in 2007. The authors conducted a framing analysis of top circulating mainstream newspapers—*USA Today, The New York Times*, and *The Washington Post*—and the same framing analysis with *The Huffington Post* and *Crooks and Liars* (liberal) and *Michelle Malkin* and *Newsbusters* (conservative). The idea is that if the MSM papers are truly objective in their reporting, then the frames would be different from either the self-described liberal or conservative blog news sources, or contain similar elements of both. The study identified the major themes in the news reports, and then identified how those themes were framed. Table 2.1 shows the results.

Of note is that although the blogs did talk about the role of the news media, all other themes covered were the same by both the MSM and the news blogs. Importantly, one can readily see the lock-step framing of the story between the "objective" hard news stories and the liberal news blogs. As pointed out in the study, it is troubling that a self-professed "non-partisan press so neatly aligns with self-professed liberal advocacy positions while concomitantly being devoid of any association with the self-professed conservative political positions. . . . Thus . . . the mainstream news media framed a very contentious issue in a manner that facilitated discussion of only one point of view."[52] Interestingly, even when other facts do happen to make it into a news story,

Table 2.1  Jena 6 Incident News Coverage Framing

| Themes | Framing: News Articles | Framing: Huffington Post and Crook and Liars | Framing: Michelle Malkin and Newsbusters |
|---|---|---|---|
| Punishment of black students | Schoolyard fight, so too harsh; unjust. Compared to noose hanging students, so too harsh; unjust | Schoolyard fight, so too harsh; unjust. Compared to noose hanging students, so too harsh; unjust | Appropriate to crime |
| Identity of attackers | School kids; youngsters Victims of racism Victims of white legal system | School kids; youngsters Victims of racism Victims of white legal system | Aggressive; prior criminal records Barker the victim |
| Description of event | Black vs. white; civil rights era Example of lingering racism | Black vs. white; civil rights era Example of lingering racism | Excuse for activists to self-promote No similarities with civil rights era |
| Role of News Media | | Not enough coverage Unconcerned with black America's plight | Stoking racial tensions Intentionally inaccurate One-sided |

*Source*: Author.

"for those stories in which a single frame thoroughly pervades the text, stray contrary opinions . . . are likely to possess such low salience as to be of little practical use to most audience members."[53] This function of frames enhancing or suppressing the salience of facts and ideas is an important element of framing: "Salience is key to any attempt to put a certain spin or interpretation on an issue, event, product or person. By highlighting or emphasizing certain aspects, or attributes, the media can influence not only what we think about, but how we think about it."[54]

In a major study I examined 116 different newspapers and almost 800 news articles dealing with controversial political issues. I looked at politicians representing both major political parties, and news coverage of those politicians in the mainstream printed press. Using framing analysis, I discovered that the frames the press constructs in their news stories act "in opposition to those who do not agree with their political agenda [and] took the form of direct opposition to the points of view expressed by [politicians] that did not comport with press ideals. This direct opposition irreparably harmed these speakers' ability to explain their point of view to the American public. Unless the reader had firsthand access to transcripts of [what these speakers said], all information was filtered through the frame of the press."[55] An important finding then is that the "context through which the statements made by these political leaders were understood changed; a new context was provided by the press which also framed the statements in such a way that the original meaning of the messages were changed. In this manner these political actors were not treated fairly as news sources, but rather they were forced into an oppositional role to that of the press."[56]

As mentioned above, it is generally agreed upon that frames define problems for us and often assign causes for those problems. Frames also suggest or imply solutions for those problems. Most all framing researchers also agree that frames relay moral judgments about the issue/event under discussion. As communication researcher Robert Entman wrote, frames take "some aspects of a perceived reality and make them more salient in a communicating text, in such a way as to promote a particular problem definition, causal interpretation, moral evaluation, and/or treatment recommendation for the item described."[57] However, whereas the aspects of problems, causes, and solutions have been examined in some detail, comparatively little has been done to examine if frames actually shape or encourage moral evaluations as opposed to elements of morality-shaping frames. Although work in moral psychology has found that one's political orientation (liberal, conservative) is reflected in the moral foundations one uses, little of this has made its way into assessment of public address or assessment of the news media. Certainly, framing is a way to determine political bias, but we can also apply the theory of moral foundations to do this due to its relationship with political values.

With this in mind, we turn to the next chapter to review the concept of moral foundations. In so doing, we will set up the necessary theoretical perspective to determine

1. If frames provide moral assessment or if morality operates independently of, and perhaps informs, frames
2. If the moral foundations of journalists correlate with a liberal political position

## NOTES

1. This figure can change based upon how examples are covered. For instance, some studies count only negative and positive statements, whereas others include neutral comments as well. For the later, estimates are around 65 percent negative coverage, higher still than any other president. For examples of these studies, see: Thomas E. Patterson, "News Coverage of Donald Trump's First 100 Days," *Shorenstein Center*, May 18, 2017, https://shorensteincenter.org/news-coverage-donald-trumps-first-100-days/; Danielle Kurtzleben, "Study: News Coverage of Trump More Negative than for Other Presidents," *NPR*, October 2, 2017, https://www.npr.org/2017/10/02/555092743/study-news-coverage-of-trump-more-negative-than-for-other-presidents; and Jennifer Harper, "Unprecedented Hostility: Broadcast Coverage of President Trump Still 90% Negative, Says Study," *The Washington Times*, October 2, 2017, https://www.washingtontimes.com/news/2018/mar/6/trump-coverage-still-90-negative-says-new-study/.

2. Peter Kafka, "Donald Trump Is Right! Coverage of His Administration Is Much More Negative Than Other Presidents," *Vox*, October 2, 2017, https://www.vox.com/2017/10/2/16401216/president-donald-trump-news-negative-pew-research-obama-bush-clinton.

3. See, for instance, Stephen J. Farnsworth and S. Robert Lichter, *Late Night with Trump: Political Humor and the American Presidency* (New York City, NY: Routledge, 2020) and Caitlin Flanagan, "How Late-Night Comedy Fueled the Rise of Trump: Sneering Hosts Have Alienated Conservatives and Made Liberals Smug," *The Atlantic*, May 2017, https://www.theatlantic.com/magazine/archive/2017/05/how-late-night-comedy-alienated-conservatives-made-liberals-smug-and-fueled-the-rise-of-trump/521472/.

4. See Abe Aamidor, Jim A. Kuypers, and Susan Wiesinger, *Media Smackdown: Deconstructing the News and the Future of Journalism* (New York: Peter Lang Publishing, 2013), 127–154.

5. Robert E. Denton and Jim A. Kuypers, *Politics and Communication in America: Campaigns, Media, and Governing in the 21st Century* (Carbondale, IL: Waveland Press, 2008), 148.

6. Rich Noyes, "Study: Economic Boom Largely Ignored as TV's Trump Coverage Hits 92% Negative," *NewsBusters*, October 9, 2018, https://www.newsbusters.

org/blogs/nb/rich-noyes/2018/10/09/study-econ-boom-ignored-tv-trump-coverage-hits-92-percent-negative.

7. Fred S. Siebert, Theodore Peterson, and Wilbur Schramm, *Four Theories of the Press* (Urbana: University of Illinois Press, 1956), 87.

8. Siebert, Peterson, and Schramm, *Four Theories of the Press*, 87, 89, and 91.

9. See Jim A. Kuypers, *Partisan Journalism: A History of Media Bias in the United States.* (Lanham, MD: Rowman & Littlefield, 2014) for extensive treatment of this movement away from objectivity.

10. Jim Lehrer, quoted in "Journalists Denying Liberal Bias, Part Two," *Media Research Center*, https://www.mrc.org/media-bias-101/journalists-denying-liberal-bias-part-two, accessed November 6, 2019.

11. "Social and Demographic Differences in News Habits and Attitudes," *American Press Institute*, March 17, 2014, https://www.americanpressinstitute.org/publications/reports/survey-research/social-demographic-differences-news-habits-attitudes/.

12. Mason Walker and Jeffrey Gottfried, "Republicans Far More Likely Than Democrats to Say Fact-Checkers Tend to Favor One Side," *Pew Research Center*, June 27, 2019, https://www.pewresearch.org/fact-tank/2019/06/27/republicans-far-more-likely-than-democrats-to-say-fact-checkers-tend-to-favor-one-side/.

13. "Social and Demographic Differences in News Habits and Attitudes," *American Press Institute*, March 17, 2014, https://www.americanpressinstitute.org/publications/reports/survey-research/social-demographic-differences-news-habits-attitudes/.

14. CNN.com, 2:10 p.m., June 14, 2019.

15. FOXNEWS.com, 2:15 p.m., June 14, 2019.

16. Samantha Schmidt and Kristine Phillips, "The Crying Honduran Girl on the Cover of Time Was Not Separated from Her Mother," *The Washington Post*, June 22, 2018, https://www.washingtonpost.com/news/morning-mix/wp/2018/06/22/the-crying-honduran-girl-on-the-cover-of-time-was-not-separated-from-her-mother-father-says/ and Amber Athey, "Everything the Media Got Wrong About the Crying Girl on the *TIME* Cover," *The Daily Caller*, June 22, 2018, http://dailycaller.com/2018/06/22/media-wrong-about-time-cover/.

17. That is, it combines the workings of a liberal democracy with capitalism in such a way that individual freedom and pluralism is supported and encouraged. A person works for him or herself, not for the state.

18. Robert E. Denton, Rhetorical Challenges to the Presidency, paper presented at the annual convention of the Southern States Communication Association, New Orleans, April 1, 2000, p. 5.

19. https://www.congress.gov/bill/108th-congress/senate-bill/3.

20. Alexandria Hein, "Photo Captures Moment Toddler's Leg Broke While on Slide with Mom," Fox News, June 27, 2018, http://www.foxnews.com/health/2018/06/27/photo-captures-moment-toddlers-leg-broke-while-on-slide-with-mom.html.

21. American Academy of Pediatrics, "Riding a Slide While on a Parent's Lap Increases the Risk of Injury," *EurekaAlert!*, September 15, 2017, https://www.eurekalert.org/pub_releases/2017-09/aaop-ras090817.php.

22. "Perceived Accuracy and Bias in the News Media," *Knight Foundation*, 2018, http://kf-site-production.s3.amazonaws.com/publications/pdfs/000/000/255/original/KnightFoundation_AccuracyandBias_Report_FINAL.pdf.

23. Interested readers can find hundreds of examples and summaries of studies here, Kuypers, *Partisan Journalism*, here, Jim A. Kuypers, *Bush's War: Media Bias and Justifications for War in a Terrorist Age* (Lanham, MD: Rowman and Littlefield, 2006), and here Jim A. Kuypers, *Press Bias and Politics: How the Media Frame Controversial Issues* (Westport, CT: Praeger, 2002). Other examples may be found here, https://www.mrc.org/special-reports/liberal-mediaevery-poll-shows-journalists-are-more-liberal-american-public-%E2%80%94-and.

24. https://news.gallup.com/poll/15370/party-affiliation.aspx.

25. Chris Cilliza, "Just 7 Percent of Journalists are Republicans: That's Far Less than Even a Decade Ago," *The Washington Post*, May 6, 2014, https://www.washingtonpost.com/news/the-fix/wp/2014/05/06/just-7-percent-of-journalists-are-republicans-thats-far-less-than-even-a-decade-ago/. Figures after 2014 are unavailable.

26. Dave Levinthal and Micheal Beckel, "Journalists Shower Hillary Clinton with Campaign Cash," *The Center for Public Integrity*, October 18, 2016, https://publicintegrity.org/federal-politics/journalists-shower-hillary-clinton-with-campaign-cash/.

27. For instance, see Kuypers, *Press Bias and Politics*; Aamidor, Kuypers, and Wiesinger, *Media Smackdown*, 127–154; and Jim A. Kuypers, "News Media Framing of the Donald J. Trump and Hillary Clinton 2016 Presidential Nomination Acceptance Speeches: Terministic Screens and the Discovery of the Worldview and Bias of the Press," in *The 2016 American Presidential Campaign and the News Media: Implications for the American Republic and Democracy*. A. Jim Kuypers, ed. (Lanham, MD: Lexington Books, 2018).

28. See the lengthy but non-exhaustive lists compiled by the Media Research Center: https://www.mrc.org/media-bias-101/journalists-denying-liberal-bias-part-one.

29. Of note is that social scientific studies of press bias often rely on word counts to make assumptions about bias and are unable to properly contextualize the usages. On this point, see note number 83 in Jim A. Kuypers, Stephen Cooper, and Matthew Althouse, "The President and The Press: A Rhetorical Framing Analysis of George W. Bush's Speech to the United Nations on November 10, 2001," *American Communication Journal* 10, no. 3 (2008), http://www.ac-journal.org/?page_id=37. For examples of academic studies arguing against liberal press bias, see Ceren Budak, Sharad Goel, and Justin M. Rao, "Fair and Balanced? Quantifying Media Bias through Crowdsourced Content Analysis," *Public Opinion Quarterly* 80, no. S1 (2016), 250–271; D. D'Alessio and M. Allen, "Media Bias in Presidential Elections: A Meta-analysis," *Journal of Communication* 50 (2000), 133–156; E. E. Dennis, "How 'liberal' Are the Media Anyway? The Continual Conflict of Professionalism and Partisanship," *Journal of Press/Politics* 2, no. 4 (1997), 115–11; D. Domke, M. D. Watts, D. V. Shah, and D. P Fan, "The Politics of Conservative Elites and the 'liberal media' Argument," *Journal of Communication* 49, no. 4 (1997), 35–59; David Niven, *Tilt? The Search for Media Bias* (Westport, CT: Praeger, 2002).

30. Slate Staff, "How *Slate* Votes," *Slate*, November 7, 2016, http://www.slate.com/articles/news_and_politics/slate_fare/2016/11/how_slate_staffers_are_voting.html.

31. "New York Times Endorsement Through the Ages," *The New York Times*, accessed, January 20, 2020, https://www.nytimes.com/interactive/2016/09/23/opinion/presidential-endorsement-timeline.html.

32. Jessica Winter, "Slate Isn't Too Liberal. But . . .," *Slate*, May 21, 2015, https://slate.com/news-and-politics/2015/05/is-slate-magazine-too-liberal-or-conservative-what-members-said-about-the-magazines-bias.html.

33. Kuypers, *Press Bias and Politics*, 246.

34. Dominic A. Infante, Andrew S. Rancer, and Deanna F. Womack, *Building Communication Theory*, 2nd ed. (Prospect Heights, Illinois: Waveland Press, 1993), 338.

35. Infante, Rancer, and Womack, *Building Communication Theory*, 338.

36. Timothy P. Carney, "Liberal News Media Bias Has a Serious Effect," *The New York Times*, December 21, 2015, https://www.nytimes.com/roomfordebate/2015/11/11/why-has-trust-in-the-news-media-declined/liberal-news-media-bias-has-a-serious-effect.

37. For a recent example with details, see: Kuypers, *Partisan Journalism*. See also, Editorial, "Media Bias: Pretty Much all of Journalism Now Leans Left, Study Shows," *Investors Business Daily*, November 16, 2018, https://www.investors.com/politics/editorials/media-bias-left-study/.

38. Shahram Heshmat, "What Is Confirmation Bias? People Are Prone to Believe What They Want to Believe," *Psychology Today*, April 23, 2015, https://www.psychologytoday.com/us/blog/science-choice/201504/what-is-confirmation-bias.

39. Dan Kahan as quoted in W.W., "Ezra Klein's Strangled Vox," *The Economist*, April 11, 2014, https://www.economist.com/democracy-in-america/2014/04/11/ezra-kleins-strangled-vox.

40. Heshmat. See also, Yoel Inbar and Joris Lammers, "Political Diversity in Social and Personality Psychology," *Perspectives on Psychological Science* 7, no. 5 (2012), 496–503; Piercarlo Valdesolo, "Fixing the Problem of Liberal Bias in Social Psychology," *Scientific American*, May 5, 2015, https://www.scientificamerican.com/article/fixing-the-problem-of-liberal-bias-in-social-psychology/; Richard E. Vatz, "Towson Professor: Higher Ed Discriminates against Conservatives," *The Baltimore Sun*, October 14, 2019, https://www.baltimoresun.com/opinion/op-ed/bs-ed-op-1015-conservative-discrimination-20191014-vv6vaj4blndgrj2mhdiwjlwtfq-story.html; Mitchell Langbert and Sean Stevens, "Partisan Registration and Contributions of Faculty in Flagship Colleges," *National Association of Scholars*, January 17, 2020, https://www.nas.org/blogs/article/partisan-registration-and-contributions-of-faculty-in-flagship-colleges.

41. Inbar and Lammers, "Political Diversity in Social and Personality Psychology," 496. These biased manifestations are seen in the communication discipline as well. See, Richard E. Vatz, "NCA's De Facto Ideological Discrimination," *WBAL*, March 9, 2011, https://www.wbal.com/article/68920/3/ncas-de-facto-ideological-discrimination. Emphasis mine.

42. Maxwell E. McCombs and Donald L. Shaw, "Agenda-Setting and the Political Process," in *The Emergence of American Political Issues: The Agenda-Setting Function of the Press*. Donald L. Shaw and Maxwell E. McCombs, eds. (St. Paul, MN: West Publishing Co., 1977), 151.

43. William A. Gamson, "News as Framing: Comments on Graber," *American Behavioral Scientist* 33 (1989), 157.

44. Jim A. Kuypers, "Framing Analysis," in *Rhetorical Criticism: Perspectives in Action*. Jim A. Kuypers, ed. (Lanham, Md: Lexington Books, 2009), 182.

45. Kuypers, "Framing Analysis," 182.

46. Peter A. Kerr and Patricia May, "Newspaper Coverage of Fundamentalist Christians, 1980–2000," *Journalism and Mass Communications Quarterly* 79 (2002), 54–72.

47. Some of these liberal privileging of usages are institutionalized in the Associated Press Stylebook. See, Ryan Saavedra, "Associated Press Now Refers To Illegal Aliens As 'Undocumented Citizens,'" *The Dailywire*, September 7, 2017, https://www.dailywire.com/news/associated-press-now-refers-illegal-aliens-ryan-saavedra.

48. Kuypers, *Partisan Journalism*, 101.

49. Gladys Engel Lang and Kurt Lang, "The Media and Watergate," in *Media Power in Politics*, Doris A. Graber, ed. (Washington, DC: Congressional Quarterly Press, 1984), 202–209.

50. Thomas E. Nelson, Rosalee A. Clawson, and Zoe M. Oxley, "Media Framing of Civil Liberties Conflict and its Effects on Tolerance," *American Political Science Review* 91, no. 3 (1997), 567.

51. As exemplified by CNN's Don Lemon. See, Ian Schwartz, "Don Lemon Defends Antifa: 'No Organization Is Perfect,'" *Real Clear Politics*, August 28, 2018, https://www.realclearpolitics.com/video/2018/08/28/don_lemon_defends_antifa_no_organization_is_perfect.html#!.

52. Adria Y. Goldman and Jim A. Kuypers, "Contrasts in News Coverage: A Qualitative Framing Analysis of 'A' List Bloggers and Newspaper Articles Reporting on the Jena 6." *Relevant Rhetoric* 1, no. 1 (2010), http://relevantrhetoric.com/Contrasts%20in%20News%20Coverage.pdf.

53. Robert M. Entman, "Framing U.S. Coverage of International News: Contrasts in Narratives of the KAL and Iran Air Incidents," *Journal of Communication* 41, no. 4 (1991), 21.

54. David Weaver, "Reply to Kosicki's Column: Framing Should not Supplant Agenda-Setting," *Communication Theory & Methodology Newsletter* (Communication Theory & Methodology Divison of the Association for Education in Journalism & Mass Communication), http://communication.sbs.ohio-state.edu/ctm/current/weaver.htm.

55. Kuypers, *Press Bias and Politics*, 198.

56. Ibid., 198.

57. Robert M. Entmann, "Framing: Toward Clarification of a Fractured Paradigm," *Journal of Communication* 43 (1993), 52.

*Chapter 3*

# Moral Foundations and Journalistic Bias

## PRIMING MORAL VALUES

There are legions of studies focusing on how news stories frame problems and their causes, and also suggest or critique solutions. What is comparatively little studied, though, is how frames convey the moral aspect of the policies, issues, and events the press covers. Framing researchers, myself included, have uncritically accepted the assertion that frames provide clues about moral judgments, and, as we will see below, that news stories also convey some aspect of this moral dimension. Yet this assumption has not been well examined. In particular, how press reports convey the moral qualities of the reporters writing the reports, or how these moral dimensions can reveal the underlying political ideologies of the reporters are questions that have not been asked. That they should be asked seems self-evident, and one way of answering them involves research in the area of moral psychology, which strongly suggests that conservatives and liberals utilize considerably different moral palettes. To the degree this is true, then, should we not find liberal reporters framing news from a liberal moral perspective? Thus, if one is going to look for political influences in the press framing of issues and events, one could also look for how the moral element is expressed by reporters in their news stories, and then see if that expression matches better a liberal, moderate, or conservative moral mindset as explained in moral psychology. Given the tension between the perceptions of the public, known effects of confirmation bias, academic studies that find evidence of bias and those that do not, and journalistic assertions about their own objectivity, using moral foundation theory allows for another venue to examine charges of liberal bias in MSM reporting.

The work of moral psychologists who have championed Moral Foundations Theory (MFT) provides a starting point for such an analysis. At its heart, MFT posits that our morality is both innate and learned.[1] We have five distinct moral foundations, expressed here as dichotomies: Care/Harm, Fairness/Cheating, Loyalty(ingroup)/Betrayal, Authority/Subversion, Sanctity/Degradation. Research into these foundations distinctly shows that liberals and conservatives prioritize them differently. The theory asserts that these "evolved moral psychological systems involve primarily fast, intuition based moral cognition in response to an appraisal of a morally-relevant situation. The intuitive moral psychological systems, though modifiable, are organized prior to experience and evolved to enable adaptive social life within and among groups."[2] Importantly, after this "intuitive (and often emotion-filled) response, slow reasoning is used primarily (post hoc) to find reasons to confirm and justify one's own intuitive reaction to the situation and to recruit/persuade others why they ought to join us in our judgment."[3] In this sense, then, we often "feel" our moral response before we reason it out; additionally, we could, if not careful, reason our way into believing our feelings in the face of contrary evidence.

According to Jonathan Haidt, MFT starts with the premise that human nature is intrinsically linked with moral elements, as well as being "moralistic, critical, and judgmental."[4] We are righteous as part of our nature; that is, we naturally view actions and events through a moral lens. Importantly, to our purpose in this book, MFT provides evidence that at times moral reasoning is not about figuring out truth, but rather used to support our "social agendas—to justify our own actions and to 'defend the teams' to which we belong."[5] When we think of moral rules, we think of those societal and cultural rules related to "justice, rights, and welfare pertaining to how people ought to relate to each other."[6] Our sense of morality, then, has a certain "innateness" about it. We have intuitions about disrespect and disgust, for instance; to the degree that this is true, we can imagine someone (including a journalist, for example) suddenly *feeling* a moral emotion about a situation or event, and then looking for evidence to support or justify that feeling. Moral reasoning often occurs *after* the moral emotion; it is "often a servant of moral emotions."[7] We are *prewired* for much of our biological behavior, and according to Haidt, we are prewired for much of our moral sensitivities as well; that is, there is a certain innate and intrinsic aspect to our possessing moral sensibilities. These initial sensitivities are subsequently modified as we grow and mature. The society in which we live influences us, as do our family, friends, experiences, and culture. *To the degree that this is true, we should find that the mainstream news media, as its own culture (and monolithically liberal in composition), would show signs of moral reasoning/judgments indicative of the liberal mind in its reporting.* There are four key principles of MFT: "(a) there is an innate 'first draft' of the moral mind organized in advance of experience; (b) this draft is 'edited' during development within a particular culture; (c) moral intuitions are nearly automatic and come first, with moral reasoning used to articulate justifications for these intuitive judgments; and (d) particular patterns of moral foundations have emerged in response to diverse social challenges."[8]

Yet how does the actual process of moral reasoning occur? How does it work? MFT likens our moral sensibilities to our taste buds, with the five moral foundations analogous to five possible moral "tastes," each of which, as mentioned above, can be stated with opposite quality.[9] Of note is that the first two moral dimensions, Care/Harm and Fairness/Cheating, are "individualizing" in the sense that they are associated with actions that protect and concern individuals. The other moral dimensions, Loyalty(ingroup)/Betrayal, Authority/Subversion, Sanctity/Degradation, are considered "binding" dimensions in that they are associated with actions that link individuals to a larger collective grouping.

Importantly for what we are doing here, it also links these receptors to political leanings in individuals, with empirical research findings indicating that liberals operate with an increased sensitivity to some receptors and decreased sensitivity to others when compared with conservatives, who tend toward a balanced palette use. Let us take a moment of look at each of these moral foundations.[10]

## Care/Harm

This "individualizing" moral foundation has to do with suffering that is not one's own. Initially, a way of ensuring children were cared for, the types of potential victims, or persons or things in need of care have grown, especially in those with liberal/progressive inclinations. This area "makes us sensitive to signs of suffering and need; it makes us despise cruelty and want to care for those who are suffering."[11] Evidence suggests that the more one identifies as liberal, the more one views this foundation *universally* applied (globally; I am my brother's keeper; it takes a village); the more conservative, the more *locally* applied (nationally, family; I am not my brother's keeper). Essentially this foundation is concerned with "the protection of the innocent or helpless, the relief of suffering, sympathy toward victims, and anger or disdain toward actors responsible for inflicting harm, emotional suffering, or violence."[12]

## Fairness/Cheating

This "individualizing" foundation developed as a way of "reaping the rewards of cooperation without getting exploited."[13] It is "related to concepts of justice, cooperation, and fair play, as well as the preferential treatment afforded some people, the denial of rights, unfair actions, and the profiting of some individuals over others."[14] There is a "reciprocal altruism" operating here, with the underlying idea of proportionality; that is, one ought to receive what one deserves based upon what one has done. Put another way, one reaps what one sows. It is about protecting one's communities as well as one's self from those who cheat or who are out for a free ride. For liberals, however, this foundation operates more around the concept of proportionality with regard to resources evenly distributed to all, regardless of one's "sowing." Thus, for liberals, the Marxist idea of "from each according to his ability to each according to his needs" may well apply here.

## Loyalty(Ingroup)/Betrayal

Humans are essentially tribal, males especially so. Loyalty, which advances group cohesion (ingroup) for survival and competition, is important for the species. This "binding" foundation asks who are team players and who are traitors, and goes a long way toward explaining our fascination with sports teams from high school to professional. We tend to wish to reward team players and ostracize and punish traitors. Moral understandings emanating from this foundation are "focused on the creation and ranking of in-groups, actions affecting a group, and fealty to one's in-group in competition with out-groups over scarce resources."[15] When engaging this foundation, the left tends to adopt a universal/global perspective and conservatives tend to adopt a national level, although both are concerned with "in group" status.

## Authority/Subversion

This "binding" foundation concerns respect for our hierarchical relationships, whether at the level of friends and family or business and societal; it "consists of notions of respect, deference and obedience toward hierarchical institutions, the fulfillment of duties, signs of respect for authority, the system's protection of subordinate individuals, and respect for social traditions."[16] As a condition of social life, human "authorities take on responsibility for maintaining order and justice."[17] The importance is especially seen when one considers that without "agreement on rank and a certain respect for authority there can be no great sensitivity to social rules."[18] Yet this authority runs both ways since superiors are looked upon to help and protect subordinates and subordinates are to work with and help superiors protect the group or tribe. Authority here is seen as "protecting order and fending off chaos."[19] Important awareness triggers for this foundation include acts of obedience/

disobedience, acts of respect/disrespect, and acts of submission/rebellion with respect to legitimate authorities. Additionally, any acts that are seen to support/subvert traditions, institutions, or values that promote stability also engage this moral dimension.

### Sanctity/Degradation

This "binding" foundation recognizes human ability to "endow ideas, objects, and events with infinite value, particularly those ideas, objects, and events that bind a group together into a single entity."[20] It "is linked to notions of both physical and spiritual purity and hygiene, along with decency standards, virtuous or uplifting actions, control of one's desires, and the feelings of disgust that accompany impure stimuli or unnatural and degrading actions."[21] Because of this, it explains why people "feel that some things, actions, and people are noble, pure, and elevated" and others "are base, polluted, and degraded."[22] Some triggers are the ideas of what is "clean" or "degraded" and actual or symbolic pollution. Feelings of disgust, even when we cannot explain them, can provide us with "valuable warning[s] that we are going too far, even when we . . . can't justify those feelings by pointing to victims."[23]

## CONSERVATIVE AND LIBERAL MORAL PERCEPTIONS

As mentioned above, liberal and conservatives exhibit different weightings related to these foundational moral receptors. This has been shown in studies focused on subjects as varied as letters to newspaper editors,[24] the debate over stem cell research,[25] preached sermons from different denominations,[26] political speeches,[27] and many more.[28] Of note is that liberals appear to operate with one overly developed moral receptor, and four weaker receptors; conversely, conservatives appear to operate using all moral foundations relatively equally, and with greater ease of movement between them. Work by Haidt, Jesse Graham, and others have rather consistently demonstrated the linkage of certain moral foundations to particular political positions.[29] This can be seen in the graph below where I present aggregate findings from MFT studies. Essentially graph 3.1 shows the relevance of a particular moral foundation to a person's decision when determining right or wrong: 0 = not at all relevant; 5= extremely relevant.

The exact numerical beginnings and endings of each foundation is not as important as the overall trajectory of where they begin and where they end. We definitely see a trend from liberals primarily engaging Care/Harm, and

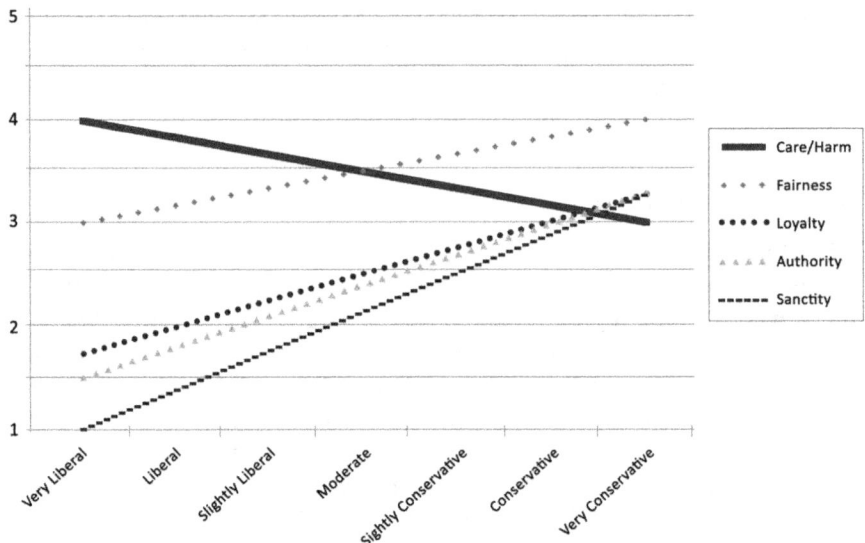

**Graph 3.1 Conservative and Liberal Moral Foundation Distribution.** *Source*: Author. Adapted from Yourmorals.com; Haidt, 2012; and Ravi Iyer, Spassena Koleva, Jesse Graham, Peter Ditto, and Jonathan Haidt, "Understanding Libertarian Morality: The Psychological Dispositions of Self-Identified Libertarians," *PLoS ONE*, vol. 7 no. 8 (2012). http://journals.plos.org/plosone/article?id=10.1371/journal.pone.0042366.

to a lesser degree, Fairness/Cheating, and conservatives more evenly using all five foundations with a slightly stronger emphasis on Fairness/Cheating. Keep in mind that liberals and conservatives see the Fairness/Cheating foundation differently. For conservatives, it tends to be based on the idea that one deserves something to the degree that one has worked for it—one reaps what one sows. It is not that they do not share, but rather a protection from those who cheat or who are out for a free ride. For liberals, this foundation operates more around the concept of proportionality with regard to resources distributed evenly to all, regardless of one's "sowing."

These conservative and liberal moral palettes are seen more clearly in figure 3.1, where the various moral foundations are shown in relative proportions to each other. As can be seen, conservatives have a more balanced approach to using all foundations than do liberals.

Of note is that the distribution of conservatives and liberals in America are unequal. Liberals make up approximately 20–25 percent of the population, moderates 35–40 percent, and conservatives around 40 percent. In relation to MFT, this means that a large majority of the population share a more greatly

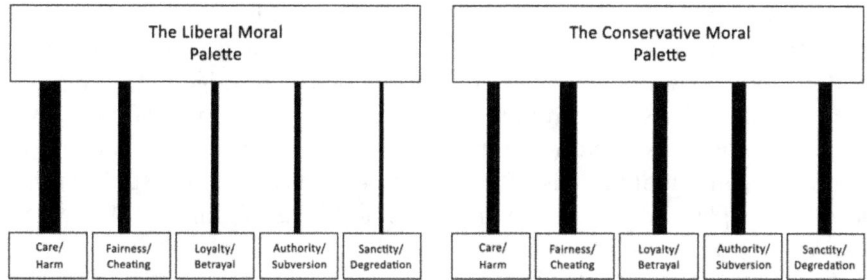

Figure 3.1 Conservative and Liberal Moral Palettes. *Source*: Author. Based on https://theindependentwhig.com/2015/03/09/this-explains-and-changes-everything/ Taken from Haidt, pp. 297 and 302, using aggregate figures from Yourmorals.com; Haidt, 2012; and Ravi Iyer, Spassena Koleva, Jesse Graham, Peter Ditto, and Jonathan Haidt, "Understanding Libertarian Morality: The Psychological Dispositions of Self-Identified Libertarians," *PLoS ONE* 7, no. 8 (2012). http://journals.plos.org/plosone/article?id=10.1371/journal.pone.0042366.

balanced use of the moral foundations. Such a distribution can be seen in graph 3.2.

That liberals and conservatives see political arguments from different moral foundations is a major component of MFT. Interestingly, evidence suggests that if liberal-supported messages are linked to nonliberal foundations that conservatives are more likely to contemplate or even support the argument, but there is little evidence available suggesting that it works the other way around, in part because liberals operate with a more limited palette of moral foundations. For instance, researchers looking at moral foundations in pro-environmental messages discovered that most are based on the Care/

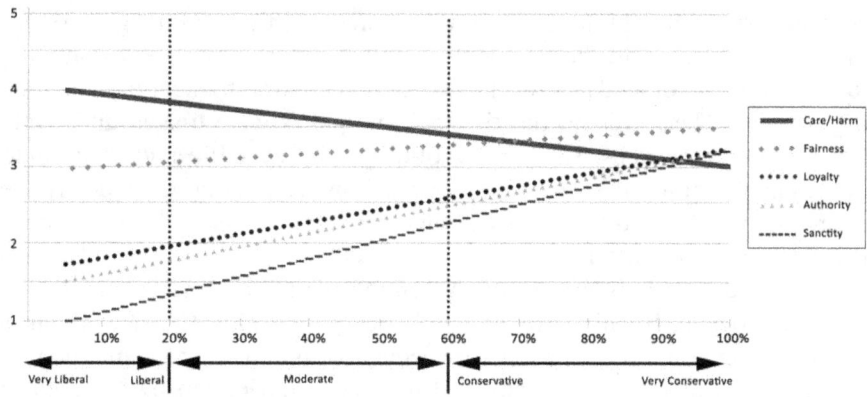

Graph 3.2 Moral Foundation Population Distribution. *Source*: Author.

Harm foundation, from liberals speaking to liberals, but not resonating well with conservatives. Yet when the messages were changed to accent purity and sanctity, conservatives were more likely to acknowledge or to agree with the message.[30] These researchers and others have noted that "political messages are more persuasive when they are framed in terms of moral intuitions that align with the intuitions of the target population."[31] Such studies might also help explain why liberals tend to see no liberal bias in MSM news yet conservatives and moderates see the liberal bias.

MFT certainly shows that by analyzing discourse we can discover linkages to certain moral foundations, and their use can suggest the source's political leanings. *So, to the degree that MFT holds true, we can see potential for looking for moral foundations in the reports of the mainstream news media to help confirm or confute what some studies have already shown: that the political identities of journalists influence the content of their news reports.*

## JOURNALISTS AND MORAL FOUNDATIONS

As mentioned earlier, there is little by way of MFT studies that examine the moral foundations of the press, although there are a few studies that use MFT in conjunction with news media analysis. One such study looked at a selection of hard news, editorials, opinion, and news analyses pieces.[32] The samples were compiled by a computer program that automatically extracted all articles from the politics section of *The New York Times*, Reuters, CBS News, and *The Washington Post*. Any named entities were removed, meaning that persons, distinct places, organizations, and so on were removed from the samples. The researchers, before the actual study, ensured that articles contained some moral information and prioritizing articles with high variance in moral content. Thus, the sample was limited and, in some ways, contrived to facilitate ease of analysis for those coding the moral foundations found in the samples. There was no mention of how quotes were treated differently from reporter assertions. The purpose of this social scientific study was not to determine moral foundations of journalists, however, but rather to determine intercoder reliability differences among coders with different levels of training when they used MFT.

Some studies examining moral foundations in relation to news stories have used the Model of Intuitive Morality and Exemplars, or MIME.[33] MIME takes as its starting point the common knowledge that moral "themes are latent in a wide range of media content," and that their impact can be assessed to some degree.[34] Importantly for us here, the "MIME suggests that, over time, consistent exposure to messages emphasizing the superiority of one moral foundation over another will increase the salience of that foundation among audiences and maintain its salience in the face of other influences. . . . Furthermore, the MIME holds that insulation from value inconsistent messages will foster polarized values within ideological groups and reduce openness to divergent views."[35] To the degree that this holds true, MIME can go a long way toward explaining confirmation bias among journalists (and any such insular group), and also show how news messages can be used by their audiences as a way of propping up their own political beliefs. It also suggests why journalists, so overwhelmingly liberal in composition, could be predisposed to inject their ideology into what should be objective news stories.

Of note is that the "MIME suggests a reciprocal relationship between basic motivations underlying moral judgment for distinct audiences and media content produced for those audiences."[36] In an interesting study by communication researchers Nicholas Bowman et al., newspaper headlines concerning Osama bin Laden's death were used to determine press-generated moral foundations. They suggested that any "differences in the frequencies of moral domains in newspaper headlines and subheads were found as a function of the political leanings of the target audience."[37] In short, these authors argued that newspapers serving a liberal audience tended to write headlines using liberal moral foundations such as Care/Harm, whereas papers serving more conservative audiences tended to use a more conservative moral foundation such as the patriotic act of killing bin Laden. However, paper identification, whether liberal leaning or conservative leaning, was not a variable, so one does not know if liberal papers were writing conservative headlines, for example.[38] The study also did not identify the moral foundations of the reporters writing the articles or of the editors creating the headlines, although the study does lend support for finding liberal moral foundations in texts written by liberals and conservative moral foundations in texts written by conservatives, if one speculates that the few conservative papers would be serving conservative audiences. That liberal papers serve more conservative areas is well known, and it would be of interest to discover if their headlines leaned right or left.

Another study of interest, by Brian J. Bowe, looked at the moral foundations in newspaper framing of the construction of Islamic mosques. Of note is that "components of media frames are influenced by the cognitions of journalists, newsroom routines and conventions, and the political and cultural contexts within which news stories are disseminated."[39] With this in mind, Bowe essentially asked how "patterns of problem definitions, causal attributions, moral evaluations [using MFT as determinant], and treatment recommendations combine to create frames in coverage of mosque building controversies."[40] His idea was to "use MFT to determine the ideological moral reasoning underpinning the frames."[41] Looking at five US daily papers, he examined "staff-produced news stories, staff editorials, and bylined columns specifically concerning mosque construction controversies."[42] A computer program-generated word counts for the moral foundations,[43] and human coders determine the other variables. This study, however, did not differentiate between journalist slant, hard news, opinion pieces, how quoted sources were placed, or how moral foundations might signal journalists' political biases. Whether the frames promoted a moral foundation or not was left undiscovered. Rather, the study only sought to identify overall frames across news stories and then to associate those frames with moral foundations in the same stories. As mentioned by Bowe, the "study . . . cannot untangle whether these were individual moral decisions made by journalists or moral positions imposed upon news content by the media routines and professional practices."[44] The study stopped far short of uncovering the moral foundations of journalists and their corresponding ideological positioning, although, and importantly, it did highlight that moral foundations exist in new narratives.

An additional study that found evidence of moral foundations in news stories looked at reporting of stem cell research in *The New York Times* between 1999 and 2010. The study focused almost exclusively on the Care/Harm and (what the authors described as) Purity/Taint dimensions, and made no differentiation between hard news and analysis, or the slant of the journalist, or how quotes and examples were positioned in the news story. Their primary focus was seeking the relationship between supporters and opponents of the research, and if their arguments were grounded in a particular moral foundation. The study authors found that in "spite of the strong relationship between the Purity foundation and stem cell attitudes at the individual level, Purity language was surprisingly uncommon in the debate. This finding has important implications for the rhetorical landscape in the United States. If partisan political actors invoke only the most widely endorsed foundations, elite rhetoric may come to be dominated by Harm and Fairness appeals."[45] These findings do lend strong evidence toward the ideological world view of journalists potentially limiting debate, since journalists do control who and what is quoted in news stories.

Since one of the four major functions of frames is asserted to be providing moral judgments, when we examine how the press frames an issue, we should be able to detect the frames pushing a moral foundation; in short, it would be the framing of a moral foundation, not a moral foundation framing a frame, as it were. Using MFT we have a ready way to discover the moral assessment once a frame has been detected. As has been shown, the press is liberal/progressive in disposition; but does this find its way into how news reports are framed? I have concluded that it does. But not everyone agrees with that assessment, as noted earlier and in the previous chapter, so another way of looking for proof is to see how evidence of moral foundations emerge from the framing of news stories. *When comparatively analyzed, will stories accurately reflect the moral foundations of those being reported upon, or will they reflect a liberal interpretation of the morality involved?* Since the focus of this book is looking at the relationship between President Trump and the MSM, do we see this with Trump coverage when we compare the moral foundations in his speeches with those in news stories about those same speeches? Additionally, do frames provide the moral dimension, or does the moral dimension inform the frames found within news stories?

## COMPARING FRAMES AND MORAL FOUNDATIONS

In order to answer these questions, as well as the questions first posed in chapter 2, in the chapters that follow I look at four key concerns addressed by President Trump: national security, the economy, the state of the American union, and immigration. The idea is to compare the frames and moral foundations found in Trump's speeches with those found in the MSM's coverage of those speeches. So, for each area I critically examine a major speech given by President Trump informed by the concepts of framing and moral foundations. I then examine the MSM coverage of each speech, using the same concepts, and then compare the results. I use *The Washington Post, The New York Times*, ABCNews.go.com, CBSNews.com, NBCNews.com, FoxNews.com, and CNN.com as the news sources. I specifically look only at hard news stories and labeled news analysis stories that focus on the speeches. By examining the frames and moral foundations in each speech and subsequent press coverage, we can begin to understand how the reporting on these speeches provides evidence of the core political values of the press.

## NOTES

1. Jonathan Haidt, *The Righteous Mind: Why Good People Are Divided by Politics and Religion* (New York City, New York: Pantheon Books, 2012).
2. Paul R. Gladden and Anthony M. Cleator, "Slow Life History Strategy Predicts Six Moral Foundations," *EvoS Journal: The Journal of the Evolutionary Studies Consortium* 9, no. 2 (2018), 44.
3. Gladden and Cleator, "Slow Life History Strategy Predicts Six Moral Foundations," 44.
4. Haidt, *The Righteous Mind*, xiii.
5. Ibid., xiv.
6. Ibid., 10.
7. Ibid., 25.
8. Brian J. Bowe and Jennifer Hoewe, "Night and Day: An Illustration of Framing and Moral Foundations in the Oklahoma Shariah Amendment Campaign," *Journalism & Mass Communication Quarterly* 93, no. 4 (2016), 971.

9. Haidt and other researchers have suggested a "provisional" sixth foundation, Liberty/Oppression. The Liberty/Oppression foundation focuses on equality and on signs of attempted domination of others. There is a certain degree of "reactance" here, where we react negatively to perceptions of "aggressive, controlling behavior" (Haidt, *The Righteous Mind*, 142). Triggers for this moral foundation are most things that are "perceived as imposing illegitimate restraints on one's liberty, including government (Haidt, *The Righteous Mind*, 174). According to Haidt, "the hatred of oppression is found on both sides of the political spectrum. The difference seems to be that for liberals . . . the Liberty/oppression foundation is employed in the service of underdogs, victims, and powerless groups everywhere" (Haidt, *The Righteous Mind*, 175). And this particularly in terms of lifestyle choices. Equality becomes sacred, moving beyond equal rights to include equal outcomes. Conservatives are less concerned with all of humanity and more concerned with country and particular groups. "For them, the Liberty/oppression foundation and the hatred of tyranny supports many of the tenets of economic conservatism," so don't tread on me with your higher taxes supporting a nanny state that also wants to oppressively regulate my small business (Haidt, *The Righteous Mind*, 175). In short, conservatives see this area as a right to be left alone by government; liberals see it as government ensuring equality. In some ways, we can see this as liberals being more concerned with lifestyle liberty here, and with concerns of social justice; conservatives more concerned with lifestyle as relates to economic liberty, and the right to keep the spoils of one's labor. This involves feelings of being dominated or oppressed. Gladden and Cleator state that the "liberty foundation focuses on personal freedom and autonomy (both economic and lifestyle-oriented freedom) and involves negative reactions to societal constraints on individual liberty and when there is an attempt to try to exert restrictive control over others" (46).

10. Although there are suggestions that there may be other moral foundations such as Liberty/Oppression, Efficiency/Waste, Ownership/Theft, and Honesty/Deception, these are only speculations at this point. Thus, we will look at only the five pairs mentioned above that are generally agreed upon as foundational. For additional thoughts on other possible foundations, see Jesse Graham, Jonathan Haidt, Sena Koleva, Matt Motyl, Ravi Iyer, Sean P. Wojcik, Peter H. Ditto, "Moral Foundations Theory: The Pragmatic Validity of Moral Pluralism," *Advances in Experimental Social Psychology* 58, no. 47 (2013), 55–130.

11. Haidt, *The Righteous Mind*, 153.
12. Bowe and Hoewe, "Night and Day," 972.
13. Haidt, *The Righteous Mind*, 153.
14. Bowe and Hoewe, "Night and Day," 972.
15. Ibid., 972.
16. Ibid., 972.
17. Haidt, *The Righteous Mind*, 143.
18. Ibid., 143.
19. Ibid., 144.
20. Ibid., 166.
21. Bowe and Hoewe, "Night and Day," 972.

22. Haidt, *The Righteous Mind*, 150.
23. Ibid., 152.
24. Bowe and Hoewe, "Night and Day," 967–985.
25. Scott Clifford and Jennifer Jerit, "How Words Do the Work of Politics: Moral Foundations Theory and the Debate Over Stem Cell Research," *The Journal of Politics* 75, no. 3 (2013), 659–671.
26. "In Religious Communities," The Righteous Mind, https://righteousmind.com/applying-moral-psych/religious-communities/, assessed June 27, 2019.
27. Jesse Graham, Jonathan Haidt, and Brian A. Nosek, "Liberals and Conservatives Rely on Different Sets of Moral Foundations," *Journal of Personality and Social Psychology* 96, no. 5 (2009), 1029–1049.
28. For more examples, go to: https://moralfoundations.org/.
29. I refrain from listing them all here. A detailed, although incomplete, source of citations for this work is listed here: https://www.moralfoundations.org/publications.
30. M. Feinberg and R. Willer, "The Moral Roots of Environmental Attitudes," *Psychological Science* 24, no. 1 (2013), 56–62.
31. René Weber, J. Michael Mangus, Richard Huskey, Frederic R Hopp, Ori Amir, Reid Swanson, Andrew Gordon, Peter Khooshabeh, Lindsay Hahn, and Ron Tamborini, "Extracting Latent Moral Information from Text Narratives: Relevance, Challenges, and Solutions," *Communication Methods and Measures* 12, no. 2–3 (2018), 2.
32. See Weber, Michael Mangus, Huskey, Hopp, Amir, Swanson, Gordon, Khooshabeh, Hahn, and Tamborini, "Extracting Latent Moral Information from Text Narratives," 119–139. The Taylor & Francis online provided pdf of this article uses page numbers 1–21, and those are the numbers used in quotes.
33. Nicholas Bowman, Robert Joel Lewis, and Ron Tamborini, "The Morality of May 2, 2011: A Content Analysis of US Headlines Regarding the Death of Osama Bin Laden," *Mass Communication and Society* 17 (2014), 639–664.
34. Weber, Mangus, Huskey, Hopp, Amir, Swanson, Gordon, Khooshabeh, Hahn, and Tamborini, "Extracting Latent Moral Information from Text Narratives."
35. Ibid.
36. Bowman, Lewis, and Tamborini, "The Morality of May 2, 2011," 640.
37. Ibid., 660.
38. A small conservative paper serving a small conservative county, for example, would have a different headline than the liberal *New York Times* serving a liberal audience, which is a variable for future study.
39. Brian J. Bowe, "Permitted to Build? Moral Foundations in Newspaper Framing of Mosque Construction Controversies," *Journalism & Mass Communication Quarterly* 95, no. 3 (2018), 786. See also Paul D'Angelo and Jim A. Kuypers, eds., *Doing News Framing Analysis: Empirical and Theoretical Perspectives* (New York: Routeledge, 2010).
40. Bowe, "Permitted to Build? Moral Foundations in Newspaper Framing of Mosque Construction Controversies," 788.
41. Ibid., 788.
42. Ibid., 789.

43. According to Bowe, "To determine moral evaluation, individual stories were analyzed using a moral foundations dictionary created for use with Linguistic Inquiry and Word Count (LIWC) software. This software counts virtue and vice terms related to the five foundations and calculates a score that is a percentage of foundation terms in each text" (p. 790). The conclusions drawn from such word counts are highly suspect as I have noted in Jim A. Kuypers, *Bush's War: Media Bias and Justifications for War in a Terrorist Age* (Lanham, MD: Rowman and Littlefield, 2006). Only through a qualitative assessment can words be fully assigned their meaning, relative strengths, and contexts.

44. Bowe, "Permitted to Build? Moral Foundations in Newspaper Framing of Mosque Construction Controversies," 801.

45. Clifford and Jerit, "How Words Do the Work of Politics: Moral Foundations Theory and the Debate Over Stem Cell Research," 669.

*Chapter 4*

# National Security

On December 18, 2017, President Trump delivered a formal speech[1] in which he introduced his administration's national security vision contained in the National Security Strategy (NSS) document.[2] The document, available to the public, is required by the 1986 Goldwater-Nichols Department of Defense Reorganization Act, which mandates that the executive branch periodically present the legislative branch an outline of the major security concerns faced by the United States and how the executive branch intends to deal with them. These documents are intentionally general in their details, and are designed to act as a foundational source while the executive branch and Congress discuss funding and actions involved with national security. These documents also serve to alert foreign governments of US military and foreign priorities without being too specific, and provide the public with the opportunity to see what a president is doing with respect to campaign promises.

The document's release is not a yearly event, and often coincides with major strategic security shifts from one presidential administration to another. For instance, in 2002 the Bush administration's document introduced the concept of "pre-emptive strikes," reflecting the administration's concern with the War on Terror. In 2010, the Obama administration released a document that emphasized greater interaction with China and Russia, and also stressed nuclear nonproliferation and climate change as national strategic priorities. In all, since 1986, seventeen documents have been produced.[3]

Previous documents had described the world stage as a "community of nations" or as the "international community." The Trump administration document introduced a new context, stressing instead that the world was a competitive arena in which "fundamentally political contests between those who favor repressive systems and those who favor free societies" occurred. In particular, the president stressed the "revisionist powers of China and Russia, the rogue states of Iran and North Korea, and transnational threat organizations, particularly jihadist terrorist groups" as threats to the security of the United States. For the Trump administration, since the days of Ronald Reagan, both parties had increasingly mischaracterized the international front. Essentially stating that because as Americans we "took our political, economic, and military advantages for granted,"[4] powers such as Russia, China, Iran, and North Korea and also terrorist groups engaged in plans to challenge our power and values, as well as those of our allies. In addition, even friendly powers took advantage of American generosity and complacency, such as the NATO nations refusing to pay their full share of costs, while America continued to pay a lion's share for the collective defense, more than all other NATO members combined.[5]

## PRESIDENT TRUMP'S SPEECH

The timing of the document's release is a first in that President Trump was the first president to publish the NSS document in his inaugural year as president. Moreover, not all presidents give an actual address along with the security document's publication, but Trump chose to deliver one at the Ronald Reagan Building and International Trade Center in Washington, D.C.

Although not a major theme within the speech, the past actions of the American people acted as a contextualizing aspect for the entire speech. In a sense, this idea exists in some ways in all the frames found within the speech. For President Trump, the foundations of his strategic vision rest with the American people, who "have always been the true source of American greatness." They have advanced American "culture" and "values," and have "fought and sacrificed on the battlefields all over the world," liberating "captive nations," and "lifted entire regions of the planet from poverty to prosperity."

### Framing

In breaking with past administrations of both political parties, President Trump was walking a rather fine line. On the one hand, he was redefining some aspects of foreign policy, taking a more confrontational stance against both Russia and China, for instance, but also staying within the mainstream of both parties on America's general role in the world. There are seven themes in the president's speech: past actions of American leaders, present American actions, the NSS, border security, economic security, national defense, and American influence.

## Past Actions of American Leaders

The NSS document represented a major break from all administrations following Ronald Reagan, and President Trump takes pains to frame the past actions of both Republican and Democrat political and business leaders. He grounds his actions in his belief in the American people, mentioned above, and the duty of American leaders to act on their behalf. With this in mind, he stresses how citizens had watched "Washington politicians presid[ing] over one disappointment after another." These leaders had forgotten "whose voices they were to respect and whose interests they were supposed to defend." Some of their failures included negotiating "disastrous trade deals that brought massive profits to . . . foreign nations, but sent thousands of America factories, and millions of American jobs, to those other countries." Moreover, these leaders had "drifted from American principles," losing "sight of America's destiny," and their "belief in American greatness."

Not only in trade, but political leaders who "engaged in nation-building abroad" failed to "build up and replenish" their own nation. The US military had been "shortchanged" with "inadequate resources, unstable funding, and unclear missions." Moreover, "very wealthy allies" were not required to "pay their fair share for defense," which placed a "massive and unfair burden on the U.S. taxpayer." In terms of defense, leaders "neglected a nuclear menace in North Korea," and made an "incomprehensibly bad deal with Iran," while terrorists were allowed to "gain control of vast parts of territory all over the Middle East."

Internally, America's energy resources were put "under lock and key," while the government also imposed "punishing regulations and crippling taxes." And "over the profound objections of the American people," their leaders left America's "borders wide open," with the result that "millions of immigrants entered illegally" with millions more entering "without the proper vetting needed to protect" Americans.

## Present Actions: America First

Linked to the present actions of the administration is the president's notion of putting "America First" in all domestic and foreign policies. It is a foundational aspect of his NSS, and is linked with the ideas he put forth that the "American people rejected the failures of the past" and "rediscovered" their "voice and reclaimed ownership" of the country. As foundational, the idea of America First means that the "first duty" of the government "is to serve its citizens," particularly those "forgotten" by past administrations; every "decision and every action" is made by "putting America first."

In some senses, the stress on present actions leads into the proposed actions of the NSS document. The Trump administration had increased American "investment" in its defense with the belief that a strong military will lead to "long and extraordinary peace." The economy had been addressed, with withdrawal from "some job-killing deals such as the Trans-Pacific Partnership" and an announcement that America would "no longer tolerate trading abuse." Immigration restrictions and "new vetting procedures" had been imposed in the name of keeping "terrorists out of the United States." Both Iran and North Korea's nuclear ambitions were being addressed, with the United States especially engaging the "Gulf states and other Muslim-majority nations" in order to "fight radical Islamist ideology and terrorist financing."

In particular, the president stresses his actions to "strengthen the NATO Alliance" and his demands for "significant increases in member contributions," because his administration would no longer allow the practice of member states remaining "delinquent" in their payments while the United States guaranteed their safety. For the president, "countries that are immensely wealthy should reimburse the United States for the cost of defending them. This is a major departure from the past, but a fair and necessary one—necessary for our country, necessary for our taxpayers."

Also stressed was the economic growth since 2016, along with the cutting of bureaucratic regulations. The Trump administration had cut "22 regulations for every one new regulation" and had also "unlocked America's vast energy resources." The economic recovery is important to the strategic plan since Trump intends the economy to "be one of America's truly greatest weapons."

## National Security Strategy

The importance of the framing of past and present actions coalesced around five "fundamental truths" at the heart of the NSS:

1. "A nation without borders is not a nation."
2. "A nation that does not protect prosperity at home cannot protect its interests abroad."
3. "A nation that is not prepared to win a war is a nation not capable of preventing a war."
4. "A nation that is not proud of its history cannot be confident in its future."
5. "And a nation that is not certain of its values cannot summon the will to defend them."

We see in these principles the four key areas addressed in Trump's NSS. Importantly, the strategy is predicated on a "principled realism" guided by "vital national interests and rooted in [American] timeless values." And as mentioned above, the strategy initiates a fundamental shift in strategic thinking, recognizing that the world has entered into a new era of competition.

The four pillars of the strategic document are essentially extensions of the policies already discussed by the president, and each is specifically framed in the speech. These four "vital national interests" are: border security, economic security, security through national defense, and security through American influence.

## Border Security

The purpose of border security is essentially to "protect the American people, the homeland, and our great American way of life." This includes securing the borders, and for the first time, a "serious plan to defend [the American] homeland." Border security calls for a border wall between Mexico and the United States, legal immigration reform, and increased support for Border Patrol agents, ICE officers, and Homeland security personnel. Included with this is the enhancement of means to confront radical Islamic terrorists, with particular emphasis on combating its spread into the United States. Cyberterrorism and social media attacks are mentioned as well.

## Economic Security

For the president, economic security is national security: "Economic vitality, growth, and prosperity at home is absolutely necessary for American power and influence abroad." This pillar emphasizes steps for ensuring economic vitality and prosperity: cutting taxes and reducing "unnecessary regulations." The president points out that it "calls for trade based on the principles of fairness and reciprocity . . . for firm action against unfair trade practices and intellectual property theft [and] for new steps to protect our national security industrial and innovation base." Additionally, this pillar calls for a reinvestment and refurbishment of America's infrastructure.

## National Defense

Peace through strength sums well the president's vision here. He stresses that "weakness is the surest path to conflict," whereas "unrivaled power is the most certain means of defense." Thus, complete modernization of the military is called for. Additionally, the strategy calls for countering cyber and electromagnetic attacks, "recognizes space as a competitive domain" and outlines new "steps to address new forms of conflict such as economic and political aggression."

*American Influence*

The president does not break new ground when he states that we should "advance American influence in the world," but does shift the focus from previous NSS documents when he suggests that "this begins with building up our wealth and power at home." This is clearly part of the America First idea, but goes beyond it as well since the president envisions America as a first among equals when he states, "America will lead again." Importantly, America First and America's strategic defense do not mean that Americans will "seek to impose [their] way of life on anyone." Rather, the United States will simply begin to "champion [its] values without apology." The document calls for "strong alliances and partnerships based on cooperation and reciprocity." Moreover, international cooperation is stressed, with the Trump administration wishing to "make new partnerships with those who share our goals, and make common interests into a common cause."

America, as a first among equals, "will pursue the vision we have carried around the world over this past year—a vision of strong, sovereign, and independent nations that respect their citizens and respect their neighbors; nations that thrive in commerce and cooperation, rooted in their histories and branching out toward their destinies."

## Moral Foundations

Almost missing from the speech is any linking to the moral foundations of Sanctity (purity)/Degradation and Authority/Subversion. In terms of sanctity, the president does mention "others who spread violence and evil around the globe" and states, "God Bless You," and in terms of authority does mention that it is an "honor" to represent the American people and that "the rule of law prevailed" throughout American history. However, these mentions are insignificant, with by far the strongest moral foundation being Loyalty(ingroup)/Betrayal, followed to a lesser degree by Fairness/Cheating and Care/Harm, using almost the same emphasis each.

*Loyalty(Ingroup)/Betrayal*

Overwhelmingly the strongest foundation, it resonated both implicitly and explicitly throughout the speech. In some ways, this makes sense in that this is a speech about national security, yet it goes deeper in that the "nation" was made to be one with its "people." The president begins by thanking those who "who devote their lives to serving our nation," and expressed thanks for being able to "represent the American people" around the world. And it is, the president stressed, "the people" who are the source of American greatness. And this greatness as a nation sees multiple expressions. For instance, "America has been among the greatest forces for peace and justice in the history of the world."

But there is Betrayal as well: elite and selfish politicians "surrendered our sovereignty to foreign bureaucrats in faraway and distant capitals." They also allowed "millions of immigrants [to enter our country] illegally [or] without the proper vetting needed to protect our security and our economy." The people "never voted for, never asked for, and never approved" such policies; instead, leaders "in Washington imposed on the country [this] immigration policy. . . . American citizens, as usual, have been left to bear the cost and to pick up the tab." These and other problems are because "our leaders drifted from American principles" and "lost their belief in American greatness."

President Trump suggests that his election is the moment that the people "reclaimed ownership of this nation" and that a fundamental change took place: "The people became the rulers of their nation again." Asserting that government leaders had usurped the power of the people, the president intoned, "The first duty of our government is to serve its citizens. . . . With every decision and every action, we are now putting America first.

Of course, there are threats to the Ingroup, the nation, and the president highlights that his administration is going after Iran and others for their "support of terrorism." This increased action includes cooperation with other nations in fighting "terrorist financing" and reclaiming "terrorist"-controlled lands. The importance of ingroup loyalty is stressed specifically in the five principles of the NSS (mentioned above), but is also applicable to other nations in that he has "a vision of strong, sovereign, and independent nations." The new NSS is "guided by our vital national interests" and operates to protect "our national interest." Moreover, Americans "will stand up for our country," and the Trump administration will use "our national strength" and "every instrument of our national power [to] protect the American people, the homeland, and our great American way of life."

He speaks specifically about his policies to "defend our homeland," stating, "we cannot secure our nation if we do not secure our borders," and that the policies are designed for "building up our wealth and power at home"; the government's "task is to strengthen our families, to build up our communities," all within a nationwide "rebirth of patriotism."

*Fairness/Cheating*

In terms of presence, the Fairness/Cheating foundation was less pronounced than Loyalty(ingroup)/Betrayal, and slightly more pronounced than Care/Harm, and also resonates throughout the speech. Starting strongly, the president states that "America has been among the greatest forces for . . . justice in the history of the world." Part of this force is linked with defense of others, and President Trump highlights a theme common in his rhetoric, that by not making other wealthy nations pay their fair share of defense, prior administrations were "putting a massive and unfair burden on the U.S. taxpayer and our great U.S. military." Thus, "We have made clear that countries that are immensely wealthy should reimburse the United States for the cost of defending them. This is a major departure from the past, but a fair and necessary one." Even less-wealthy nations receiving aid are expected to chip in, and the president uses Pakistan as an example: "And we make massive payments every year to Pakistan. They have to help." He asks other nations to "shoulder their fair share of responsibility for our common security," but within a context of "strong alliances and partnerships based on cooperation and reciprocity."

Trade is a topic that receives special treatment, and the NSS encourages fairness in trade practices as part of America's security. Thus, the president withdrew "the United States from job-killing deals such as the Trans-Pacific Partnership and the very expensive and unfair Paris Climate Accord." His administration "will no longer tolerate trading abuse," but instead will promote "trade based on the principles of fairness and reciprocity." He specifically "calls for firm action against unfair trade practices."

*Care/Harm*

Although not part of the planned speech, the president began his speech by expressing "deepest sympathies" to family who lost loved ones in a recent Amtrak train derailment.[6] As he begins discussion of the NSS document itself, the president relates specifically that it is about "America's security," that "America has been among the greatest forces for peace . . . in the history of the world," and that a strong military will "hopefully lead to long and extraordinary peace." He sees a primary task of his administration as protecting America from those who "attack our nation or threaten our society," and that his goal is to "preserve peace through strength."

Part of his administration's care for the nation involved actions such as withdrawing from "job-killing deals such as the Trans-Pacific Partnership and the very expensive and unfair Paris Climate Accord."[7] Such actions were taken to minimize harm, and the United States would "no longer tolerate trading abuse."

The president takes time to specifically list harms against the American people: "Washington politicians presided over one disappointment after another," and they "negotiated disastrous trade deals" that ruined American factories and cost American jobs. This same group "engaged in nation-building abroad" but did "not build up the nation's own infrastructure." The internal harm continued with this group's imposition of "punishing regulations and crippling taxes" and leaving "our borders wide open." Moreover, they "neglected [the] nuclear menace in North Korea" and made an "incomprehensibly bad deal with Iran" and emboldened ISIS and "others who spread violence and evil around the globe." Because of leaders' abuse, "our citizens lost something as well. The people lost confidence in their government and, eventually, even lost confidence in their future."

**Trump Summary**

The Trump speech framed seven key themes and conveyed three moral foundations. In terms of frames: the Past Actions of American Leaders was essentially relaying that leaders of both political parties had hurt Americans with bad policies; Present American Actions focused on the idea of "America First," meaning that Americans' interests should come first in all policy decisions foreign and domestic; the NSS was framed as revolving around five fundamental truths, the four pillars of national security, and a focus on national interest instead of global development; Border Security involved securing the nation, particularly the border, cybersecurity, and stopping terrorist threats; Economic Security involved highlighting the importance of economic vitality through cutting taxes and regulations, necessary for America's security; National Defense involved investing further in the military, and the idea of peace through strength; and American Influence involved advancing American interests and values globally but starting at home.

In terms of the moral foundations, overwhelmingly the president stressed the Loyalty(ingroup)/Betrayal foundation. Through this foundation Trump stressed the people of the nation, and his actions as loyal to them and the principles of the country; betrayal was expressed in terms of past policy-makers of both parties engaging in questionable activities that did not benefit "the people," but other nations and elite (implied) interests. The next two foundations were roughly co-equal in emphasis, although Fairness/Cheating was slightly stronger in emphasis. Here the president stressed fairness in terms of policies affecting the people, and also foreign nations and interests "paying their fair share" and not taking advantage of America. Part of the strength of the Care/Harm foundation was due to the very nature of the speech—security. The president's policies were designed to "care" for the American people, keeping them safe (economically and physically).

## Chapter 4

## PRESS RESPONSE

### Framing

Very little was reported about strength through prosperity, the three threats, the four pillars as such, Islamic terrorists, or Pakistan.[8] A notable exception were those articles published the day before the speech that were based upon an interview provided by three anonymous senior administration officials; those articles did mention the four pillars. The main themes expressed in the news stories, in order of strength, are: the president's speech about the report versus the report itself, the new realm of cyber warfare/social media, revisionist powers Russia and China, allegations about Putin/Trump/2016 election, and "America First."

### *The Speech Versus the Report Itself*

This was a large and powerful frame through which news audiences were invited to view the roll out of the security document. Although the press did mention some differences between the Obama security document and the Trump document (such as Obama putting in climate change as a security issue and Trump taking it out, the new focus on cybersecurity, and labeling Russia and China strategic competitors), less was said about how America's security strategy had changed than what the press perceived as differences between the speech and the strategy document itself. The additional focus on this aspect may have been enhanced because of the press conference given by three "anonymous" "Trump administration officials," with both this pre-speech discussion and the document being released before Trump gave his speech.

CNN exemplified this frame, calling attention to what it perceived as differences between the original document and Trump's speech: "When President Trump delivered a speech Monday about the strategy . . . he did invoke the phrase 'radical Islamic terrorism' despite the fact that the phrase doesn't appear anywhere in the lengthy strategy document. He did not, however, echo any of the document's criticism of Russia in his remarks."[9]

The speech was literally reclassified by the press: "And while Trump repeated some core aspects of the foreign policy strategy document . . . he reserved much of his address for touting domestic economic growth and lambasting his predecessors for damaging American security."[10] In this sense the speech was described as a "campaign address," with Trump offering a "laundry list of accomplishments and a reiteration of his view that Americans have been left behind as a result of decisions made by past administrations, including on immigration, the Iran nuclear deal, and trade pacts."[11] All this boiled down to the president framing "his foreign policy as an extension of his populist economic message, lambasting past presidents and trumpeting his own achievements during a speech meant to outline the guiding principles of his national security strategy."[12]

Other examples of the perceived dichotomy focused on Russia. The idea was linked with Democrat allegations that the Trump campaign colluded with Russia to win the 2016 election. CNN, for example, noted that Trump had highlighted cooperation with Russia about planned terrorist attacks in St. Petersburg, which it characterized as "a softer approach than what's contained within the national security strategy. . . . The document describes China and Russia as 'revisionist powers' who 'want to shape a world antithetical to US values and interests.'"[13] For *The New York Times*, while "outlining his first national security strategy, President Trump sought to distinguish himself as a commander in chief who is breaking records and setting precedents."[14] It followed this up with contorted and often overly literalist interpretations, attempting to discredit Trump's claims with such characterizations as "falsely," "misleadingly," "exaggerated," and "erroneous."[15] Others echoed this framing, accusing Trump of placing "himself at the center of a new national security strategy . . . casting his election as a pivot from failed policies pushed by his predecessors and presenting his 'America First' doctrine as the organizing principle for U.S. engagement around the world."[16]

Similar to CNN, *The New York Times* also sought to drive a wedge between Trump and the document, calling it a "mixed message."[17] For the *Times*, the document "warns of a treacherous world in which the United States faces rising threats from an emboldened Russia and China, as well as from what it calls rogue governments, like North Korea and Iran."[18] And herein lies the contrast for the *Times*, which is representative of the general framing in this theme:

> The report says with Cold War urgency, the government must put "America First," fortifying its borders, ripping up unfair trade agreements and rebuilding its military might.
>
> But in his speech announcing the strategy, Mr. Trump struck a much different tone. Instead of explaining the nature of these threats, he delivered a campaign like address, with familiar calls to build a wall along the southern border with Mexico and a heavy dose of self-congratulation for the bull market, the low jobless rate and tax cuts. . . . "America is in the game, and America is going to win," he said. . . .
>
> The document's call to push back against China on trade is familiar from the campaign, but its description of the challenge posed by Russia seems at odds with Mr. Trump's own refusal to criticize Mr. Putin for his seizure of Crimea, his efforts to destabilize Ukraine and his violations of a key nuclear treaty with the United States.

The disconnect between the president's speech and the analysis in his administration's document attests to the broader challenge his national security advisers have faced, as they have struggled to develop an intellectual framework that encompasses Mr. Trump's unpredictable, domestically driven and Twitter-fueled approach to foreign policy. The same confusion has confronted foreign governments trying to understand Mr. Trump's conflicting signals.[19]

Other stories used the idea of "mixed signals" since Trump's tone toward Russia and China in public and in his speech did not completely match the hard tone in the document itself: "The softer-than-expected speech capped a year of mixed signals on how the Trump administration plans to handle Beijing, raising more questions about the future of U.S. China ties."[20]

However, this frame went beyond just this aspect, in that the press made the speech about its perception of Trump and not the policy as expressed in the document or in the speech. As an example, "The gap between what Trump has said on China and what he has done is the source of much debate here—and Monday's speech did little to change that."[21] Another example, "And there's nothing in the document that can address the personality of Trump himself, who is known for changing his mind, altering policy via tweet and placing too much emphasis on his personal powers of persuasion. But, at least, the rest of the U.S. government is now working off the same sheet of paper when it comes to China."[22]

Whereas the other press outlets made it about Trump, this lone Fox News story offered a contrast, providing insight into how the same event could be reported using a different frame for the same theme. For this article, it was about the policy, not Trump:

> President Trump on Monday unveiled a national security strategy that enshrines his "America First" approach into U.S. policy, stressing American strength and economic security and putting rivals like China and Russia on notice. "America is in the game and America is going to win," Trump said, making clear that the United States will stand up for itself even if that means acting unilaterally or alienating others on issues such as trade, climate change and immigration. Trump said the U.S. faces "an extraordinarily dangerous world" and one of his goals is to make sure the U.S. is "leading again on the world stage." "America is coming back, and America is coming back strong," he said.[23]

## Cyber Warfare/Social Media

One element of the new security strategy involved the United States upgrading its cyber defenses, including social media dimensions. For the news media, "Trump . . . did refer to 'new domains such as cyber and social media' that might be used to attack the U.S. But he did not explicitly refer to Russian meddling in last year's election. He focused instead on how a CIA tip had helped prevent a terrorist attack in the Russian city of Saint Petersburg, which Putin had called to thank him for on Sunday."[24] Of note is that the press did relay that the document "singled out Russia as interfering in the domestic political affairs of countries around the world, using 'modernized forms of subversive tactics,' including cyber weapons, covert operations, state-funded media and 'paid social media users or "trolls."'"[25]

However, the framing focus was in pointing out that "the document did not make explicit reference to Russia's interference . . . in the [2016] U.S. presidential elections, during which American intelligence agencies have said many of those tools were employed."[26] As *The New York Times* wrote, "Mr. Trump . . . spoke of how Russia and China 'seek to challenge American influence, values and wealth.' But he made no mention of Russian interference in the 2016 presidential election, even though the document itself makes fleeting reference to 'Russia using tools in an attempt to undermine the legitimacy of democracies.'"[27]

Thus, the document was used to highlight the press version of Russian meddling in the election. However, although the security document itself casts a wide net concerning cyber threats,[28] and did focus forcefully on Russia, most of the news sources used its mention to focus on Russia's involvement with the 2016 presidential election only. CNN used the cyber section of the document itself to call attention to the difference between it and Trump's public statements on Russia: "Trump's strategy also goes far further [*sic*] than the President publicly has in calling out destabilizing Russian behavior across the globe, including its violations of Ukrainian and Georgian sovereignty. The document calls attention to Russian attempts to meddle in democracies and makes clear that the US is keeping a wary eye on Russian influence campaigns even though Trump has repeatedly cast doubt on the US intelligence community's conclusion that Russia meddled in the 2016 US election."[29]

Although some, such as CNN above, mentioned in passing that the document described "Russian aggression against its neighbors . . . 'its invasions of Georgia and Ukraine,'" they primarily focused on the document's linking of "Russia's 'information operations'" to a broader campaign to influence public opinion across the globe, in particular to the 2016 election: "This, of course, is similar to the US intelligence community's conclusions that Russia meddled in the 2016 American presidential election."[30]

*The New York Times* exemplifies well the overall press frame here of describing the very real threat of cyber weapons and diminishing Trump's positions: "The document described the problems facing the nation rather than prescribing solutions. [T]the document reads . . . 'the use of cyber-tools have allowed state and nonstate competitors to harm the United States across various domains.' But the document deals with the subject at some remove, not dwelling on how Russia used cyber-techniques in an attempt to interfere with the 2016 election. And it does nothing to describe any broad national strategy to guard against meddling in future elections."[31]

*The Washington Post* also provides an example of this extended framing: "Trump has publicly complimented . . . Putin, calling him 'very smart,' and has sought a better relationship with Russia. . . . He has been openly skeptical of U.S. intelligence findings that Russia mounted a systematic effort to undermine the 2016 presidential election. But Trump has not reversed congressional sanctions on Russia over its actions in Ukraine, as Putin hoped he would. The strategy document released Monday skirts the issue of Russia's involvement in the presidential election. 'Through modernized forms of subversive tactics, Russia interferes in the domestic political affairs of countries around the world,' the document says."[32] Additionally, the press often pushed this frame well beyond the US intelligence community's assessment of Russian interference in the 2016 general election, making implications designed to diminish Trump's credibility: "Mr. Trump made no mention of Russian interference in the 2016 election, which United States intelligence agencies concluded was intended to help him win. He focused instead on a phone call on Sunday from Mr. Putin, who thanked him for [helping] them foil a terrorist plot in St. Petersburg."[33]

Thus, almost all importance for cybersecurity was reduced to allegations of Russian meddling, and, for some, to help Trump win, thus highlighting how what Trump and the document did *not* mention acted to hurt Trump.

*Revisionist Powers Russia and China*

Although both the strategic document and Trump spoke of numerous threats beyond Russia and China—North Korea, Iran, Pakistan, Islamic terrorism, and so on—the press primarily focused on conveying the document and speech as recategorizing Russia and China as "revisionist powers," and as threats to the United States,[34] something again different from the Obama document.

When mentioned, the frame was remarkably consistent, summed well here by ABC News:

> "Whether we like it or not, we are engaged in a new era of competition," Trump said in his speech. "We recognize that weakness is the surest path to conflict and unrivaled power is the most certain means of defense." Both China and Russia were listed among three key challenges to the U.S., and Trump referred to them as "revisionist powers," putting them alongside "rogue regimes" like North Korea and Iran. Trump said the U.S. would seek to build a "great partnership" with the countries but always on conditions that prioritized U.S. interests.[35]

The reply from Russia and China was also remarkable in the consistency of its reporting. China was shown as saying the strategy was a "victory for hardliners," and called for "the U.S. to 'abandon its Cold War mentality and zero-sum game concept,' warning that failure to do so 'would only harm itself as well as others.'"[36] A standard Russian quote was that a "spokesman for Russian President Vladimir Putin told reporters . . . that the document had a 'clearly imperial nature' and demonstrated a reluctance to abandon the idea of a 'unipolar world.'"[37]

Of course, in a departure from the Obama document, both countries were described as "rival powers" by Trump, and the press did relay this. Yet this was the main focus of the press, to the detriment of sharing other major threats as defined by both Trump and the security document:

> China will remain a key target of the administration's focus on guarding US economic security, and Trump's national security strategy repeatedly calls out abusive Chinese trade practices, such as its theft of US companies' intellectual property. Trump's strategy also goes far further [sic] than the President publicly has in calling out destabilizing Russian behavior across the globe, including its violations of Ukrainian and Georgian sovereignty. The document calls attention to Russian attempts to meddle in democracies and makes clear that the US is keeping a wary eye on Russian influence campaigns even though Trump has repeatedly cast doubt on the US intelligence community's conclusion that Russia meddled in the 2016 US election.[38]

The narrowing of threats reflects the reporting prior to the president's speech, primarily. Russian meddling in the 2016 election and concerns about unfair Chinese trade practices: "China as key national security concerns. The strategy document required by congressional mandate reflects Trump's focus on trade since coming into office, and while it does not threaten the use of tariffs as Trump has, it makes clear the US will ensure that trade is 'fair and reciprocal.' 'The United States will no longer turn a blind eye to violations, cheating, or economic aggression,' the document says."[39] Fox News also took this tack, writing, "China and Russia 'challenge American power, influence, and interests, attempting to erode American security and prosperity.'"[40]

This frame also highlighted not only the document categorizing China and Russia as "rival powers" but as "strategic competitors." Consider this representative example from *The Washington Post*:

> Although you wouldn't know it from his speech, President Trump's first ever National Security Strategy (NSS) places the United States in a new posture vis-à-vis China, a much harder line . . . . China [has]twice as many mentions compared with the Obama administration's. . . . And while the Obama strategy focused on engagement and cooperation with China, the Trump team

concentrated on identifying the mounting threats posed by China. . . . The Trump strategy calls out China for a range of malicious practices, warns about China's international expansion and commits the United States to competing with and even combating China on every conceivable playing field. "China is seen as a strategic competitor because China competes effectively across the political, economic, military and informational domains in ways probably not duplicated by our other competitors," a senior administration official said.[41]

*Putin/Trump/2016 Election*

As can be seen from the above, there is a Russian thread running through most of the frames found within the reporting on the unveiling of the national security document. The document touched on many threats beyond Russia, but the press stressed Russia and Trump, castigating Trump for not focusing enough on it: "While the national security strategy document refers to Russia nearly two dozen times, criticizing its meddling in other countries' affairs and its attempts to undermine the US, Trump referenced Russia only once, alongside China, when he called both 'rival powers.' Trump then pivoted to his call with . . . Putin on Sunday to discuss intelligence cooperation that thwarted a terrorist attack in Russia."[42] This highlighted press focus on Russia conveyed an even greater sense of the importance of Russia than its importance in the document itself. In short, although Russia is seen as a threat in the document, the press makes the country seem an even greater threat, and then makes it seem as if Trump is ignoring that threat: "That is why the strategy document is unequivocal about the threat to democracies posed by Russian influence operations, even if that is not a message that President Trump always wants to hear."[43]

CNN provides a representative example of this:

> Other aspects of the strategy seem discordant with Trump's own insistence that ties with Russia be improved. While the President's strategy doesn't directly address Russian attempts to influence the US presidential election last year, it does make reference more broadly to attempts by Moscow to interfere in democratic contests. "Today, actors such as Russia are using information tools in an attempt to undermine the legitimacy of democracies," the document reads. "The American public and private sectors must recognize this and work together to defend our way of life." Trump did not mention those lines during his remarks, instead sticking to broad declarations of American superiority on the global stage.[44]

This framing was consistent through the coverage. For example, this from Fox News: "Trump did not discuss Russian meddling in the 2016 election during his remarks, though the document also notes that 'actors such as

Russia are using information tools in an attempt to undermine the legitimacy of democracies.'"[45] From *The Washington Post*: "Trump has publicly complimented Russian President Vladimir Putin, calling him 'very smart,' and has sought a better relationship with Russia after years of worsening ties under Obama. He has been openly skeptical of U.S. intelligence findings that Russia mounted a systematic effort to undermine the 2016 presidential election."[46] Most, including Fox News, highlighted Trump's relationship with Putin: "Russian President Vladimir Putin called him over the weekend to thank the CIA for help in stopping a terror plot in St. Petersburg. 'They were able to apprehend these terrorists before the event with no loss of life, and that's a great thing and the way it's supposed to work,' said Trump."[47]

## *America First*

The press never fully defined America First, but half of the articles did reference it in reports. Although mentioning the concept, CNN, like others, failed to explain beyond this description: "makes clear that 'America First' is more than just a campaign slogan but now a guiding force in the US's foreign policy making."[48] Another CNN report simply characterized the plan as, "unsurprisingly, an unabashedly 'America First' strategy that . . . is full of insights into how Trump's national security advisers see the world."[49] And as in this *Washington Post* example, no explanation for the concept was provided, even when acknowledged as central to the strategy: "presenting his 'America First' doctrine as the organizing principle for U.S. engagement around the world."[50]

Those that did offer a brief explanation generally presented a negative frame of the concept. For instance, "Trump's strategy in part also affirmed a vision of the world that aligns with one often expressed by Russian diplomats, in which states unabashedly pursue their own national interests without expressing concern for universal values. It also offered an implicit rejection of the emphasis on global cooperation that has been attributed to the foreign policy of . . . Barack Obama."[51] CBS News called it an "ideology."[52]

One aspect of the policy that generally was relayed, as in this example by Fox News, was Trump's assertion "that [although] 'America First' does not mean 'America Alone',," although it was primarily Fox alone that added that "the national security strategy makes clear that the United States will stand up for itself even at the cost of alienating allies."[53] Fox News also suggested that Trump's strategy "enshrines his 'America First' approach into U.S. policy. . . . 'America is in the game and America is going to win,' Trump said, making clear that the United States will stand up for itself even if that means acting unilaterally or alienating others on issues such as trade, climate change and immigration."[54]

## Moral Foundations

Overwhelmingly the major moral foundation conveyed by the press was the Care/Harm foundation. This is followed by the Fairness/Cheating foundation, which in turn is followed by the Loyalty(ingroup)/Betrayal foundation.

### Care/Harm

The press did relay some of Trump's Care moral foundation, most notably that "he emphasized 'protecting the homeland and American people.'"[55] Additionally, the press, as noted above, made frequent references to Russia and China and, in so doing, also relayed Trump's touchstone of Harm: "sharp references to Russia and China, which 'challenge American power, influence, and interests, attempting to erode American security and prosperity. They are determined to make economies less free and less fair...'."[56] His focus on stopping terrorists fit here as well.[57]

In terms of Care, the president was quoted as "defend[ing the] interest of American people. . . [and their] prosperity."[58] He wished to "revitalize the American economy, rebuild our military, defend our borders, protect our sovereignty and advance our values,"[59] and in international relations he "will attempt to build a great partnership with those and other countries, but in a manner that always protects our national interest."[60] Moreover, in seeking to revamp the nation's nuclear arsenal, Trump "calls those weapons 'the foundation of our strategy to preserve peace and stability by deterring aggression against the United States.'"[61] This "Preserving peace through strength" line was frequently used by the press.[62]

Yet Trump also conveyed Harm that could befall the United States, and some of this was relayed as well through quotes or paraphrases: National Security Advisor H.R. "McMaster described China's economic aggression as a threat that is . . ."[63] The administration recognizes that "weakness is the surest path to conflict and unrivaled power is the most certain means of defense."[64] And that "he's going to stand up for America no matter who threatens America."[65] And of course, China and Russia were depicted as threats that are "developing advanced weapons and capabilities that could threaten our critical infrastructure and our command and control architecture."[66] The president warned of "cyber-enabled economic warfare"[67] and that the "American public and private sectors must recognize the threat and work together to defend our way of life."[68]

Except for the "homeland" comments and Russia and China challenging American power, the other examples were minimal in terms of presence. Far more common was press re-emphasis and interpretation. That Trump did not include climate change as a security threat in the document was the single most press-generated moral foundation in this area. Fox News actually used the words of President Obama, who described climate change as an "urgent and growing threat to our national security."[69] Following this was Trump's "arguing that the US's economic security is fundamental to national security."[70] Russia and China are "attempting to erode American security and prosperity."[71]

CNN minimized Care with regard to Russia writing that Trump "referenced Russia only once, alongside China, when he called both 'rival powers.' Trump then pivoted to his call with Russian President Vladimir Putin on Sunday to discuss intelligence cooperation that thwarted a terrorist attack in Russia. The President also did not refer to Russia's influence campaigns as referenced in the national security strategy document," so, because he did not stress what the reporter thought should be emphasized, the document would not be realized.[72] And Trump "also emphasizes the importance of cybersecurity and immigration enforcement."[73]

One reason that this foundation was so influential in news discourse was the simple fact that the National Security document was about threats to the United States, and reporting of necessity had to convey that. Here are examples of this:

1. "The strategy outlined three major threats to the United States [and] outlined four pillars of the national security strategy to deal with those threats . . ."[74]
2. Russia was relayed as saying that it "could, 'not agree with such an attitude towards our country as a "threat to U.S. security,"' as Mr. Trump stated."[75]
3. "The strategy document is unequivocal about the threat to democracies posed by Russian influence operations . . ."[76]
4. "The strategy offered little else to counter the types of threats and techniques . . . utilized by Russia in influencing the 2016 election."[77]
5. The National "strategy is clear about the threat to the United States posed by cyber intrusions."[78,79]
6. "National Security document team concentrated on identifying the mounting threats posed by China."[80]
7. China made "implied military threats to persuade other states."[81]
8. China's activities in the "China Seas flouts international law, threatens the free flow of trade."[82]
9. "Trump . . . does not consider climate change a threat to U.S. national security."[83]

Other examples of this foundation are found not within single quotes but rather scattered throughout press reporting and within a variety of specific topics. Some examples:

1. China "warning that failure to [recognize it as an equal] 'would only harm [the United States] as well as others.'"[84]
2. "The Chinese side is willing to have peaceful coexistence."[85]
3. "Repeatedly calls out abusive Chinese trade practices . . ."[86]
4. "The president also called out previous American 'leaders, so many who forgot whose voices they were to respect and whose interest they were supposed to defend.' He was criticizing past administrations for interventionist foreign policy that wasted taxpayer dollars and neglected the needs of Americans at home."[87]
5. Part of National security is protecting America from North Korea.[88]
6. "The strategy document is unequivocal about the threat to democracies posed by Russian influence operations, even if that is not a message that President Trump always wants to hear."[89]
7. Trump as part of his campaign "lambasting his predecessors for damaging American security."[90]
8. "Trump determined that a major address would help underscore the document's adherence to his campaign promises of protecting American interests."[91]
9. "The United States will unilaterally defend its sovereignty."[92]
10. "Trump's doctrine holds that nation-states are in perpetual competition and that the U.S. must fight on all fronts to protect and defend its sovereignty from friend and foe alike. While the administration often says that 'America First' does not mean 'America Alone,' the national security strategy makes clear that the United States will stand up for itself even at the cost of alienating allies."[93]
11. Trump's document points out cooperation with partners who "are calling for a rejection of Islamist extremism and violence."[94]
12. "Must defend our National Security Innovation Base (NSIB) against competitors."[95]

Of note, however, is that although the discussion did bring in the Care/Harm foundation, that the press injected a strong sense of Harm into the discourse, that was not in the document or the speech. It, essentially, added that President Trump was not caring for America, but rather harming it:

1. In terms of Russian cyber-warfare (and election meddling, with the implication that Trump benefited or even colluded): "Instead of explaining the nature of these threats, he delivered a campaignlike address."[96]
2. When relaying Russian concerns about the security document, "incorrectly painted Russia as a threat to the national security."[97]
3. When Trump links economic security to national security: "Yet many of the trade tactics he has advocated could end up hurting the U.S. economy."[98]

4. The "strategy document is unequivocal about the threat to democracies posed by Russian influence operations, even if that is not a message that President Trump always wants to hear."[99]
5. "President Trump did mention the importance of 'new domains such as cyber and social media' that could be used to attack or threaten the United States, but the strategy offered little else to counter the types of threats and techniques the intelligence community says were utilized by Russia in influencing the 2016 election. Trump's strategy also does not consider climate change a threat to U.S. national security, as President Obama's national security strategy did."[100]
6. "He focused instead [of on Russian election meddling] on how a CIA tip had helped prevent a terrorist attack."[101]
7. The Communist Chinese are viewed as a threat, but only because Trump makes it so: "After Trump signed a law this month that opened the way for U.S. Navy ships to visit Taiwan, a Chinese diplomat quoted by state media said the mainland would attack the day that happened."[102]
8. Another instance of this: "The document asserts that Russia and China "want to shape a world antithetical to U.S. values and interests," which seems quite at odds with the President's own enthusiastic embrace of Russia."[103]

*The Washington Post* voiced a key news media distinction in this foundation:

> "A nation that does not protect prosperity at home cannot protect its interests abroad," Trump said. "A nation that is not prepared to win a war is a nation not capable of preventing a war. A nation that is not proud of its history cannot be confident in its future. And a nation that is not certain of its values cannot summon the will to defend them." [An source] argued that "what's missing from this document is any emphasis that the U.S. has to promote democracy and human freedom, which most American presidents . . . have felt was important. He's weakening us on these essential foundations of American power."[104]

## *Fairness/Cheating*

The single most prevalent grounding of this moral foundation was relayed through Trump's comment about trade with Russia and China: "which 'challenge American power, influence, and interests, attempting to erode American security and prosperity.' Both countries . . . 'are determined to make economies less free and less fair.'"[105] Fairness referred primarily to trade, although some mention of mutual defense reciprocity was also relayed. With regard to trade, Trump was shown as making "clear the US will ensure that trade is 'fair and reciprocal' [and] 'will no longer turn a blind eye to violations, cheating, or economic aggression.'"[106]

Stressing a campaign theme, some outlets focused on what they labeled "familiar aspects of Trump's political agenda, including his insistence that trade with other countries be fair and reciprocal."[107] Continuing along these lines, "the president emphasized his view that the United States has been cheated and taken advantage of abroad while its citizens were ill-served at home—a situation he said his security plan would seek to reverse."[108] Some outlets did mention Trump saying he would be "ripping up unfair trade agreements,"[109] with most relaying simply that he "called for 'firm action against unfair trade practices and intellectual property theft.'"[110]

In terms of America's allies, Trump was depicted in two ways, one relaying that the document stressed "'Advancing American influence abroad' through strong alliances based on reciprocity, with partners paying their fair share."[111] And the other demeaning that assertion: "'We have made clear that countries that are immensely wealthy should reimburse the United States for the cost of defending them,' Mr. Trump said. 'This is a major departure from the past, but a fair and necessary one.' The notion that allies do not share the costs of hosting American troops abroad is inaccurate. His emphasis on a dollar-for-dollar 'reimbursement' also mischaracterizes the relationship between the United States and its allies. 'That would be mercenary.'"[112]

*Loyalty(Ingroup)/Betrayal*

Although this moral foundation was present, Trump's press conveyed use of it was relegated almost exclusively to his use of "America First" policy, but not in the speech. Rather it was assumed and assigned meaning by the press: The document was "in keeping with his 'America First' policy. 'Our new strategy is based on a principle of realism guided by our national interests and rooted in our timeless values. This strategy recognizes that, whether we like it or not, we are engaged in a new era of competition,' Trump said."[113] However, this policy was never explained by the press, and confusion about its meaning was evident in that the press was unable to consistently characterize it, so it was alternately described as a policy, an "approach,"[114] a "strategy,"[115] a "campaign slogan,"[116] a "campaign theme,"[117] a "doctrine,"[118] and an "ideology."[119] Beyond this, Trump's insistence on securing the American border was relayed: "a nation without borders is not a nation."[120]

Other foundational markers were mixed throughout the press reporting. Elements from China to terrorism threatening the homeland were present, with no consistent single thread expressed:

1. Trump, on the homeland, "warns of a treacherous world in which the United States faces rising threats from an emboldened Russia and China."[121]

2. Relaying China's criticisms: "It is selfish to put your national interest above other countries' interest and the mutual interest of the international community. It will lead the United States to isolationism."[122]
3. With regard to terroristic threats to the homeland: "To confront the threat of jihadist terrorism."[123]
4. And there was a mention of Trump's call for "and a rebirth of patriotism . . ."[124]

**Press Summary**

The news media framed six key themes and conveyed three moral foundations. In terms of frames, The President's Speech About the Report Versus the Report Itself theme was essentially cast as Trump's tone versus the document's tone, and Trump was soft on Russia, but the document was not. Additionally, the speech was cast derisively as a (Trump self-aggrandizing) domestic campaign speech, and not about the document. The theme of the New Realm of Cyber Warfare/Social Media was framed as the document and Trump not specifically calling out Russia for interference in 2016 election; Trump was wrong for this, and lacked credibility. The theme of the Revisionist Powers Russia and China was framed so as to generally exclude other threats mentioned by Trump and the document, that is, Russia for election meddling and China for unfair trade. Additionally, they were implied to be not as bad a threat as Trump said. The theme of Allegations About Putin/Trump/2016 Election was framed so as to maximize the charge that Trump had not focused enough on Russian election interference. The press relayed beyond the document's tone that Russia was extremely dangerous, but that Trump diminished this. Finally, the theme of "America First" was framed to relay the president's assertion that America was to be first but not alone, yet also conveyed strong confusion about its meaning: campaign slogan, doctrine, strategy, ideology, and so on. It was not defined, and was implied to be a selfish concept

In terms of moral foundations, the news media overwhelmingly stressed the Care/Harm foundation. President Trump was relayed as wanting to protect the homeland and the American people, depicting Russia and China as trying to hurt America, and stressing peace through strength. News reports did convey security threats to the United States and, in a limited way, the Trump idea that economic security is national security. However, Trump was morally depicted as hurting the country by leaving out climate change, as not truly caring for the United States, but hurting it by ignoring Russian election meddling, understating the Russian cyber threat, overstating the China threat, and not imposing American values on other nations as part of the security document. To a much lesser degree, the news media relayed the Loyalty(ingroup)/Betrayal foundation, and here it conveyed in an ill-defined manner Trump's America First concept, as well as general threats to the homeland. Just following this foundation was the Fairness/Cheating foundation. Here Russia and China were depicted as cheating to get ahead, with Trump focusing on wanting fair trade with China, but this was reduced to a campaign theme. And, implied, making other countries pay their fair share was wrong.

## NOTES

1. Donald J. Trump, "Remarks by President Trump on the Administration's National Security Strategy," White House, December 18, 2017, https://www.whitehouse.gov/briefings-statements/remarks-president-trump-administrations-national-security-strategy/.

2. Available here: https://apps.npr.org/documents/document.html?id=4332188-Trump-s-National-Security-Strategy-Dec-2017. Referred to as National Security Document. Accessed July 8, 2019.

3. All documents available here: http://nssarchive.us/.

4. National Security Document.

5. Amanda Macias, "The US Spent $686 Billion on Defense Last Year—Here's How the Other NATO Countries Stack Up," *CNBC*, July 6, 2018, https://www.cnbc.com/2018/07/03/nato-spending-2017.html and Lucie Béraud-Sudreau and Nick Childs, "The US and its NATO Allies: Costs and Value," *International Institute for Strategic Studies*, July 9, 2018, https://www.iiss.org/blogs/military-balance/2018/07/us-and-nato-allies-costs-and-value.

6. Lauren Meltzer, "Amtrak Train Derailment: At least 3 Killed in Washington State Crash," December 18, 2017, https://www.cbsnews.com/news/washington-train-derailment-today-multiple-dead-injured-amtrak-501-high-speed-train-derails-seattle/.

7. As can be seen here, sometimes the same statement can fall into two moral foundations.

8. There were a total of eighteen articles that reported following President Trump's speech and six that reported on the administration's presentation by three anonymous senior officials.

9. Peter Bergen, "Trump's New Strategy: Russia Is an Actual Threat," CNN, December 19, 2017. CNNWR00020171219edcj004sa obtained from factiva.com.

10. Kevin Liptak, "Trump Unveils National Security Plan, Blasts Previous Presidents," CNN, December 18, 2017. CNNWR00020171218edci00bhx obtained from factiva.com.

11. Liptak, "Trump Unveils National Security Plan, Blasts Previous Presidents."

12. Ibid.

13. Ibid.

14. Linda Qiu, "Trump Inaccurately Claims 'Firsts' in Defense Speech," *The New York Times*, December 18, 2017. NYTFEED020171219edcj000xd obtained from factiva.com.

15. Barnini Chakraborty, "Trump Unveils National Security Strategy: 'America is Going to Win,'" FOX News, December 18, 2017, https://www.foxnews.com/politics/trump-unveils-nationalsecurity-strategy-america-is-going-to-win.

16. Anne Gearan and Steven Mufson, "Trump Sets Out National Security Strategy of 'principled realism' and Global Competition," *The Washington Post*, December 19, 2017. WPCOM00020171218edci005pm obtained from factiva.com.

17. Mark Landler and David E. Sanger, "Trump Delivers a Mixed Message on His National Security Approach," *The New York Times*, December 18, 2017. NYTFEED020171218edci00234 obtained from factiva.com.

18. Landler and Sanger, "Trump Delivers a Mixed Message on His National Security Approach."

19. Ibid.

20. Emily Rauhala and Andrew Roth, "China Left Wondering What 'America First' Foreign Policy Actually Means," *The Washington Post*, December 20, 2017. WPCOM00020171219edcj001xh obtained from factiva.com.

21. Rauhala and Roth, "China Left Wondering What 'America First' Foreign Policy Actually Means."

22. Josh Rogin, "Trump's National Security Strategy Marks a Hawkish Turn on China: The Document Makes the Harder U.S. Stance on China Official and Public," *The Washington Post*, December 19, 2017. WPCOM00020171219edci00002 obtained from factiva.com.

23. Chakraborty, "Trump Unveils National Security Strategy."

24. Patrick Reevell, "Russia Calls Trump's National Security Strategy 'imperialist,'" ABC News, December 19, 2017, https://abcnews.go.com/US/trumps-national-security-strategyemphasizes-competition-prosperity-home/story?id=51860497.

25. Reevell, "Russia Calls Trump's National Security Strategy 'imperialist.'"

26. Ibid.

27. Landler and Sanger, "Trump Delivers a Mixed Message on His National Security Approach."

28. Only one of the news articles covered actually went into any detail of the proposed changes: Bergen, "Trump's New Strategy."

29. Jeremy Diamond, "5 Things to Know about Trump's National Security Strategy," CNN, December 18, 2017. CNNWR00020171218edci00bq9 obtained from factiva.com.

30. Bergen, "Trump's New Strategy."

31. Landler and Sanger, "Trump Delivers a Mixed Message on His National Security Approach."

32. Gearan and Mufson, "Trump Sets Out National Security Strategy of 'principled realism' and Global Competition."

33. Andrew E. Kramer, "Russia and China Object to New 'America First' Security Doctrine," *The New York Times*, December 19, 2017. NYTFEED020171219edcj00731 obtained from factiva.com.

34. For instance, Kramer, "Russia and China Object to New 'America First' Security Doctrine."
35. Reevell, "Russia Calls Trump's National Security Strategy 'imperialist.'"
36. Ibid.
37. Ibid.
38. Diamond, "5 Things to Know about Trump's National Security Strategy."
39. Ibid.
40. Jonathan Lemire and Hope Yen, "Trump Doctrine: Economy Security Is National Security," FOX News, December 18, 2017, https://www.foxnews.com/us/trump-doctrine-economic-securityis-national-security.
41. Rogin, "Trump's National Security Strategy Marks a Hawkish Turn on China."
42. Diamond, "5 Things to Know about Trump's National Security Strategy."
43. Bergen, "Trump's New Strategy."
44. Liptak, "Trump Unveils National Security Plan, Blasts Previous Presidents."
45. Lemire and Yen, "Trump Doctrine: Economy Security Is National Security."
46. Gearan and Mufson, "Trump Sets Out National Security Strategy of 'principled realism' and Global Competition."
47. Lemire and Yen, "Trump Doctrine: Economy Security Is National Security."
48. Diamond, "5 Things to Know about Trump's National Security Strategy."
49. Bergen, "Trump's New Strategy."
50. Gearan and Mufson, "Trump Sets Out National Security Strategy of 'principled realism' and Global Competition."
51. Reevell, "Russia Calls Trump's National Security Strategy 'imperialist.'"
52. Margaret Brennan and Jillian Hughes, "Trump to Unveil National Security Strategy," CBS News, December 18, 2017, https://www.cbsnews.com/news/trump-to-unveil-national-security-strategy/.
53. Lemire and Yen, "Trump Doctrine: Economy Security Is National Security."
54. Chakraborty, "Trump Unveils National Security Strategy."
55. Sarah Kolinovsky, "Trump's National Security Strategy Emphasizes Competition and Prosperity at Home," ABC News, December 18, 2017, https://abcnews.go.com/US/trumps-nationalsecurity-strategy-emphasizes-competition-prosperity-home/story?id=51860497. See also, Anne Gearan, "National Security Strategy Plan Paints China, Russia as U.S. Competitors," *The Washington Post*, December 18, 2017. WPCOM00020171218edci001rx obtained from factiva.com; Gearan and Mufson, "Trump Sets Out National Security Strategy of 'principled realism' and Global Competition"; Lemire and Yen, "Trump Doctrine: Economy Security Is National Security"; Jaccqueline Alemany, "Trump Outlines New National Security Strategy," CBS News, December 18, 2017, https://www.cbsnews.com/news/live-trump-delivers-national-security-strategyspeech-live-stream/.
56. Brennan and Hughes, "Trump to Unveil National Security Strategy"; Rauhala and Roth, "China Left Wondering What 'America First' Foreign Policy Actually Means"; Chakraborty, "Trump Unveils National Security Strategy"; "China Reacts to Trump's National Security Strategy," CBS News, December 19, 2017, https://www.cbsnews.com/news/donald-trump-china-national-security-strategy-victoryhardliners-us-isolationism/; Alemany, "Trump Outlines New National Security Strategy."

57. Alemany, "Trump Outlines New National Security Strategy." See also, Chakraborty, "Trump Unveils National Security Strategy."

58. Gearan and Mufson, "Trump Sets Out National Security Strategy of 'principled realism' and Global Competition." See also, Gearan, "National Security Strategy Plan Paints China, Russia as U.S. Competitors," and Gearan and Mufson, "Trump Sets Out National Security Strategy of 'principled realism' and Global Competition."

59. Chakraborty, "Trump Unveils National Security Strategy."

60. Liptak, "Trump Unveils National Security Plan, Blasts Previous Presidents."

61. Landler and Sanger, "Trump Delivers a Mixed Message on His National Security Approach."

62. Kolinovsky, "Trump's National Security Strategy Emphasizes Competition and Prosperity at Home"; Bergen, "Trump's New Strategy"; Gearan, "National Security Strategy Plan Paints China, Russia as U.S. Competitors"; Gearan and Mufson, "Trump Sets Out National Security Strategy of 'principled realism' and Global Competition." Lemire and Yen, "Trump Doctrine: Economy Security Is National Security"; Alemany, "Trump Outlines New National Security Strategy."

63. Kolinovsky, "Trump's National Security Strategy Emphasizes Competition and Prosperity at Home."

64. Reevell, "Russia Calls Trump's National Security Strategy 'imperialist.'"

65. Rebecca Shabad, "H.R. McMaster says Trump Administration Will Confront Russia's 'Destabilizing Behavior,'" CBS News, December 19, 2017, https://www.cbsnews.com/news/hrmcmaster-donald-trump-administration-will-confront-russia-destabilizing-behavior/.

66. Chakraborty, "Trump Unveils National Security Strategy."

67. Rogin, "Trump's National Security Strategy Marks a Hawkish Turn on China."

68. Bergen, "Trump's New Strategy."

69. Chakraborty, "Trump Unveils National Security Strategy." See also, Gearan, "National Security Strategy Plan Paints China, Russia as U.S. Competitors"; Landler and Sanger, "Trump Delivers a Mixed Message on His National Security Approach"; Lemire and Yen, "Trump Doctrine: Economy Security Is National Security"; Bergen, "Trump's New Strategy"; Diamond, "5 Things to Know about Trump's National Security Strategy"; Alemany, "Trump Outlines New National Security Strategy."

70. Diamond, "5 Things to Know about Trump's National Security Strategy." See, too: Gearan and Mufson, "Trump Sets Out National Security Strategy of 'principled realism' and Global Competition"; Chakraborty, "Trump Unveils National Security Strategy"; Lemire and Yen, "Trump Doctrine: Economy Security Is National Security."

71. Diamond, "5 Things to Know about Trump's National Security Strategy"; Chakraborty, "Trump Unveils National Security Strategy"; Landler and Sanger, "Trump Delivers a Mixed Message on His National Security Approach."

72. Diamond, "5 Things to Know about Trump's National Security Strategy." See also: Kramer, "Russia and China Object to New 'America First' Security Doctrine"; Liptak, "Trump Unveils National Security Plan, Blasts Previous Presidents."

73. Diamond, "5 Things to Know about Trump's National Security Strategy." See also: Gearan, "National Security Strategy Plan Paints China, Russia as U.S. Competitors."

74. Kolinovsky, "Trump's National Security Strategy Emphasizes Competition and Prosperity at Home."

75. "Russia Blasts Trump's 'Imperial' National Security Strategy," CBS News, December 19, 2017, https://www.cbsnews.com/news/russia-donald-trump-imperial-national-security-strategy/.

76. Bergen, "Trump's New Strategy."

77. Kolinovsky, "Trump's National Security Strategy Emphasizes Competition and Prosperity at Home."

78. Bergen, "Trump's New Strategy."

79. Landler and Sanger, "Trump Delivers a Mixed Message on His National Security Approach."

80. Rogin, "Trump's National Security Strategy Marks a Hawkish Turn on China."

81. Ibid.

82. Bergen, "Trump's New Strategy."

83. Kolinovsky, "Trump's National Security Strategy Emphasizes Competition and Prosperity at Home."

84. Reevell, "Russia Calls Trump's National Security Strategy 'imperialist.'" See, too: Kramer, "Russia and China Object to New 'America First' Security Doctrine."

85. "China Reacts to Trump's National Security Strategy."

86. Diamond, "5 Things to Know about Trump's National Security Strategy."

87. Alemany, "Trump Outlines New National Security Strategy."

88. Shabad, "H.R. McMaster says Trump Administration Will Confront Russia's 'Destabilizing Behavior.'" See also, Lemire and Yen, "Trump Doctrine: Economy Security Is National Security."

89. Bergen, "Trump's New Strategy."

90. Liptak, "Trump Unveils National Security Plan, Blasts Previous Presidents."

91. Ibid.

92. Lemire and Yen, "Trump Doctrine: Economy Security Is National Security."

93. Ibid.

94. Ibid., and also Chakraborty, "Trump Unveils National Security Strategy."

95. Rauhala and Roth, "China Left Wondering What 'America First' Foreign Policy Actually Means."

96. Landler and Sanger, "Trump Delivers a Mixed Message on His National Security Approach."

97. Rauhala and Roth, "China Left Wondering What 'America First' Foreign Policy Actually Means."

98. Gearan and Mufson, "Trump Sets Out National Security Strategy of 'principled realism' and Global Competition."

99. Bergen, "Trump's New Strategy."

100. Kolinovsky, "Trump's National Security Strategy Emphasizes Competition and Prosperity at Home."

101. Reevell, "Russia Calls Trump's National Security Strategy 'imperialist.'"

102. "China Reacts to Trump's National Security Strategy."

103. Bergen, "Trump's New Strategy."

104. Gearan and Mufson, "Trump Sets Out National Security Strategy of 'principled realism' and Global Competition."

105. Brennan and Hughes, "Trump to Unveil National Security Strategy." See, too: Rauhala and Roth, "China Left Wondering What 'America First' Foreign Policy Actually Means"; Landler and Sanger, "Trump Delivers a Mixed Message on His National Security Approach." Kramer, "Russia and China Object to New 'America First' Security Doctrine"; Chakraborty, "Trump Unveils National Security Strategy"; Lemire and Yen, "Trump Doctrine: Economy Security Is National Security."

106. Diamond, "5 Things to Know about Trump's National Security Strategy."

107. Liptak, "Trump Unveils National Security Plan, Blasts Previous Presidents."

108. Gearan and Mufson, "Trump Sets Out National Security Strategy of 'principled realism' and Global Competition."

109. Landler and Sanger, "Trump Delivers a Mixed Message on His National Security Approach." See also, Gearan and Mufson, "Trump Sets Out National Security Strategy of 'principled realism' and Global Competition."

110. Lemire and Yen, "Trump Doctrine: Economy Security Is National Security."

111. Kolinovsky, "Trump's National Security Strategy Emphasizes Competition and Prosperity at Home."

112. Qiu, "Trump Inaccurately Claims 'Firsts' in Defense Speech." Of course, reimbursement for costs is not the same as payment for services, a point omitted by the press.

113. Kolinovsky, "Trump's National Security Strategy Emphasizes Competition and Prosperity at Home."

114. Reevell, "Russia Calls Trump's National Security Strategy 'imperialist.'"

115. Bergen, "Trump's New Strategy"; Chakraborty, "Trump Unveils National Security Strategy."

116. Landler and Sanger, "Trump Delivers a Mixed Message on His National Security Approach."

117. Gearan and Mufson, "Trump Sets Out National Security Strategy of 'principled realism' and Global Competition."

118. Ibid.

119. Alemany, "Trump Outlines New National Security Strategy."

120. Ibid.

121. Landler and Sanger, "Trump Delivers a Mixed Message on His National Security Approach."

122. "China Reacts to Trump's National Security Strategy."

123. Diamond, "5 Things to Know about Trump's National Security Strategy"; Bergen, "Trump's New Strategy."

124. Liptak, "Trump Unveils National Security Plan, Blasts Previous Presidents."

*Chapter 5*

# The Economy

On December 18, 2017, President Trump delivered a formal speech[1] at the World Economic Forum Congress Centre in Davos, Switzerland. The yearly event, colloquially known as DAVOS, attracts political, industry, media, science, and other leaders to discuss world economic strategy. Bill Clinton, in 2000, was the last American president to visit the Davos event, so Trump's presence was an anticipated moment, both for the very presence of an American president and because he had campaigned against globalism—a concept embraced by most at the event, which represents global elitism on a large scale. It was, in some sense, entering the lion's den for Trump, not only because of his anti-globalist positions, but because he was expected to promote trade deals with America. Both American and international news media were attentive.

## PRESIDENT TRUMP'S SPEECH

In a few instances, the speech offers something one would hear at a pep rally. The president is enthusiastic in giving an international declaration: America is open for business. "The world is witnessing the resurgence of a strong and prosperous America. I'm here to deliver a simple message: There has never been a better time to hire, to build, to invest, and to grow in the United States. America is open for business, and we are competitive once again."[2] In this cheerleading mode, he continues, "Now is the perfect time to bring your business, your jobs, and your investments to the United States." And much of the speech is designed to explain this. In a large sense, the speech conveys that "There has never been a better time to come to America," and that "America is the place to do business." And it shares this call to action, "So come to

America, where you can innovate, create, and build." This is the idea running through his address, and informs all of the framing of other themes.

## Framing

There are four main themes running throughout the president's speech. By far the strongest is Reforms/Results. This is followed in descending order of stress with the New Competitive Model, the American People, and Dangers in the World.

### Reform/Results

This theme speaks to both attempted reforms and results of Trump administration policy changes. The president describes the steps taken during his first year as "extraordinary strides" to restore the American dream of "a great job, a safe home, and a better life for [one's] children." Highlighting the strong economic growth since taking office, he states, "Consumer confidence, business confidence, and manufacturing confidence are the highest they have been in many decades." In particular, "Small-business optimism is at an all-time high," and this helped in the creation of "2.4 million jobs." Trump takes time to highlight not only that unemployment numbers have decreased since taking office, but that "African American unemployment has reached the lowest rate ever recorded in the United States, and so has unemployment among Hispanic Americans."

In terms of specific policy changes, he lists "fairly" enforcing laws, "dramatic" tax cuts "to make America competitive," and the elimination of "burdensome regulations at a record pace." In short, his administration is reforming the bureaucracy to make it lean, responsive, and accountable." These changes are highlighted in the speech, especially a key element of Trump's presidency to date, the Tax Cuts and Jobs Act of 2017,[3] which, according to President Trump, contained the "most significant tax cuts and reform in American history." Citing "massive" tax cuts for "the middle class and small businesses," the president also highlights the lowering of the "corporate tax rate from 35 percent, all the way down to 21 percent." (Or tied for third highest rate in the world to approximately ninetieth.) In addition to tax reform, he highlights regulatory reform, stating that "now is the perfect time to bring your business, your jobs, and your investments to the United States," because "we have undertaken the most extensive regulatory reduction ever conceived." Highlighting this reduction, he states that the target goal was the elimination of two old regulations for each one new regulation, but then relays how his administration had "cut 22 burdensome regulations for every 1 new rule,"[4] with the result that America is "freeing our businesses and workers so they can thrive and flourish as never before," and that creates an "environment that attracts capital, invites investment, and rewards production."

In addition to the specific domestic reforms, he highlights changes to America's approach to international trade, specifically addressing international concerns about his anti-globalist stance. Stressing that trade must promote "broadly shared prosperity and rewards to those who play by the rules," the president continues, stating his administration will "enforce [America's] trade laws and restore integrity to [America's] trading system." In an international setting, "fair and reciprocal trade can . . . create a system that works not just for the U.S. but for all nations."

All of these reforms are, of course, intertwined with the idea of America being open for business: "America is roaring back, and now is the time to invest in the future of America."

## Competitive Model

The call for increased business with America is made within a new competitive model. Rather than a zero-sum game, the president suggests that strong, independent nations who, along with America, will be the key "for a future in which everyone can prosper, and every child can grow up free from violence, poverty, and fear." This was stated within the context of the president's policy of "America First," something critics of the president viewed with alarm. Addressing this, the president states, "But America first does not mean America alone. When the United States grows, so does the world. American prosperity has created countless jobs all around the globe, and the drive for excellence, creativity, and innovation in the U.S. has led to important discoveries that help people everywhere live more prosperous and far healthier lives."

Healthy trade is promoted as a cornerstone of prosperity for the Trump administration, and he stresses this well in his speech, stating that, "the United States is prepared to negotiate mutually beneficial, bilateral trade agreements with all countries." For the president, "we are all stronger when free, sovereign nations cooperate toward shared goals and they cooperate toward shared dreams." In this sense, the competitive model involves more than just seeking trade and profit. It involves leaders looking out for the people of their countries: "Each of you has the power to change hearts, transform lives, and shape your countries' destinies. With this power comes an obligation, however—a duty of loyalty to the people, workers, and customers who have made you who you are." These are obligations that are not exclusionary; they do not separate nations, but allow for the building of strong nations who can work together for mutual benefit. With this in mind, President Trump states, together then "let us resolve to use our power, our resources, and our voices, not just for ourselves, but for our people—to lift their burdens, to raise their hopes, and to empower their dreams; to protect their families, their communities, their histories, and their futures."

## American People

The important element of Trump administration reforms is not so much about improving the business environment as it is improving the lives of the American people. For example, the president calls regulation "stealth taxation," saying that "unelected bureaucrats [have] imposed crushing and anti-business and anti-worker regulations on our citizens with no vote, no legislative debate, and no real accountability." Thus, for him and his policies, the idea of America First is rooted in his ideals about America: "I believe in America. As President of the United States, I will always put America first, just like the leaders of other countries should put their country first also." Putting America First means, "Just like we expect the leaders of other countries to protect their interests, as President of the United States, I will always protect the interests of our country, our companies, and our workers."

The policy of America First is intertwined with the competitive model. The importance of this interrelationship with the economic recovery and expansion, as well as its relationship to America's international agenda, is an idea stressed by Trump as he taps into the leadership roles and abilities of those in the immediate audience: "To be successful, it is not enough to invest in our economy. We must invest in our people. When people are forgotten, the world becomes fractured. Only by hearing and responding to the voices of the forgotten can we create a bright future that is truly shared by all."

Ultimately, the president's economic model is rooted in the American people: "The nation's greatness is more than the sum of its production. A nation's greatness is the sum of its citizens: the values, pride, love, devotion, and character of the people who call that nation home." Success necessitates cooperation, and far from saying America will act alone in the world, the president invites other nations to "become part of this incredible future we are building together."

## Dangers

The president did not deliver an entirely "feel good" or pep rally–style speech. He made it clear that the world faces dangers to its prosperity; this included many of those repeatedly stressed by American presidents such as "rogue regimes [and] terrorism" but also "revisionist powers, those nations such as North Korea and Iran who seek to undermine the world order." To better combat such attempts, he asks "friends and allies to invest in their own defenses and to meet their financial obligations. Our common security requires everyone to contribute their fair share." Additionally, he wishes to "unite all civilized nations in our campaign of maximum pressure to de-nuke the Korean Peninsula," and to "confront Iran's support for terrorists" and its push to "obtain nuclear weapons."

But in addition to these threats from revisionist nations and terrorists, President Trump includes piratical trade practices that undermine free and equitable trade for all and insists that there can be no "free and open trade if some countries exploit the system at the expense of others. We support free trade, but it needs to be fair and it needs to be reciprocal. Because, in the end, unfair trade undermines us all." And because of this, the United States would "no longer turn a blind eye to unfair economic practices, including massive intellectual property theft, industrial subsidies, and pervasive state-led economic planning. These and other predatory behaviors are distorting the global markets and harming businesses and workers, not just in the U.S., but around the globe."

## Moral Foundations

Four moral foundations were present. One, Fairness/Cheating, is slightly more powerful than the others, followed by Care/Harm and Loyalty(ingroup)/Betrayal possessing relatively the same strength. Authority/Subversion was minimally present.[5]

### Fairness/Cheating

Running strongly throughout all of the speech was the idea of fair trade and opportunities. It is essentially unfair that "unelected bureaucrats" are imposing "crushing and anti-business and anti-worker regulations on our citizens with no vote, no legislative debate, and no real accountability." The push against this anti-trade contingent is made strongly in the speech, "We are reforming the bureaucracy to make it lean, responsive, and accountable. And we are ensuring our laws are enforced fairly." Additionally, to counter the anti-business element, the Trump administration is "creating an environment that attracts capital, invites investment, and rewards production" in large part through making "domestic reforms to unleash jobs and growth." Additionally, and speaking to both the domestic and international audience, the administration is "working to reform the international trading system so that it promotes broadly shared prosperity and rewards to those who play by the rules."

Essentially President Trump argues that both America and the world "cannot have free and open trade if some countries [most notably Communist China] exploit the system at the expense of others. We support free trade, but it needs to be fair and it needs to be reciprocal. Because, in the end, unfair trade undermines us all." Ultimately, he argues that his administration has attacked "unfair economic practices" and is "insisting on fair and reciprocal trade."

*Care/Harm*

Harm is not heavily stressed, although it is presented as linked with bureaucratic red tape. President Trump asserts that "unelected bureaucrats" who are "all over the place" have continually made it increasingly difficult for businesses to prosper. Additionally, "predatory behaviors [by some countries and businesses] are distorting the global markets and harming businesses and workers, not just in the U.S., but around the globe."

His primary moral focus appears to be on how his administration's policies act to care for the American people, and by extension, in some ways, for the peoples of the world. They "advance prosperity, security, and peace," and have "created 2.4 million jobs" through tax cuts "for the middle class and small businesses to let working families keep more of their hard-earned money." The policies on energy use act to "provide affordable power to our citizens and businesses, and to promote energy security for our friends all around the world." And linking the American policies here specifically to helping other countries, such as the Ukraine, the president states that no "country should be held hostage to a single provider of energy."

Economic goals do not take place in a vacuum, and this is highlighted in the speech when the president states, "We cannot have prosperity without security. To make the world safer from rogue regimes, terrorism, and revisionist powers, we are asking our friends and allies to invest in their own defenses and to meet their financial obligations." He asks specifically for joint actions to "Unite all civilized nations" in confronting rogue nations and providing security to the world. The end result should be for "every child [to] grow up free from violence, poverty, and fear." But he also makes clear that his first priority is protecting America, and that such protection includes securing the border, stating that he will "protect our nation. We will defend our citizens and our borders." His policies have been enacted for "securing our immigration system, as a matter of both national and economic security."

*Loyalty(Ingroup)/Betrayal*

This moral foundation in intertwined with Fairness and Care, and is linked strongly, in keeping with President Trump's policy of America First, to the

American people. It is also linked, however, with the civilized and rule following nations of the world. Trump is at DAVOS to "represent the interests of the American people and to affirm America's friendship and partnership in building a better world." Moreover, his administration's economic policies are "lifting up forgotten communities, creating exciting new opportunities, and helping every American find their path to the American Dream." Moreover, his administration is "committed to developing [America's] workforce [and is] lifting people from dependence to independence."

Importantly, and explaining his idea behind his administration's policy of America First, President Trump shares, "I believe in America. As President of the United States, I will always put America first, just like the leaders of other countries should put their country first also." And here the idea of ingroup helps others beyond American shores: "But America first does not mean America alone. When the United States grows, so does the world. American prosperity has created countless jobs all around the globe." In a particularly telling example of ingroup attention, he states, "A nation's greatness is the sum of its citizens."

*Authority/Subversion*

Authority does not necessarily mean authoritarian, and here we see Authority being linked strongly with Loyalty(ingroup), and for Trump, it is linked to the people. Pointedly his foundational use of Subversion is not enjoined with opposition to his policies, but to "state-led economic planning." Although President Trump does promote his role as leader of the American people—as "President of the United States, I will always protect the interests of our country, our companies, and our workers"—he includes this into the Loyalty(ingroup)/Authority mix and asserts it directly at the group elite global leaders: "Each of you has the power to change hearts, transform lives, and shape your countries' destinies. With this power comes an obligation, however—a duty of loyalty to the people, workers, and customers who have made you who you are." Additionally, the president enjoins the world leaders to "use our power, our resources, and our voices, not just for ourselves, but for our people—to lift their burdens, to raise their hopes, and to empower their dreams; to protect their families, their communities, their histories, and their futures."

**Trump Summary**

The president's speech framed four key themes and conveyed four moral foundations. In terms of frames, Reforms/Results essentially relayed that tax and regulation cuts were excellent for trade, the economy was roaring back to life, and that Trump was focusing on fair trade for all. The New Competitive Model relayed that America first is not America alone, that it is healthy for independent nations to put their people first, trading as equals, because a nation's people should come first. The American People frame sought to convey that the purpose of reform is primarily to improve lives of Americans, to invest in the people; this is the concept of America First. The Dangers in the World frame was direct in confronting that which could derail prosperity: terrorism, rogue nations, revisionist powers (Russia, China); moreover, this frame highlighted unfair trade practices, and insisted that there must be common security with all paying their fair share.

In terms of the moral foundations, overwhelmingly the president stressed the Fairness/Cheating foundation. He categorized unelected bureaucrats (the Bureaucracy) as inherently unfair, so his policies minimizing regulations to allow businesses to work more efficiently, benefiting more Americans, is fair. His administration is working to stop unfair trade practices to insure greater prosperity for all. In short, stop "unfair economic practices" and insist "on fair and reciprocal trade." The next two foundations were roughly coequal in emphasis. In terms of the Care/Harm foundation, the president stressed that predatory trade practices and unelected bureaucrats are harming Americans. The actions of the administration are meant to care for and to protect first the American people, and tangentially for the peoples of the world. Better trade and better security, including the border, are a priority for the administration, but can also be had by all. To effect this, others must care for their people first as well, and part of this is by participating in mutually beneficial security arrangements. The Loyalty(ingroup)/Betrayal foundations are conveyed through Trump working to better the lives of the American people. The people come first, as part of his America First policy. Policies are in place to lift up Americans and their communities. For Trump, "A nation's greatness is the sum of its citizens." Although strongly American for the ingroup, Trump also enlarges America First to embrace the idea of "not America alone," stating that other nations should put their people first, and come together to mutually beneficial arrangements for all civilized nations. Finally, the foundation of Authority/Subversion has subversive elements in the sense of "state-led economic planning." Trump does speak of his authority as the leader of the American people, but imparts this to all the leaders at DAVOS, insisting that with "this power comes an obligation . . . a duty of loyalty to the people, workers, and customers who have made you who you are." Leaders are in a position of power, of authority, to work for their people.

## PRESS RESPONSE

### Framing

*America First*

The America First policy was used by Trump during his 2016 campaign, and has come to be the cornerstone of his foreign policy.[6] Even as he refers to it, controversy swirls around it, so he does take the time to interweave, as shown above, explanations of it in his addresses. The press, when referring to it, usually ignore these references, and instead simply reiterate the term, sometimes even redefining it, at times with hostility.[7] Although Trump calls it a policy, the press usually does not. For example, ABC related it to a campaign, writing, "Trump's 'America First' *platform*."[8] Others suggested that he was "making the case for ["defending" ] his 'America First' *agenda* . . . taking his sales pitch on the U.S. economy to the alpine ski village."[9] For CBS News, President Trump was "touting his 'America First' *message*."[10] No mention of what America first means was made. CNN focused on, "tailored his 'America First' *message* to the Davos crowd."[11] And also that Trump "pushed his 'America First' *message* abroad."[12] And that he "touted" his "America First" *agenda*."[13] NBC suggested that Trump was using the speech to both invite foreign investment and to "insist that his 'America First' *vision* doesn't equate with isolationism."[14]

Although some did relay that he "highlighted his 'America First' policy," these moments were minimally expanded, usually only to add, "he will says [*sic*] that he will always put America first, but he says, 'America First does not mean America alone.'"[15] And "the president delivered a mostly mild address, insisting that 'America First' did not mean 'America alone' and that his country's economic success was a boon to the rest of the world."[16] Some did expand beyond this, providing excerpts: "'As president of the United States, I will always put America first, just like the leaders of other countries should put their countries first also,' Trump . . . told the crowd. 'But "America First" does not mean America alone,' Trump added."[17] Along these same lines *The New York Times* wrote, "Mr. Trump reassured the world's political and financial leaders that his 'America First' agenda was not a rejection of international cooperation. The combative nationalist gave way to the let's-make-a-deal businessman, as he invited them to invest in what he called a resurgent United States. 'I believe in America,' Mr. Trump told a jampacked auditorium on the last day of the annual World Economic Forum in Davos. 'As president of the United States, I will always put America first, just like the leaders of other countries should put their country first also. But America first does not mean America alone. When the United States grows, so does the world.'"[18]

The contrast between Trump's "combative nationalism" and business concerns was highlighted in a kinder manner by *The Washington Post*, which noted that he was "wrapping his 'America first' message of sovereignty in a salesman's offer to other nations and businesses." The article continued, relaying:

> Trump's keynote address to the World Economic Forum was a gentler delivery of his trademark economic populism and the trade protectionism on which he campaigned. His invitation for mutual economic advancement was an implicit answer to criticism that he is leading a retreat from U.S. global leadership. "I believe in America. As president of the United States, I will always put America first. Just like the leaders of other countries should put their countries first. But America first does not mean America alone," Trump said.[19]

CNN offered its own interpretation of Trump's America First policy while also mentioning the contrast with Trump's populist message and global concerns: "And while the president did tout the commercial benefits of his 'America First' agenda—a climate of competitive taxes and relaxed regulations—he downplayed the resentments and anger that have colored his previous assessments of the global financial elite."[20]

*Populism/Globalism*

Running throughout this frame was the sense that globalism is a good and that nationalism/populism is a negative. The press did note that Trump had "toned down his populist rhetoric. . . . 'The speech had a very strong domestic focus.'"[21] And that he had "donned a salesman's hat . . . rather than using the platform . . . to rail against globalization."[22] Additionally, the contrast between Trump as populist and the global concerns of DAVOS went well beyond the mainstream media (MSM) frame of America First, in some cases implying that Trump was responsible for division in the world: "The theme of this year's summit is 'Creating a Shared Future in a Fractured World,' an acknowledgement of some of the nationalist and populist forces Trump has channeled in the United States and their impact on globalization."[23] Additionally, it was made to seem as if Trump was the only concern at DAVOS: "Trump's presence also loomed large over the gathering ahead of the event: The World Economic Forum's annual Global Risk Report analyzing long-term worldwide risk warned that 'charismatic strongman politics is on the rise across the world,' citing Trump's 'America First' platform. The report also argued that Trump's fulfillment of unilateralist campaign promises to withdraw from the Trans-Pacific Partnership and Paris climate agreement contributed to the "erosion of institutions of multilateral dialogue and decision-making."[24]

In some ways the press set this up. For instance, *The Washington Post* wrote, "The business elite viewed President Trump's inauguration and nationalistic brand of politics with high anxiety."[25] And that participants had "been awaiting Trump's remarks to the World Economic Forum with a sense of dread, fearing he'd use the platform to shame global elites in the same manner he railed against them during his populist presidential campaign."[26] This contrast was routinely pushed: "Donald J. Trump the candidate denounced what he called 'the false song of globalism.' A year after taking office, President Trump came on Friday to tell the elites at Davos, who composed the song, that maybe they could still perform in harmony."[27] However, this was qualified, with the implication being that Trump was opportunistically changing his "rhetoric": "That did not mean Mr. Trump has joined the globalism chorus. He has spent much of the last year trying to dismantle the international political and economic system represented by the Davos consensus. . . . But his unlikely visit to Davos was meant to be a shift in tone from his populist, protectionist rhetoric."[28] *The Washington Post* presented it this way, "A gentler delivery of his trademark economic populism and the trade protectionism on which he campaigned. His invitation for mutual economic advancement was an implicit answer to criticism that he is leading a retreat from U.S. global leadership."[29]

The idea of selling America, that Trump was acting the part of salesman, was frequently seen: "Sounding more like the businessman he used to be than the outspoken populist he has become . . . [he] said he favored free trade, provided that abusive trade practices by other countries were curbed. But almost completely missing from his remarks was the sometimes confrontational nationalism of his election campaign and many of his tweets."[30] In another example, Trump was depicted as "dispensing with the blood-and-soil nationalism of his last major address in Europe, Trump instead framed his presidency as that of a deregulating, tax-cutting business titan. Many in the gathering of high-flying executives and financiers lapped it up."[31]

## Open for Business

"'America is open for business,' he said."[32] This frame is linked with Trump's salesman pitch mentioned above. Essentially, it conveyed the more enthusiastic elements of Trump's speech, but in essence did so without context or explanation, so Trump was basically portrayed as making a claim, but then his reasons for doing so are not shared with readers. Some examples:

1. "Sounding at moments like the president of a local chamber of commerce, Trump declared 'there has never been a better time to do business in America.'"

2. Trump was "telling business and political leaders the United States 'is open for business. Now is the perfect time to bring your business, your jobs, your investments to the United States,' he said. 'When the United States grows, so does the world.'"[33]
3. "'The world is witnessing the resurgence of a strong and prosperous America. . . . There has never been a better time to hire, to build, to invest and to grow in the United States,' he says. . . . 'America is open for business and we are competitive once again.'"[34]

Although "open for business" was strongly linked with growth in Trump's speech, only a few articles mentioned some positive aspects of growth, although when more than just the simple claim was presented, the evidence was minimized:

3. "'America is open for business and we are competitive once again,' declared Trump, touting strong gains in the stock market since his election and other economic gains."[35]
4. "Pointing to his administration's successful push to cut regulations and enact a tax reform package, Trump told the group of foreign bankers and dignitaries that 'there has never been a better time to invest, build and grow in the United States.'"[36]

## Trade

The international trade system, and America's role in it, was another major theme of the news media here. Essentially, this frame was the result of reporting Trump's statements on trade, but also were intertwined with the Open for Business frame mentioned above. Trump was reported as saying that the "international system 'needs to be fair . . . unfair trade undermines us all.'"[37] Trump's idea of fairness was also relayed: "The U.S. won't turn a 'blind eye' to unfair trade practices, Trump declared, while expressing a willingness to enter agreements that benefit all parties. Trump's remarks were eagerly anticipated for any clues they might offer on the direction of American trade policy, which has taken a more combative stance in recent weeks. President Trump last week approved tariffs on imported solar equipment and watching machines, raising concerns about U.S. protectionism."[38] Additionally, "He insisted Friday that trade relationships must be fair and what he calls 'reciprocal,' but he did not dwell on the theme that the United States routinely gets the short end of the international trade stick."[39] The Trump administration idea of enforcement and fair trade was relayed: "'We will enforce our trade laws and restore integrity to the trading system. Only by insisting on fair and reciprocal trade can we create a system that works not just for the U.S. but for all nations,' he says, adding that the U.S. will work on 'mutually beneficial' trade agreements including with those countries that were members of the Trans-Pacific Partnership (TPP)."[40]

*Attacking the Press*

During an after-speech interview with Schwab, President Trump mentioned the contrast of positive press he received as a businessman with the negative press he had received both as candidate and president. Half of the news articles made mention of his "attack" on the press: "He could not resist a jab at the 'fake' media."[41] However, CBS news was only one of the three articles that mentioned this was in the question-and-answer session following the speech, and perhaps had the most neutral presentation of the exchange: "He also said that he has benefited from friendly press coverage as a businessman, but when he became president, he realized how 'fake' the press can be."[42] ABC news also mentioned this, but added what turns out to be an extreme minority response: "Some attendees in the audience booed when he criticized media coverage of his administration in a brief question and answer session following his speech."[43] *The New York Times* also wrote that he "could not resist referring to 'fake news' outlets in a brief question-and-answer session after his speech. 'It wasn't until I became a politician that I realized how nasty, how mean, how vicious, and how fake the press can be,' he said."[44]

Of note is that only a few of the over 1,000 in attendance live "booed," even as some in the press played this moment up while driving the overall negative tone of this frame:

1. CNN wrote, "Deriding the 'nasty, mean, and fake' news media, Trump drew boos and hisses from the crowd."[45]
2. And in a different CNN report: "Deriding the 'nasty, mean, and fake' news media, Trump drew boos and hisses from the crowd of global elites, a break from the otherwise polite reception he received here at the yearly summit for the world's ultra-wealthy."[46]
3. And in another CNN report: "Crowd boos as Trump calls media 'fake.'"[47]
4. NBC News wrote: "He also hit a familiar anti-media note: 'It wasn't until I became a politician that I realized how nasty, how mean, how vicious and how fake press can be,' he said. The comments prompted boos from members of the crowd."[48]
5. *The Washington Post* also reported in this manner, "a dig at the 'nasty' press, which drew boos from the audience."[49]
6. Also from *The Washington Post*, "He drew hisses and boos, as well as some laughter, when he told World Economic Forum founder Klaus Schwab that 'it wasn't until I became a politician that I realized how nasty, how mean, how vicious and how fake the press can be.'"[50]

CNN specifically related an anti–climate change activist saying that only about 20–30 percent of attendees applauded Trump, even as the video tape suggests a much higher percentage and also shows numerous attendees giving a standing ovation.[51]

Trump's actual remarks present greater insight into the intentionally negative tone of this press frame.

> The other thing is, I've always seemed to get, for whatever reason, a disproportionate amount of press or media. (Laughter.) Throughout my whole life—somebody will explain someday why—but I've always gotten a lot. (Laughter.) And as businessman I was always treated really well by the press. The numbers speak and things happen, but I've always really had a very good press. And it wasn't until I became a politician that I realized how nasty, how mean, how vicious, and how fake the press can be. As the cameras start going off in the background. (Laughter.)

So, whereas some in the media framed reception of Trump's remarks negatively, when one reads the official transcript or listens to the tape, that while there are a couple of boos, there is more laughter, and some applause as well.[52]

## Moral Foundations

News media moral foundations fell into three groups. First, Loyalty (ingroup)/Betrayal was the largest concentration of moral statements, far out sizing in emphasis the other two groups. Care/Harm and Fairness/Cheating were considerably smaller, although with about coequal representation.

### *Loyalty(Ingroup)/Betrayal*

The president was depicted as a nationalist who supports America: "I believe in America"[53] and as relaying that America was again ascendant: "The world is witnessing the resurgence of a strong and prosperous America. . . . There has never been a better time to hire, to build, to invest and to grow in the United States. . . . America is open for business and we are competitive once again."[54] The nationalistic sentiment was highlighted here: "As president of the United States, I will always put America first, just like the leaders of other countries should put their countries first also." Few included the extension to this by relaying, "'But "America First" does not mean America alone,' Trump added."[55]

Although the words of the president were conveyed, the media presented a different sense of morality than Ingroup, actually inferring a Betrayal of the global. How Trump used his policy phrase, "America First" was taken to task: "President Trump plans to make the case for his "America First" agenda."[56] And implying criticism, Trump was depicted as having "defended his 'America First' policy agenda" in his speech.[57] He was relayed as taking "a less aggressive stance than some anticipated in touting his 'America First' message, saying leaders of other countries should also look after their nation's interest."[58] And only because he was in the heart of globalism did he, hypocritically, tailor "his 'America First' message to the Davos crowd, and toned down his populist rhetoric."[59] In so doing, he was "dispensing with the blood-and-soil nationalism of his [previous] major address in Europe."[60] Even so, the America First policy was depicted as a betrayal to a news media-supported globalism. For instance, ABC News reported that globalists "analyzing long-term worldwide risk warned that 'charismatic strongman politics is on the rise across the world,' citing Trump's 'America First' platform."[61] Set up as harmful, it was thus a betrayal. The media highlighted "Trump's continued skepticism about international arrangements that he sees as infringements on U.S. sovereignty."[62] The news media downplayed Trump's claims of being for the people, impugning such claims as "faux populism," asserting without evidence a growing American disapproval of Trump's economic agenda. "It's not an America First agenda, it's a Billionaires First agenda."[63]

Even though some in the news media relayed the positive aspects of the Trump tax reductions, "now corporations are paying bonuses and boosting wages for American workers,"[64] the overwhelming sense was of betrayal of liberal moral principles: Trump acted to "implement . . . protectionist and isolationist economic policies."[65] Immigration was specifically brought into the mix by the media, and although his immigration proposal was minimally described as being portrayed by Trump as "in the interest of economic and national security,"[66] the press countered this with warnings of "some wariness about [his] presidential style and apprehension about his stance on immigration."[67] This included bringing in critics of "Trump's move to end the Deferred Action for Childhood Arrivals, the Obama-era program protecting immigrants."[68] And it also included linking economics to other media-highlighted issues in order to show Trump as a betrayer of America: "'I strongly disagree with President Trump's reaction to the events that took place in Charlottesville,' [said a critic.] 'Constructive economic and regulatory policies are not enough and will not matter if we do not address the divisions in our country.'"[69]

## Care/Harm

Although Trump was depicted as nationalistic, his message to work with other countries for mutual security was sometimes relayed: "Calling on other countries to work together in the fight against ISIS and to address North

Korea's nuclear program, Trump said 'our common security requires everyone to contribute their fair share.'"[70] Trade, which sometimes fell within this context, was also highlighted, particularly his specific call to fight against the harm caused by others' 'Predatory behaviors' that are "distorting global markets."[71] Trump's concerns about Communist China being a "direct threat" were relayed, a threat characterized by China's "technology transfers, by disrespect for intellectual property rights, by commercial espionage, by all kinds of bad things."[72]

In addition to relaying these aspects of Trump's Care foundation (mainly the Harm that others could do to the United States), the media did relay some random aspects of Trump's Care foundation, such as one instance of wishing to work with Palestinians to "come to the table to negotiate peace with Israel."[73] Or, in one instance, "J.P. Morgan says it will spend $20 billion over five years to raise hourly pay of its workers and open new branches in the U.S."[74] But such instances were unusual, since the overall sense was of a minimization of any Caring component to the Trump rhetoric. For example, one article suggested that in President Reagan's time, "working-class Americans were struggling and beginning to give up hope." And for "Trump . . . inequality had skyrocketed, working-class Americans felt abandoned and many despaired." But then, it suggested, neither president really had anything to do with the positive economy following their policy initiatives, only that "maybe it's just the jolt of change itself that counts. Maybe the economy just needs a good hard kick from time to time to get the engine to turn over and the thing going forward again."[75] And often the Care foundation was evoked to show Harm:

1. "worldwide risk" because of nationalistically inclined "charismatic strongman politics," of which "Trump's 'America First' platform" figures prominently.[76]
2. Trump's "withdraw from the Trans-Pacific Partnership and Paris climate agreement" causing harm.[77]
3. Trump as "a danger to the world."[78]

*Fairness/Cheating:*

One area in which the media conveyed a better sense of President Trump's moral foundations was in his sense of Fairness: "The international system 'needs to be fair . . . unfair trade undermines us all.'"[79] And another instance commonly used is: "We support free trade, but it needs to be fair and it needs to be reciprocal because, in the end, unfair trade undermines us all. The United States will no longer turn a blind eye to unfair economic practices."[80] These commonly coalesced into something along these lines: "The U.S. won't turn a 'blind eye' to unfair trade practices, Trump declared, while expressing a willingness to enter agreements that benefit all parties."[81] Another variation of this is: "'We will enforce our trade laws and restore integrity to the trading system. Only by insisting on fair and reciprocal trade can we create a system that works not just for the U.S. but for all nations,' he says, adding that the U.S. will work on 'mutually beneficial' trade agreements including with those countries that were members of the Trans-Pacific Partnership (TPP)."[82]

This sense of cooperative fairness was also shared by relaying Trump's call for "other countries to work together in the fight against ISIS and to address North Korea's nuclear program":

1. "our common security requires everyone to contribute their fair share."[83]
2. "all countries should contribute 'their fair share' when it comes to common security.[84]
3. "He insisted Friday that trade relationships must be fair and what he calls 'reciprocal.'"[85]
4. And a lone quote: "Stay optimistic. I think the [Trump] administration is fighting for fairness."[86]

However, the press did not expand on Trump's ideas, and when not conveying the president's own words, the press was generally negative, focusing on its perceptions of inequalities. For instance, tax cuts would "worsen inequality."[87] And Obama "addressed global challenges such as climate change and widening inequality,"[88] but Trump did not.

## Press Summary

The news media framed five key themes and conveyed three moral foundations. In terms of frames, America First was undefined within the frame, with the news media showing confusion about its status—policy, slogan, agenda, and so on—even as through the framing it implied it was wrong because it promotes nationalism. The theme of the Populism/Globalism was framed to highlight globalism as a good, with nationalism and populism as negative forces harmful to the United States and the movement toward globalism. Trump was in DAVOS "selling" America, being a salesman, so hypocritically downplayed his anti-globalism. In terms of the framing of "Open for Business," the press conveyed this using only Trump's assertions, so minimal evidence provided for his making the claim. He was playing the role of the "salesman," related to the above. The theme of Trade did relay Trump's comments that trade must be fair, and that he sought for predatory practices to be ended. Finally, the theme of Attacking the Press was framed as Trump finding it irresistible to attack the press, and that it was a deliberate moment in the speech that was received with condemnation—boos.

In terms of moral foundations, the news media overwhelmingly stressed the Loyalty(ingroup)/Betrayal foundation. Although the words of the president were conveyed, the media presented a different sense of morality than the president's ingroup, actually inferring his betrayal of the global. He was depicted as scaling back his nationalistic rhetoric only because he was in the heart of the globalist community. Thus, for the press, there was a clear clash between Trump's *American* Ingroup Loyalty and the news media *globalist* Ingroup Loyalty, with Trump made to be betrayer, not those who put global interests ahead of American interests: he betrayed globalist ideals to "implement . . . protectionist and isolationist economic policies" which ultimately benefited, according the press, a privileged few instead of the people (of the world). The next strongest foundation was Care/Harm. Although some aspects of Trump's Care foundation were relayed, stronger was the Harm foundation, with China and unfair trade practices harming the United States. But, ultimately, Trump and his policies were characterized as causing Harm, regardless of the empirical data on the economy. Finally, the Fairness/Cheating foundation did most accurately reflect Trump's foundational aspects, although not quite. The foundational "fairness" in trade was well conveyed by the news media, although with a stress on cooperative fairness through a willingness to enter into larger, multinational trade agreements. Thus, not related to Loyalty to America/People (Trump), but rather Loyalty to the global (Press). However, when not conveying the president's own words, the press was generally negative, focusing on inequalities such as what the news media believed about the tax cuts, and immigration concerns.

## NOTES

1. Donald J. Trump, "Remarks by President Trump to the World Economic Forum [Davos, Switzerland,]" January 26, 2018, https://www.whitehouse.gov/briefings-statements/remarks-president-trump-world-economic-forum/.

2. "Donald Trump Speaks at Davos 2018," YouTube.com, accessed July 13, 2019, https://www.youtube.com/watch?v=UT7GlaDc060.

3. See, https://www.irs.gov/newsroom/tax-cuts-and-jobs-act-a-comparison-for-businesses; https://taxfoundation.org/final-tax-cuts-and-jobs-act-details-analysis/; and https://www.heritage.org/taxes/report/analysis-the-2017-tax-cuts-and-jobs-act.

4. Clyde Wayne Crews, "Trump Exceeds One-In, Two-Out Goals On Cutting Regulations, But It May Be Getting Tougher," *Forbes*, October 23, 2018, https://www.forbes.com/sites/waynecrews/2018/10/23/trump-exceeds-one-in-two-out-goals-on-cutting-regulations-but-it-may-be-getting-tougher/#5f1205803d40.

5. Just barely present was Sanctity/Degradation, which does play a role in the speech when the president explains his policies as an attempt to "restore integrity to our trading system." Moreover, he explains that "We cannot have free and open trade if some countries exploit the system at the expense of others."

6. There were a total of twenty articles that reported following President Trump's speech.

7. Griff Witte and Michael Birnbaum, "A Year of Trump's 'America First' Agenda Has Radically Changed the US Role in the World," *The Washington Post*, January 20, 2018, https://www.washingtonpost.com/world/a-year-of-trumps-america-first-agenda-has-radically-changed-the-us-role-in-the-world/2018/01/20/c1258aa6-f7cf-11e7-9af7-a50bc3300042_story.html?utm_term=.d378a790de86; see also, https://www.whitehouse.gov/search/?s=america+first.

8. Benjamin Siegel, "Trump Addresses Business Leaders at Davos: 'Now is the time to invest in the future of America,'" ABC News, January 26, 2018, https://abcnews.go.com/Politics/trump-addresses-business-leaders-davos-now-time-invest/story?id=52629607. Emphasis mine.

9. Benjamin Siegel, "Trump Touts Relationship with May, Threatens Palestinian Aid at Davos Gathering of Global Elite," ABC News, January 25, 2018, https://abcnews.go.com/Politics/trump-touts-relationship-threatens-palestinian-aid-davos-gathering/story?id=52591507. Emphasis mine.

10. "Stocks Rise as Trump Declares America 'open for business,'" CBS News, January 26, 2018, https://www.cbsnews.com/news/stock-futures-rise-as-trump-declares-america-open-for-business/ Emphasis mine.

11. Alanna Petroff and Ivana Kottasová, "What Davos Thought of Trump's Speech," CNN, January 26, 2018, https://www.cnn.com/2018/01/26/politics/read-trump-davos-speech/index.html. Emphasis mine.

12. "Trump Swaggers into Davos Ready to Take on the World," CNN, January 25, 2018, https://www.cnn.com/2018/01/25/politics/donald-trump-davos-speech/index.html. Emphasis mine.

13. "Trump Swaggers into Davos Ready to Take on the World."

14. Adam Edelman, "Trump to Davos: 'America First Does Not Mean America Alone,'" NBC News, January 26, 2018, https://www.nbcnews.com/politics/donald-trump/trump-tells-davos-crowd-america-first-does-not-mean-america-n841306. Emphasis mine.

15. Rebecca Shabad, "Trump Says 'America is open for business' in Address to World Economic Forum at Davos," CBS News, January 26, 2018, https://www.cbsnews.com/news/trump-davos-world-economic-forum-speech-davos-2018-01-26-live-stream/.

16. Ishaan Tharoor, "Trump Enters the Davos Club by Charming the Plutocrats," *The Washington Post*, January 26, 2018, https://www.washingtonpost.com/news/worldviews/wp/2018/01/26/trump-enters-the-davos-club-by-charming-the-plutocrats/?utm_term=.b26134c35e4f.

17. Edelman, "Trump to Davos."

18. Tom Brenner, "A Sober Trump Reassures the Davos Elite," *The New York Times*, January 26, 2018, https://www.nytimes.com/2018/01/26/world/europe/donald-trump-davos-speech.html.

19. Anne Gearan and Heather Long, "Trump Encourages a Buy-American Brand of Globalism at Davos," *The Washington Post*, January 26, 2018, https://www.washingtonpost.com/politics/trump-encourages-a-buy-american-brand-of-globalism-at-davos/2018/01/26/3e991bf6-0220-11e8-8acf-ad2991367d9d_story.html?utm_term=.0f516edcb5d8.
20. "Trump Swaggers into Davos Ready to Take on the World."
21. Petroff and Kottasová, "What Davos Thought of Trump's Speech."
22. "Trump Swaggers into Davos Ready to Take on the World."
23. Siegel, "Trump Addresses Business Leaders at Davos."
24. Ibid.
25. Heather Long and Tory Newmyer, "Trump Wins Over Global Elites at Davos: All it Took Was a $1.5 Trillion Tax Cut," *The Washington Post*, January 25, 2018, https://www.washingtonpost.com/business/economy/trump-wins-over-global-elites-at-davos-all-it-took-was-a-15-trillion-tax-cut/2018/01/25/3c688624-0201-11e8-8acf-ad2991367d9d_story.html.
26. "Trump Swaggers into Davos Ready to Take on the World."
27. Brenner, "A Sober Trump Reassures the Davos Elite."
28. Ibid.
29. Gearan and Long, "Trump Encourages a Buy-American Brand of Globalism at Davos."
30. "Trump, in Davos Speech, Sticks to Script as He Declares America Open for Business," *The New York Times*, January 26, 2018, https://www.nytimes.com/2018/01/26/business/davos-world-economic-forum-trump.html.
31. Tharoor, "Trump Enters the Davos Club by Charming the Plutocrats."
32. Edelman, "Trump to Davos."
33. Siegel, "Trump Touts Relationship with May, Threatens Palestinian Aid at Davos Gathering of Global Elite."
34. Shabad, "Trump Says 'America is open for business' in Address to World Economic Forum at Davos."
35. "Stocks Rise as Trump Declares America 'open for business.'"
36. Edelman, "Trump to Davos."
37. Siegel, "Trump Touts Relationship with May, Threatens Palestinian Aid at Davos Gathering of Global Elite."
38. "Stocks Rise as Trump Declares America 'open for business.'"; see also, Edelman, "Trump to Davos"; "Trump Swaggers into Davos Ready to Take on the World."
39. Gearan and Long, "Trump Encourages a Buy-American Brand of Globalism at Davos."
40. Shabad, "Trump Says 'America is open for business' in Address to World Economic Forum at Davos."
41. Brenner, "A Sober Trump Reassures the Davos Elite."
42. Shabad, "Trump Says 'America is open for business' in Address to World Economic Forum at Davos."
43. Siegel, "Trump Touts Relationship with May, Threatens Palestinian Aid at Davos Gathering of Global Elite."
44. "Trump, in Davos Speech, Sticks to Script as He Declares America Open for Business."

*The Economy* 89

45. Petroff and Kottasová, "What Davos Thought of Trump's Speech."
46. "Trump Swaggers into Davos Ready to Take on the World."
47. Terry Moran, "Analysis: It's the 'economy, stupid'. And Right Now, the Trump Economy Is Blasting Off," ABC News, January 26, 2018, https://abcnews.go.com/Politics/analysis-economy-stupid-now-trump-economy-blasting-off/story?id=52632659.
48. Edelman, "Trump to Davos."
49. Tharoor, "Trump Enters the Davos Club by Charming the Plutocrats."
50. Gearan and Long, "Trump Encourages a Buy-American Brand of Globalism at Davos."
51. Petroff and Kottasová, "What Davos Thought of Trump's Speech." See also, as one example, "Donald Trump Speaks at Davos 2018," YouTube.com, accessed July 13, 2019, https://www.youtube.com/watch?v=UT7GlaDc060.
52. "Donald Trump Speaks at Davos 2018," YouTube.com, accessed July 13, 2019, https://www.youtube.com/watch?v=UT7GlaDc060.
53. Siegel, "Trump Addresses Business Leaders at Davos"; see also, Brenner, "A Sober Trump Reassures the Davos Elite."
54. Shabad, "Trump Says 'America is open for business' in Address to World Economic Forum at Davos."
55. Edelman, "Trump to Davos." See also, Brenner, "A Sober Trump Reassures the Davos Elite."
56. Rick Klein, "The Note: Davos Will Test Dealmaker in Chief's Ability to Negotiate Fractured Global Relationships," ABC News, January 25, 2018, https://abcnews.go.com/Politics/note-davos-test-dealmaker-chiefs-ability-negotiate-fractured/story?id=52593385.
57. Siegel, "Trump Addresses Business Leaders at Davos."
58. "Stocks Rise as Trump Declares America 'open for business.'"
59. Petroff and Kottasová, "What Davos Thought of Trump's Speech."
60. Tharoor, "Trump Enters the Davos Club by Charming the Plutocrats."
61. Siegel, "Trump Touts Relationship with May, Threatens Palestinian Aid at Davos Gathering of Global Elite."
62. Gearan and Long, "Trump Encourages a Buy-American Brand of Globalism at Davos."
63. Tharoor, "Trump Enters the Davos Club by Charming the Plutocrats."
64. Moran, "Analysis: It's the 'economy, stupid.'"
65. Edelman, "Trump to Davos."
66. Ibid.
67. Long and Newmyer, "Trump Wins Over Global Elites at Davos."
68. Ibid.
69. Ibid.
70. Siegel, "Trump Addresses Business Leaders at Davos."
71. Charles Riley, "'Predatory Behaviors' Are Distorting Global Markets," CNN, January 26, 2018, https://money.cnn.com/2018/01/26/news/economy/trade-trump-davos/index.html. See also, Brenner, "A Sober Trump Reassures the Davos Elite" and Edelman, "Trump to Davos."
72. Riley, "'Predatory Behaviors' Are Distorting Global Markets."

73. Siegel, "Trump Touts Relationship with May, Threatens Palestinian Aid at Davos Gathering of Global Elite."
74. Moran, "Analysis: It's the 'economy, stupid.'"
75. Ibid.
76. Siegel, "Trump Touts Relationship with May, Threatens Palestinian Aid at Davos Gathering of Global Elite."
77. Ibid.
78. Long and Newmyer, "Trump Wins Over Global Elites at Davos."
79. Siegel, "Trump Addresses Business Leaders at Davos."
80. Brenner, "A Sober Trump Reassures the Davos Elite."
81. "Stocks Rise as Trump Declares America 'open for business.'" See also, Edelman, "Trump to Davos" and Riley, "'Predatory Behaviors' Are Distorting Global Markets."
82. Shabad, "Trump Says 'America is open for business' in Address to World Economic Forum at Davos."
83. Siegel, "Trump Addresses Business Leaders at Davos."
84. Shabad, "Trump Says 'America is open for business' in Address to World Economic Forum at Davos."
85. Gearan and Long, "Trump Encourages a Buy-American Brand of Globalism at Davos."
86. Long and Newmyer, "Trump Wins Over Global Elites at Davos."
87. Ibid.
88. Tharoor, "Trump Enters the Davos Club by Charming the Plutocrats."

*Chapter 6*

# The 2019 State of the Union

The State of the Union message to Congress is a Constitutionally prescribed action for American presidents to perform; he must, "from time to time give to the Congress information on the state of the Union and recommend to their consideration such measures as he shall judge necessary and expedient." Since George Washington's first message, some presidents have delivered it orally before Congress and others have simply sent a written missive. In more recent times, presidents have used the opportunity, in the words of President Truman, as "an unexcelled means 'for the President to tell Congress and the people what this country is up against and what should be done about it.' [Moreover, with] its great publicity value and with its potentially mammoth national and international television-radio audience, the Annual Message has become one of the most important rhetorical instruments available to the President."[1] The tradition of national broadcast and regular formal addresses really began with Franklin Roosevelt, who addressed Congress while simultaneously having his message broadcast by radio.

Aside from the above, another important aspect of the address is that in politically fractured times, with news cycles on different items throughout the year, and spatting political parties and disputes taking national attention in different directions, that this is the one night of the year that all eyes are on the president and on what he says; in that sense, there is a unity of the nation of sorts, even if only of its attention. Although no real consensus exists about whether the president or the press sets the policy or value agenda here, certainly one fact is clear: only the president gives this uniquely constitutionally mandated address. For a moment, the nation and news are focused upon its contents; it is widely read and broadcast. In 1966, this rhetorical opportunity to focus the nation's attention was seen for what it was, and opposition parties began an official response to the address.

## PRESIDENT TRUMP'S SPEECH

President Trump's second State of the Union address[2] attracted almost forty-seven million viewers and was the third longest recorded at eighty-two minutes.[3] This does not, however, tell us much about the amount of content since stops for applause and introductions of guests add to the overall length as delivered. By word count, President Trump had 5,540 words, well below Obama's average of 6,824 but above Bush's average of 5,184.[4] As a major political event, it was broadcast live by ABC, CBS, CNN, CNNe, FOX, FOX BUSINESS, FOXNC, MSNBC, NBC, PBS, TELEMUNDO, and UNIVISION, not to mention scores of lesser streaming services. Print news coverage was nationwide.

Minimized in mainstream news coverage, with most outlets not even mentioning it, was the overwhelmingly positive reception the speech received from those who watched it. One exception to this was CBS which relayed, in one story only, that "seventy-six percent of Americans who tuned in to President Trump's State of the Union address . . . approved of the speech. . . . Just 24 percent disapproved."[5] Buried in the story was important information that although 97 percent of Republicans approved of the speech, 82 percent of Independents, and even 30 percent of Democrats approved. Importantly, in relation to the press framing of this speech we will discuss later, "fifty-six percent of Americans who watched . . . feel the president's speech will do more to unite the country, rather than divide it, although 36 percent don't think it will change things much."[6] *Which means that only 8 percent of those watching felt the speech had a "divisive" edge to it.* Moreover, the poll found that pluralities of Americans (70 percent or better) approved of the president's proposed policies in the areas of immigration, troop withdrawal from the Middle East, and the US-North Korean summits.[7]

### Framing

There were six major themes addressed in the speech: Framing of Facts, Illegal Immigration, the Economy, National Security, Health Care, and a Call for Collective Political Action. Certainly, there were more topics covered, and arguably there could be more or fewer themes as well. These represent, however, what appear to be the central themes as represented in the entirety of the speech, including emphasis placed in both text and delivery.

#### *Framing of Facts*

All State of the Union addresses share administrative and legislative achievements, and these achievements are accompanied by supporting facts. Of note is that the president's list of facts was primarily nonpartisan, although not exclusively. For instance, Trump did make reference to the Republican's contentious, partisan tax cut: "We passed a massive tax cut for working families and doubled the child tax credit." Almost all the Democrats in attendance voted against this; all Democratic presidential primary contenders have promised to repeal it. Two more moments stand out: "We eliminated the very unpopular Obamacare individual mandate penalty" and "My administration has cut more regulations in a short period of time than any other administration during its entire tenure."

Yet aside from these points, most other accomplishments were framed as Trump administration policies acting against the neglect of presidents of both parties, and were listed as facts: the economic boom, 5.3 million new jobs, of which 600,000 were new manufacturing jobs. Rising wages for blue-collar workers, unemployment lower than anytime in past fifty years, with blacks and Americans of Hispanic and Asian descent having the lowest unemployment rate ever recorded. And "the energy revolution, with America now the number-one producer of oil and natural gas anywhere in the world." Trump presents this as "our economy is the envy of the world, our military is the most powerful on Earth . . . and America . . . is again winning each and every day. The state of our union is strong."

Addressing hope for bipartisan actions from Congress, the president remarks, "Believe it or not, we have already proven that that's possible. In the last Congress, both parties came together to pass unprecedented legislation to confront the opioid crisis, a sweeping new farm bill, [and] historic VA reforms." Although in a controversial manner, the president did address the problem of partisan action: "An economic miracle is taking place in the United States, and the only thing that can stop it are foolish wars, politics, or ridiculous partisan investigations," adding, if "there is going to be peace and legislation, there cannot be war and investigation."

## *Illegal Immigration*

Trump spends approximately 7 percent of the speech focused on the above-mentioned bipartisan areas and extends with, "Republicans and Democrats must join forces again to confront an urgent national crisis." Among the most prominent of those mentioned, the president singles out "ending illegal immigration and putting the ruthless coyotes, cartels, drug dealers, and human traffickers out of business." Trump proposes this specifically as a moral issue, stating, "The lawless state of our southern border is a threat to the safety, security, and financial wellbeing of all America. We have a moral duty to create an immigration system that protects the lives and jobs of our citizens." But this is not just about those seeking illegally to enter the United States, but also an "obligation to the millions of immigrants living here today who followed the rules and respected our laws. Legal immigrants enrich our nation and strengthen our society in countless ways." In this sense, he speaks to legal immigrants presently in the country, and the importance of controlling the border to their well-being and success.

He also frames allowing continued illegal immigration as "very cruel," and then spends almost 10 percent of his speech detailing problems with America's southern border, of which illegal immigration is just one problem among many. No other issue in the speech receives such detailed treatment. Problems are legion, and framed as "wealthy politicians and donors push[ing] for open borders while living their lives behind walls, and gates, and guards." He stresses that it is "working-class Americans" who pay the price for this with "reduced jobs, lower wages, overburdened schools, [overcrowded] hospitals . . . increased crime, and a depleted social safety net." Additionally, "One in three women is sexually assaulted on the long journey north," with smugglers using "migrant children . . . to exploit our laws and gain access to our country. Human traffickers and sex traffickers take advantage" of the border situation to "smuggle thousands of young girls and women into the United States and to sell them into prostitution and modern-day slavery." Moreover, "innocent Americans are killed by lethal drugs that cross our border." And "countless Americans are murdered by criminal illegal aliens" including those by the "savage gang, MS-13 . . . ."

Trump pushes for Congress to act immediately on a "common sense proposal," moving beyond a simple wall to include "humanitarian assistance, more law enforcement, drug detection, [and a] crack down on child smuggling." He notes that most of the present members of Congress from both parties had previously, before he was president, voted for a wall. Additionally, he points out that his plan is not for a "simple concrete wall," but rather a "smart, strategic, see-through steel barrier," and that "border agents will determine where it is needed." Pointing to San Diego and El Paso as examples, he declares: "Simply put: Walls work, and walls save lives." Trump ends his immigration section with, "let's work together, compromise, and reach a deal that will truly make America safe." Obviously illegal immigration is singled out for a sizable portion of the speech, but other areas are framed strongly as well.

*The Economy*

America's economy is highlighted as a positive force, and is additionally framed in future terms, focusing in on trade with China, a new the North American Free Trade Agreement (NAFTA), and infrastructure renewal. China in particular is called out for "targeting our industries and stealing our intellectual property...." The president calls this "the theft of American jobs and wealth." Importantly, he does not set this up as a "war" with China, instead explaining that he respects Communist Chinese President Xi, and that he does not "blame China for taking advantage" of the United States, but instead blames America's "leaders and representatives for allowing this travesty to happen." He argues for "a new trade deal with China," one that "must include real, structural change to end unfair trade practices, reduce our chronic trade deficit, and protect American jobs."

Describing NAFTA as a "catastrophe that is responsible for hurting so many working Americans," the president calls for a new NAFTA, the United States-Mexico-Canada Agreement (the USMCA).[8] He envisions the new deal as one that will bring "back our manufacturing jobs in even greater numbers, expand American agriculture, protect intellectual property, and ensure that more cars are proudly stamped with our four beautiful words: 'Made in the USA.'"

## National Security

The president links a strong military with advancing America's security interests. Negotiating with North Korea, and withdrawal from the INF Treaty with Russia are part of this. Venezuela is singled out for special attention since the United States had officially recognized the government led by opposition leader Juan Guaido: "We stand with the Venezuelan people in their noble quest for freedom, and we condemn the brutality of the Maduro regime, whose socialist policies have turned that nation from being the wealthiest in South America into a state of abject poverty and despair." And linking national security to a repudiation of socialism, he declares, "we are alarmed by the new calls to adopt socialism in our country." Highlighting that "America was founded on liberty and independence, and not government coercion, domination, and control," he affirms, "We are born free and we will stay free. Tonight, we renew our resolve that America will never be a socialist country."

Concerning the Middle East, the president mentions his administration's recognition of Jerusalem as Israel's capital, but primarily focuses in on America being involved in fighting in the Middle East for almost nineteen years at great cost: over 7,000 American lives, over 52,000 wounded, and over $7 trillion spent. This not without success, though, in that the military has "liberated virtually all the territory from the grip of those blood thirsty monsters [ISIS]," that with the final work being done with our allies it is "time to give our brave warriors in Syria a warm welcome home." Additionally, the president is focusing on bringing the troops stationed in Afghanistan home, and "preventing another war, which is why the US must stand up to Iran now." Focusing in on the dangers Iran presents, he proclaims that the United States "will not avert our eyes from a regime that chants 'Death to America' and threatens genocide against the Jewish people. We must never ignore the vile poison of anti-Semitism, or those who spread its venomous creed. With one voice, we must confront this hatred anywhere and everywhere it occurs."

## Healthcare

Healthcare is primarily framed into a future setting, although the president does refer to his administration's determination to lower prescription drug prices: "It's unacceptable that Americans pay vastly more than people in other countries for the exact same drugs, often made in the exact same place. This is wrong, this is unfair, and" he states in a bipartisan invitation, "together we will stop it." He specifically asks "Congress to pass legislation that finally takes on the problem of global freeloading and delivers fairness and price transparency for American patients."

A number of other healthcare-related issues are offered as potential bipartisan areas of actions: HIV research, childhood cancer, nationwide paid family leave, and, in general, lowering "the cost of healthcare" and protecting "patients with preexisting conditions." Also related to healthcare but certain to prompt Democrat resistance, "prohibiting late abortion of children who can feel pain in the mother's womb."

## Call for Collective Action

Besides the sense of all Americans wanting to win for their country, a major unifying element was the "majesty of America's mission and the power of American pride," which was linked with the past, notably World War II, but also linked with movement into the future and the identification of problems with the current political climate. The political climate surrounding the speech was addressed through framing a call for collective action. Certainly, there are moments of partisan accomplishments—the tax cuts, deregulation—nevertheless, these are accomplishments of President Trump's administration and are appropriate to mention in the speech. Although such partisan moments do slightly diminish the calls for unity, they are not, however, so powerful that they overshadow the calls for bipartisan and collective American action on a number of fronts. The president begins his speech with, "We meet tonight at a moment of unlimited potential. As we begin a new Congress, I stand here ready to work with you to achieve historic breakthroughs for all Americans." To attempt a collective spirit, the president later brings up Americans fighting for freedom in World War II, liberating concentration camps, and then circles back to consistent American greatness in fighting for great causes: "Everything that has come since—our triumph over communism, our giant leaps of science and discovery, our unrivaled progress towards equality and justice—all of it is possible thanks to the blood and tears and courage and vision of the Americans who came before."

Speaking directly to Congress he enjoins cooperation when he states, "Think of this Capitol. Think of this very Chamber, where lawmakers before you voted to end slavery, to build the railroads and the highways, and defeat fascism, to secure civil rights, and to face down evil empires. Here tonight, we have legislators from across this magnificent republic. Together, we represent the most extraordinary nation in all of history." Importantly, he asks, "What will we do with this moment? How will we be remembered?" The president wishes members of Congress to look "at the opportunities before us. Our most thrilling achievements are still ahead. Our most exciting journeys still await. Our biggest victories are still to come. We have not yet begun to dream." In another unifying attempt, he offers this thought: "We must choose whether we are defined by our differences or whether we dare to transcend them. We must choose whether we squander our great inheritance or whether we proudly declare that we are Americans." Attempting an inspirational mode, he affirms, "We do the incredible. We defy the impossible. We conquer the unknown." He then proceeds to spur Congress to collective action:

> This is the time to reignite the American imagination. This is the time to search for the tallest summit and set our sights on the brightest star. This is the time to rekindle the bonds of love and loyalty and memory that link us together as citizens, as neighbors, as patriots. This is our future, our fate, and our choice to make. I am asking you to choose greatness. No matter the trials we face, no matter the challenges to come, we must go forward together. We must keep America first in our hearts. We must keep freedom alive in our souls. And we must always keep faith in America's destiny that one nation, under God, must be the hope and the promise, and the light and the glory, among all the nations of the world.

## Moral Foundations

All five moral foundations are present in the president's speech, although not to the same degree. By far the most prominent moral foundation was that of Loyalty(Ingroup)/Betrayal. This was followed by Care/Harm, with Fairness/Cheating a close third. Sanctity/Degradation and Authority/Subversion, although present, were not strongly drawn upon like the others.

### *Loyalty(Ingroup)/Betrayal*

Throughout the speech, President Trump used this foundational touchstone to infuse all his policies with purpose. He particularly stresses the "fellow citizens" who are "watching us now, gathered in this great chamber, hoping that we will govern not as two parties but as one nation." He presents his policy proposals, whether in actuality or not, as the "agenda of the American people." The purpose of his policies was clearly expressed: "to defend American jobs and demand fair trade for American workers"; "to create an immigration system that is safe, lawful, modern"; "and to pursue a foreign policy that puts America's interests first." He insists his policies will make "our families stronger" and "communities safer." The foundational unit of Loyalty is America, and he makes it clear that "America saved freedom, transformed science, redefined the middle class, and, when you get down to it, there's nothing anywhere in the world that can compete with America."

Illegal and legal immigration are linked with the foundation of Loyalty, and thus the president speaks of the need to "secure our very dangerous southern border" and "ending illegal immigration" as parts of this foundation. He expands beyond the dangers of illegal immigration to embrace legal immigration, explaining, "This includes our obligation to the millions of immigrants living here today who followed the rules and respected our laws. Legal immigrants enrich our nation and strengthen our society in countless ways." When the president asks Congress "to defend our very dangerous southern border out of love and devotion to our fellow citizens and to our country," he is enacting the Loyalty foundation (and others as well). Showing legal immigration as part of an Ingroup Loyalty, Trump introduces a special guest, an ICE Officer brought to America as a child: "When Elvin was a boy, he and his family legally immigrated to the United States from the Dominican Republic."

Repeatedly throughout the speech were small references touching upon this foundation: "global freeloading" on prescription drugs that impacts "American patients"; touching upon both nation and family, "a plan for nationwide paid family leave, so that every new parent has the chance to bond with their newborn child"; "our triumph over communism"; he believes that we should "declare that we are Americans"; that this "is the time to rekindle the bonds of love and loyalty and memory that link us together as citizens, as neighbors, as patriots"; that "we must go forward together"; and his belief that together we can forge "America's destiny [as] one nation."

Although most groundings to this foundation were positive, some references brought up attacks on such Loyalty, with "We must be united at home to defeat our adversaries abroad"; "violent terrorists attacked the USS Cole"; and "confront the world's leading state sponsor of terror: the radical regime in Iran."

*Care/Harm*

Although not quite as strong as the Loyalty foundation, the Care foundation nevertheless had considerable presence throughout all the president's policy proposals. Unlike other foundations, however, there was a clear delineation between the positive and negative spheres of moral implications, between the

Care aspect and the Harm aspects. Americans were being harmed by reckless policies of both parties, so new policies to "care" for them were being advanced. Even past actions of the nation were linked with this foundation, as in World War II when America acted "to save our civilization from tyranny."

One can see readily the more Caring side of the foundation in numerous areas such as the president's proposals on healthcare reform, particularly those "to reduce the price of healthcare and prescription drugs" and provide "access to lifesaving cures," as well as with his admonition to Congress to work together to make American "communities safer" and to "heal old wounds." On the subject of immigration, the president could not have been clearer when he asserts: "This is a moral issue. The lawless state of our southern border is a threat to the safety, security, and financial wellbeing of all America. We have a moral duty to create an immigration system that protects the lives and jobs of our citizens." Within this context, he asks Congress to "defend our very dangerous southern border out of love and devotion to our fellow citizens and to our country" and to "create an immigration system that is safe, lawful, [and] modern," one that would put "the ruthless coyotes, cartels, drug dealers, and human traffickers out of business." The rest of the policies mentioned were also linked to this foundation. The president desires to "reach a deal that will truly make America safe"; "work to defend our people's safety"; "end unfair trade practices, reduce our chronic trade deficit, and protect American jobs"; "protect American security"; work for "peace on the Korean Peninsula."

In terms of Harm, the president relayed the dangers of illegal immigration, particularly the "extremely high rates of violent crime." He introduced a guest who had suffered at the hands of an illegal immigrant: "Debra Bissell. Just three weeks ago, Debra's parents, Gerald and Sharon, were burglarized and shot to death in their Reno, Nevada home by an illegal alien." Speaking to those who would not confront illegal immigration, he suggests, "Tolerance for illegal immigration is not compassionate; it is actually very cruel," and "until we secure our border, they're going to keep streaming right back in."

Sprinkled throughout the speech were small references to Harm, such as avoiding war with North Korea, and references to Congressional Democrats: "If there is going to be peace and legislation, there cannot be war and investigation"; avoiding "foolish wars"; condemnation of the "brutality of the [Socialist] Maduro regime"; and condemnation of Iran: "We will not avert our eyes from a regime that chants 'Death to America' and threatens genocide against the Jewish people."

*Fairness/Cheating*

Similar in size and scope to Care/Harm, the president links most of his policies to the moral foundation of Fairness. "Things" were or were not "fair."

For instance, judicial nominations stalled in the Senate, some for over a year: "which is unfair to the nominees and very unfair to our country." His focus on "groundbreaking criminal justice reform" and the introduction of guest Alice Johnson to highlight the "disparities and unfairness that can exist in criminal sentencing, and the need to remedy this total injustice." Sentencing laws that "wrongly and disproportionately harmed the African American community" were also singled out.

Immigration was particularly framed this way, in that illegal immigration was inherently unfair while his plan was fair to legal immigrants: "Wealthy politicians and donors push for open borders while living their lives behind walls, and gates, and guards. Meanwhile, working-class Americans are left to pay the price for mass illegal migration." However, his plan "includes our obligation to the millions of immigrants living here today who followed the rules and respected our laws." Other polices were also linked to this foundation: "end unfair trade practices"; the unacceptability of Americans paying "vastly more than people in other countries for the exact same drugs. . . . This is wrong, this is unfair"; "global freeloading" and the new trade policies that aim to deliver "fairness and price transparency for American patients." Even in security matters, the president insists that the "United States was being treated very unfairly by friends of ours" and that he wanted to ensure that "other nations . . . pay their fair share."

*Sanctity(Purity)/Degradation*

Although this foundation existed at several points in the speech, it is most easily identified with the issue of abortion: "Lawmakers in New York cheered with delight upon the passage of legislation that would allow a baby to be ripped from the mother's womb moments from birth"; "the Governor of Virginia . . . states he would execute a baby after birth"; "Let us work together to build a culture that cherishes innocent life"; "And let us reaffirm a fundamental truth: All children—born and unborn—are made in the holy image of God."

In other areas, the president relays that "tens of thousands of innocent Americans are killed" as a result of an unsecure southern border, and that his policies are working to put "sadistic traffickers . . . behind bars." Moreover, "We must never ignore the vile poison of anti-Semitism, or those who spread its venomous creed"; that we can work to make "our faith deeper"; and "that one nation, under God" is still our creed.

*Authority/Subversion*

This foundation was not as strongly present as the other four, and was not present throughout the speech like the others, either. Although strongly asserted here—"America was founded on liberty and independence, and not government coercion, domination, and control"—it existed primarily in the area of immigration. For instance, "the lawless state of our southern border"; "they have to come in legally."

## Trump Summary

The president's speech framed six key themes and conveyed all five moral foundations. In terms of frames, the Framing of Facts involved how the president conveyed factual information about policies and statistics about the state of America. Some of these, particularly those pertaining to future polices, were stated as potential areas of agreement. Some accomplishments were relayed that were partisan, such as the tax cuts, but these were part of the list of accomplished items, and not dwelled upon. Illegal Immigration was framed as an expansive, urgent, moral issue; it was framed as cruel if allowed to continue. The frame stressed stopping illegal immigration as a moral act, while concomitantly protecting legal immigrants. Trump emphasized his wall as not concrete, but rather a euphemism for something far beyond a simple physical barrier. The theme of the Economy was framed to emphasize the positive growth since Trump taking office and its continuation into the future. Communist China was conveyed as a problem for the economy, and had taken advantage of weak American leadership. The emphasis was on stopping this immediately. Old trade deals that disadvantaged America must be eliminated and replaced with better ones. National Security as framed into a simple structure: strong military = American security. Importantly, security means freedom, not socialism. America has been too long in the Middle East, and Trump emphasizes bringing troops home as soon as possible. Moreover, national security involves confronting totalitarianism and hatred. Healthcare involves primarily the administration fighting for lower costs. It was emphasized that it was unfair for Americans to pay for the world's healthcare. Healthcare, in particular, was relayed as an area for potential bipartisan action. Finally, the president did frame this speech as a call for Collective Action; he pointed out that Americans have come together before (World War II, fall of Communism) and can do so again.

In terms of the moral foundations, overwhelmingly the president stressed the Loyalty(ingroup)/Betrayal foundation, integrating these moral touchstones within the sharing of policy and also helping to contextualize other moral foundations. This foundation is squarely focused on America as the basic Loyalty unit. Both legal and illegal immigration policies are linked with this foundation, with legal immigration as advancing Ingroup participation, whereas illegal immigration and its supporters would be betraying the American ideal. The Care/Harm foundation was not quite as strong of a presence as Loyalty(ingroup)/Betrayal, and consisted of clearly delineated divisions between Care aspects and Harm aspects. Many of the president's policies, such as reduction of illegal immigration, have their roots in the Harm portion of this foundation; without change, Americans would continue to be hurt. Thus, those who do nothing to stop this, and other harms, were actually being cruel. The Fairness/Cheating foundation was approximately the same strength of presence as Care/Harm, and is found linked with most of the president's policies. For the president, "things" in the country were or were not "fair," and actions were taken on that basis. So, for instance, illegal immigration was unfair to legal immigrants and American citizens, so must be stopped. The same existed for unfair trade practices, as well as other actions that hurt the American people. The Sanctity/Degradation foundation is primarily associated with the sanctity and innocence of life taken by abortion. It is also found throughout the speech at points, particularly with immigration and innocent lives lost and the sadism of traffickers across the border. Finally, the Authority/Subversion foundation was minimally present, but did resonate in areas such as the lawless southern border and the idea that immigrants needed to come into the United States legally.

## PRESS RESPONSE

As expected with a wide-ranging State of the Union address, the news media response also revealed the wide range of facts and issues.[9] Sprinkled throughout the press response were criticisms of the speech and a negative mischaracterization of Trump's approval numbers going into the speech, which, although never reaching the level of a frame, did contribute to the overall negative tone of the coverage. Criticisms of the speech included its content, with the press pushing an interpretation that wanted more focus on less controversial issues: for instance, "The president had five lines . . . on . . . infrastructure and 80 lines . . . on . . . immigration and a border wall. It should have been reversed."[10] No matter that Americans place illegal immigration at the number two of noneconomic issues facing the nation.[11] It was a "searing speech" for the press, with President Trump being characterized as "awkward," and a "disrupter"[12] Although all presidents highlight their accomplishments, the press termed President Trump's highlights as "Braggadocia"[13] and "boasting."[14]

In terms of approval numbers, the press felt that Trump "came into the evening at one of the weakest moments of his presidency"[15] "with the approval of just 37 percent of the public."[16] Although some felt that "Trump has overseen a strong economy for two years . . . his job approval remains at historic lows and his personal favorability is dismal."[17] This would continue as far as the press was concerned.[18] In effect, he has a "sagging popularity."[19] This point was made again by anonymous political advisors who suggested that the start of 2019 was a "political loser," and that "the president's ratings have plunged while Democrats and the president's potential legal problems seized headlines."[20] Of note, at that very date, Rasmussen's Daily Presidential Tracking Poll had Trump at 48 percent approval, with Obama also at 48 percent at the comparable time in his presidency.[21]

## Framing

The press reporting on the address fell into six general areas, but not with the same emphasis. Three themes—Women, Abortion, and Socialism—were present, but almost as a brief injection of press opinion rather than a full-blown frame. These themes were akin to a momentary snapshot within the speech, each framed, but of a minor nature. There were, however, three themes of note—Unity and Division, the "Wall"/Illegal Immigration, and the ongoing Mueller Investigation—that dominated the MSM coverage of the address. In the remainder of this section on the press responses, we turn to three minor themes of note: Women, Abortion, and Socialism. Following this, we look at the major themes of Unity and Division, the "Wall"/Illegal Immigration, and the ongoing Mueller Investigation.

### Minor Themes
### Women

Trump noted the 100th-year anniversary of Congress passing legislation eventually giving women the right to vote. His words were generally conveyed: "No one has benefited more from our thriving economy than women, who have filled 58 percent of the newly created jobs last year." And also, "All Americans can be proud that we have more women in the workforce than ever before. . . . [W]e also have more women serving in Congress than ever before. And congratulations, that's great." Reporting on this ran from more neutral to denigrating. In terms of the more neutral, the president was described as giving "a shout out to the record number of women elected to Congress, promoting members from both sides to break out in "USA!" chants as female members celebrated on the floor."[22] Trump also "earned some rare approval from Democrats when he celebrated the record number of women elected to Congress in last year's midterm elections. . . . Democratic women, wearing white to honor the suffragette movement, stood and cheered, including some of Trump's staunchest foes. . . . A chant of 'U-S-A! U-S-A!' broke out."[23]

The more neutral framing changed, however, when CNN, *The Washington Post*, and *The New York Times* described the moment as the president being "confronted by . . . dozens of female Democratic lawmakers. . . . [They] stood stone-faced during the overwhelming majority of Trump's speech. . . . But when Trump touted gains by women in the workforce and in Congress, [they] began to whoop and cheer—though they appeared to be congratulating each other, not applauding the President."[24] Along these same lines, when "Trump mentioned that 58% of newly created jobs had been filled by women, female Democratic lawmakers . . . stood and cheered, effectively claiming the President's applause line for themselves."[25] The framing of the bipartisan applause line as a partisan moment was ubiquitous in the reporting:

> The one big Democratic applause line of the night came at Republican expense. As the president was extolling the economy and the new jobs it had created for women in particular, Democratic applause became a crescendo as they realized that some of those new jobs were in the House of Representatives, where Democratic women had taken the place of ousted Republicans. They cheered and cheered. Mr. Trump then urged them to remain standing as he noted "we have more women serving in the Congress than ever before." He was right, but the increased numbers were on the Democratic side, where women were outfitted in white in tribute to the suffragists of a century ago; House Republicans saw a decline in their women membership in the election.[26]

*The Washington Post* devoted an entire article to argue in a hard news piece that, "Trump's celebration of women during the State of the Union wasn't quite as lofty as it seemed" and that any applause was "done ironically."[27]

## Abortion[28]

This theme showed considerably less press neutrality than that dealing with Women above. The most neutrally framed example, and least representative of the overall tone, was ABC reporting that the president had referenced "embattled Virginia Gov. Ralph Northam's controversial comments about third trimester abortions" and then followed that with Northam's remarks without commentary.[29] That was one article, which ABC followed up with an entire article on the issue, and citing those who support Virginia and New York abortion laws, to argue in a hard new piece that what President Trump was saying was wrong.[30] CBS also devoted an entire article as a hard news story, but nevertheless offered interpretive commentary, and used as its one cited source pro-choice abortion provider Planned Parenthood.[31] Fox News was similar here, although it brought in the possible overturning of *Roe v. Wade*.[32]

Others simply explained away the president's comments, of which this excerpt is representative: "Trump also homed in on the issue of abortion . . .

as an attempt to jolt enthusiasm among his evangelical base. Trump drilled down, accusing Virginia Gov. Ralph Northam of saying 'he would execute a baby after birth.' Trump appeared to be referring to controversial comments Northam offered on a radio show in which [sic] he described the birth of a 'nonviable' fetus or infant with 'severe deformities.'"[33] The article continues, providing Northam's statement, "The infant would be delivered. The infant would be kept comfortable. The infant would be resuscitated if that's what the mother and the family desired. And then a discussion would ensue between the physicians and the mother."[34] Then came the recontextualization of Trump's comment: "Northam was referring to the decision between a physician and parents about whether to resuscitate an infant in that condition. The governor's office said Northam's comments were taken out of context and said: 'The governor's comments were limited to the actions physicians would take in the event that a woman in those circumstances went into labor.'"[35] Some articles simply stated, however, that Trump was wrong without offering any evidence.[36]

Socialism

President Trump briefly but strongly described Socialism. ABC listed this as one of seven "Memorable Lines" from the address: "Here, in the United States, we are alarmed by new calls to adopt socialism in our country. America was founded on liberty and independence—not government coercion, domination and control. We are born free, and we will stay free. Tonight, we renew our resolve that America will never be a socialist country."[37] What was not mentioned by almost all who reported on this was that while Republicans cheered wildly, Democrats remained largely silent and stony-faced, with few joining Republicans in applause, and even fewer standing. The closest that any article came to mentioning this important information was from Fox: "And the House Speaker applauded briefly when Trump asserted that the U.S. would never become a socialist country, even as many Democrats remained expressionless."[38]

Some outlets pushed back, reframing the president's remarks: ABC, for instance, devoted an entire article to this speech line, quoting Representative Ocasio-Cortez as saying that it "stiffened her resolve to push socialist policies, such as her proposal to increase tax marginal rates on the very wealthy. 'I think it was great. I think he's scared,' [she] said. 'I thought it was fabulous because it shows that we've gotten under his skin. He sees that everything is closing in on him. He knows that he's losing the battle of public opinion.'" The article continued its positive framing of socialism, highlighting both Ocasio-Cortez and "Democratic Rep. Rashida Tlaib . . . both members of the Democratic Socialists of America, a group that's not a formal political party but believes in socialism over capitalism. They support socialist-backed policies such as free public college for all and single payer health care."[39]

Some sought to depict the president's concerns about socialism as unfounded, and that Democrats were not embracing it: "Mr. Trump also sought to frame the opposition Democrats as too extreme, suggesting that the country was in danger of a socialist takeover."[40] The *Washington Post* made it seem that *only* the "squad-of-four"[41] Democrats were being targeted by Trump's statement, and that Democrats generally supported what he said: "He took a sidelong slap at Democrats—whom he often accuses of encouraging socialism. . . . 'Here, in the United States, we are alarmed by new calls to adopt socialism in our country,' Trump said. 'America was founded on liberty and independence. . . . Tonight, we renew our resolve that America will never be a socialist country.' That brought Republicans and some Democrats to their feet, though not the liberal Democrats Trump probably had in mind."[42]

This is an important historic moment since it was the first time the term "socialism" was used in a State of the Union address, and thus is a monumental laying down of the gauntlet. Instead of explaining it as such, the news media explained it away as an "eye-rolling" moment: "In the audience were some of the top contenders vying for a chance to face off against Trump in 2020, and their campaigns quickly turned the candidates' eyerolling and headshaking into fundraising and social media fodder. He seemed to target some of them by saying he was 'alarmed' by new calls to adopt socialism."[43]

*Major Themes*

Division, Not Unity

Overwhelmingly, the dominant frame advanced by the press was one of division in the Legislature and the country, with President Trump speaking in front of a deeply divided Congress with partisans on both sides. This division was attributed completely to President Trump: "Trump opened and closed his remarks with pleas for unity, an unusual message for a president who relishes political combat. But he offered little in the way concessions, suggesting instead that unity means opponents come to his position. 'We must go forward together. We must keep America first in our hearts,' he concluded, referencing his controversial campaign slogan."[44] The press made it clear, "Compromise means everyone needs to line up behind him and embrace some of the most polarizing goals of his presidency at home and abroad. The calls for unity appeared oddly dissonant from the President's fervent appeals to his base on immigration, abortion and a vow to make sure America never becomes a 'socialist country.'"[45]

Others continued along the same lines: "President Trump delivered a message of bipartisan unity . . . in the new era of divided government, but signaled that he would continue to wage war for the hardline" policies he endorses.[46] Some termed this "conciliation and confrontation,"[47] with the "speech veer[ing] between calls for unity and bipartisan cooperation and Republican red meat on abortion, immigration, taxes, deregulation and anti-communism."[48] *The Washington Post* pushed this even further, writing that "President Trump confronted a split Congress . . . delivering a dissonant State of the Union address, interspersing uplifting paeans to bipartisan compromise with chilling depictions of murder and ruin."[49] Ultimately, for the press, the state of division was all President Trump's fault: "The president's call for compromise and comity struck many as particularly hollow after two years of angry tweets, recriminations and personal attacks that continued almost up until the speech. Democrats just weren't buying it."[50]

Part of this was attributed to the recent government shutdown, which was also completely attributed to President Trump, who remains "unrepentant and defiant. And while he says he's open to compromise and national unity—it must be on his terms."[51] Additionally, his "calls for conciliation—which did not address his role in inflaming partisan divisions—were met with mostly stone-faced silence from Democrats, who bitterly oppose most of his agenda and whose memories are still fresh with the 35-day government shutdown."[52]

The press mentioned frequently the partial Federal government shutdown[53] in what is one of the two most powerful frames in coverage—Division/Unity and Illegal Immigration. In terms of the shut down and division, "President Donald Trump . . . gave his second State of the Union address . . . one week after he originally was invited to deliver it but didn't because of the longest-ever government shutdown."[54] The shutdown was, however, President Trump's fault, with, for instance, "air traffic controllers who went unpaid during the government shutdown" being highlighted.[55] And with "the longest government shutdown in U.S. history over and another potential one around the corner, Trump will need to try to bring both parties in Congress together before funding runs out again."[56] But this is made to seem impossible with the press framing the entire situation as divisive, with Trump offering little. CNN in particular offers a centered look at the framing by the press on division, arguing that the president's speech floundered,

> with appeals to bipartisanship giving way to divisive policy pitches and stern warnings aimed at discouraging Democratic investigations into his administration. "An economic miracle is taking place in the United States—and the only thing that can stop it are foolish wars, politics or ridiculous partisan investigations," Trump said, as Pelosi visibly scoffed behind him. Even most Republicans sat silent. "If there is going to be peace and legislation, there cannot be war and investigation. It just doesn't work that way!"[57]

Much stress was put on the fact that the president mentioned his signature call for a wall in his address. For instance, NBC highlighted Xavier Becerra's Spanish-language rebuttal: "'Who would believe that the state of our union would be driven by President Trump's obsession to build a wall that no experts want?' Becerra said, noting that Trump in his address did not repeat his campaign promise that Mexico would pay for the wall. 'How can it be that the state of our young, rich and strong nation is now disorder, tension, hostility?' he added."[58] Others also emphasized that Trump "used the speech to continue his push the divisive issue that was at the center of the shutdown impasse—a border wall with Mexico."[59]

Two areas in particular were focused on when framing the president as divisive: the shutdown, but primarily "the wall." And by asking still for the wall, the president was framed as engaging in "confrontation" and, at the same time, hypocritically presenting "himself as a leader who could work across party lines even as he pressed lawmakers to build a wall along the nation's southwestern border that leaders of the newly empowered congressional Democrats have adamantly rejected."[60] For *The Washington Post* it was even worse, since the president's "speech came at one of the most acrimonious moments of his presidency. Both parties are deeply divided over his demand to construct a border wall—and leaders still are reeling from the partial government shutdown that ended late last month, which at 35 days was the longest in U.S. history."[61]

As the above examples indicate, although quotes are in place, there are few instances provided by the press of the numerous areas in the speech that offer opportunities for bipartisan efforts. Some, although mentioning the president's "pledge to work together on prescription drug prices, infrastructure and fighting cancer and HIV/AIDS," asserted that "Trump offered few signs of flexibility on the political disputes that tear at national unity."[62] There was little in the way of press framing to suggest that compromise was actually a possibility or even a true element of the speech. However, Democrat actions were offered in contrast, and offered without comment or rebuttal as correct: "Democrats have promised they will use new investigative powers to probe everything from Trump's tax returns to his policy decisions to members of his Cabinet. Special counsel Robert Mueller is also still pursuing his investigation stemming from Russian interference in the 2016 election."[63] Whereas the President is "once again" going back to divisive issues, Democrats are simply "doing their job."[64]

## Wall and Illegal Immigration

As seen above, a substantial part of the division the press frames is linked to President Trump's campaign promise to secure the southern border, of which building a wall is a central component. For the press, it is this insistence of honoring this pledge that is causing division, rather than Democrats' unyielding opposition to any compromise. CNN, for instance, pointedly wrote, "He deliberately stoked fresh tensions with Democrats over his border wall, using rhetoric that may make it more difficult to forge a compromise to defuse a standoff that is threatening to cause a second government shutdown."[65] Very often a deliberate motive was ascribed to the president here: "The president knows full well that the immigration issue as he presents and champions it will only divide America even more and appeal only to a subset of Americans."[66] And, "the President once again sought to portray the situation on the southern border as an 'urgent national crisis' that he said threatened the security of 'all of America.' He renewed his demand for a border wall in a lengthy and severe section of his speech devoted to immigration. Despite the partisan jabs, Trump sought to portray his agenda—one frequently defined by deeply divisive policies—as a nonpartisan venture."[67]

Moreover, the press refused to accurately portray the wall, calling it "the divisive issue that was at the center of the shutdown impasse"[68] and continuing to describe it as only a concrete barrier: a "'big, beautiful' concrete wall [that] Trump promised voters."[69] ABC News presented a commonly reported aspect of the address, the brief mention of the wall, instead of reporting on the overall package of illegal immigration reduction proposals: "The president did not take the politically inflammatory step of declaring a 'national emergency' to bypass Congress and get his border wall built. He called the situation on the border an 'urgent national crisis,' though he outlined no new path to avoid a second shutdown in his quest for a wall—beyond saying that it will go up."[70] The idea floated by President Trump before the speech, that he would consider declaring a national emergency to help build the wall, was also part of this framing: "During the speech, the president stopped short of declaring a national emergency to obtain funds to build a wall. . . . 'In the past, most of the people in this room voted for a wall, but the proper wall never got built. I will get it built,' he said prompting applause from Republicans. However, he did not directly threaten another government shutdown."[71]

A few articles did share the president's words beyond a brief snippet:

> The president . . . sought to paint undocumented immigrants who cross the southern border, often seeking asylum, as an invading force prone to violent crime. 'As we speak, large, organized caravans are on the march to the United States,' Trump said, adding that he 'just heard' that Mexican cities were trying to rid their communities of migrants by directing truckloads of them to areas along the border where there is little protection. 'This is a moral issue,' Trump said. 'The lawless state of our southern border is a threat to the safety, security and financial wellbeing of all Americans.' He added, 'Tolerance for illegal immigration is not compassionate. It is actually very cruel.'[72]

But then such quotes were undercut by the press with, as we will see in the conclusion, unproven, arguable, and even incorrect assertions: "Illegal border crossings are down significantly from their historic peaks, and some research indicates that undocumented immigrants commit crimes at lower rates than U.S. citizens do. Still, Trump has claimed that only a border wall would be effective in keeping out the migrants, many of whom are families with children."[73] Although not in every frame associated with this speech, only Fox News offered a more inclusive framing of the president's stand on the wall: "The president called for unity—but at the same time, did not back down from his insistence that Congress fund border security measures including a border wall."[74] Thus, instead of being divisive, the president was not backing down from trying to obtain what he promised during his campaign. Moreover, Fox was almost alone in highlighting the important distinction between a concrete wall and a "smart wall," quoting the president wanting to "'work together, compromise and reach a deal that will truly make America safe.' [This] includes 'humanitarian assistance, more law enforcement, drug detection,' a way to close 'loopholes that enable child smuggling,' and 'plans for a new physical barrier or wall.' 'This is a smart, strategic, see-through steel barrier—not just a simple concrete wall,' he explained."[75] Besides Fox News, there was only a brief mention by a *Washington Post* reporter who called attention to the context of the president's comments on the wall: "While the president emphasized the wall in a substantial section of his speech, he didn't talk about it in terms of an ultimatum. Instead, he pitched it as something he wanted."[76]

## Mueller Investigation

Amid the then ongoing Mueller investigation and Democrats' call for extensive congressional investigations of President Trump, the president briefly appealed for a renewed focus on governing, not investigations. The press latched onto this small portion of his speech (approximately .004 percent) and presented a pervasive, strong, and consistent frame of the investigations. A common refrain was that President Trump had declared: "'An economic miracle is taking place in the United States—and the only thing that can stop it are foolish wars, politics or ridiculous partisan investigations,' the president said. 'If there is going to be peace and legislation, there cannot be war and investigation. It just doesn't work that way!'"[77] This would be followed with statements that "Trump did not mention special counsel Robert Mueller's ongoing probe into Russian interference in the 2016 presidential election, but some Congressional Democrats saw the comment as an attempt to undermine Mueller's probe."[78] For the press, the president's statement was a "warning," a "threat."

In some cases, the president's comments about partisan investigations were linked with Richard Nixon and Watergate, with *The Washington Post* even devoting an entire story to this analogy.[79] For instance:

> The President responded with a threat, warning that a flurry of investigations against him and even the congressional oversight he never faced from the Republican House could derail economic growth and threaten the best job creation in decades. In an echo of President Richard Nixon who declared in 1974, that "one year of Watergate is enough," Trump warned: "If there is going to be peace and legislation, there cannot be war and investigation." Lawmakers in the House of Representatives offered an eloquent picture of how his speech was likely to be received in the country."[80]

And a litany of quotes taken from congressional Democrats' Tweets were provided as partial evidence for the country's response:

1. "The President should not be attempting to undermine the Special Counsel's investigation during the #SOTU."
2. "Mueller's investigation must be allowed to continue without obstruction."
3. "Not partisan investigations. It's #Mueller, a Republican, the southern district of New York, Republican, [and eastern] district of Virginia, Republican. #TrumpRussia #TrumpLies."
4. "Protecting the Mueller investigation is a bipartisan issue. We will protect the investigation so truth can come to light."
5. "There's nothing ridiculous about investigating crimes, Mr. President. No one, not even you, is above the law. Mueller's investigation must be completed with without obstruction."[81]

Although NBC News mentioned the small phrase as stating the president "decried 'ridiculous partisan investigations,' possibly a reference to special counsel Robert Mueller," it, like the others, did not mention Democratic promises to unleash a torrent of investigations on the president; thus, through omission, the press mitigates their role in the divisive nature of DC as explained above.[82]

The press also framed this area as "Mr. Trump himself recognized their ascension with his plea for Democrats not to pursue investigations of his administration. There was zero chance of them complying with that request. 'We are not here to play,' Representative Mary Gay Scanlon . . . said. . . . 'We are here to be serious.'"[83] The press made it seem as if all Democrats were in unison here, quoting one and then saying that person "spoke for many of his colleagues when he called it 'totally outrageous' for the president to use his nationally televised speech to try to undermine the special counsel's investigation into Russian interference in the 2016 election and multiple inquiries that Democrats are now beginning into the Trump administration."[84]

## Moral Foundations

The press overwhelmingly grounded its moral appeals in the Care/Harm Foundation. This was followed by a considerably weaker Loyalty(ingroup)/ Betrayal foundation, and an even weaker Fairness/Cheating foundation. Both the Authority/Subversion and Sanctity(purity)/Degradation foundations were present, but only minimally so, and in extremely limited circumstances.

### *Care/Harm*

Only a minimal amount of the Care foundation upon which President Trump based his speech were relayed, perhaps most by this phrase: "If there is going to be peace and legislation, there cannot be war and investigation."[85] Additionally, his mentioning of the abortion issue conveyed this foundation as well: "To defend the dignity of every person, I am asking Congress to pass legislation to prohibit the late-term abortion of children who can feel pain in the mother's womb."[86] Except for FOX News, there was a sense of diminishment, disagreement, or derision provided with the quotes. Trump was described minimally as trying to avert war through engaging in "'bold new diplomacy [with his] historic push for peace on the Korean Peninsula,'"[87] and his assertion that if he "had not been elected President of the United States, we would right now, in [his] opinion, be in a major war with North Korea,"[88] was essentially described as touting.[89] And his focus on bringing troops home after eighteen years of war—"It is time to give our brave warriors in Syria a warm welcome home"—and working to "destroy the remnants of ISIS" was met with protestations that ISIS was essentially winning and he erroneously states that the "Taliban had been forced to bargain for peace."[90]

And of course, his description of "the situation on the southern border as an 'urgent national crisis' that he said threatened the security of 'all of America'"[91] was relayed, as was, in a considerably more limited sense, his description of it as a "a moral issue": "'The lawless state of our southern border is a threat to the safety, security and financial wellbeing of all Americans.' He added, 'Tolerance for illegal immigration is not compassionate. It is actually very cruel.'"[92] As will be seen, the overwhelming response of the press was to minimize and undercut these claims, except for Fox News which provided counterclaims but also more detail than the others by sharing that, "'walls work and walls save lives,' Trump said. . . . 'So let's work together, compromise and reach a deal that will truly make America safe.'"[93] "I am asking you to defend our very dangerous southern border out of love and devotion to our fellow citizens and to our country."[94]

Even as some of what the president said was relayed, and interpreted as shown above, overall the press conveyed its interpretations of the president's statements, not the president's statements in their own force. So, in the president's speech he might have conveyed a Care foundation, but after recontextualization by the press, it became a Harm foundation, with the president depicted as harming America. Even as most all conveyed his important foundation line of "If there is going to be peace and legislation, there cannot be war and investigation,"[95] they undercut this by describing it as almost wishful thinking, by describing the president as "wanting" to be a leader who brought "peace," but who never will.[96] Instead, he was the leader who caused "bitter wounds."[97] And one who responds with an "unmistakable threat to the new Democratic House majority over impending oversight investigations into . . . alleged corruption in the administration."[98]

It was the issue of immigration that saw the largest share of Care/Harm foundational examples. Speaking of Trump's relaying the effectiveness of walls, the press characterized the success of the border wall in the San Diego area as Harmful: "House Speaker Nancy Pelosi, [for example,] has called such a wall an 'immorality.'"[99] Specifically, "The hardened border . . . pushed migrants to remote areas that are more dangerous [for them to cross]"[100]; therefore, how could Trump "continue to wage war for the hardline immigration policies,"[101] such as choosing "to cage children and tear families apart."[102]

Other issues were covered as well, with the same use of the Care/Harm part of the foundation—Democrats Care, Trump Harms:

1. "'President Trump must now take concrete steps to work with Democrats to strengthen the health and economic security of families across America,' Ms. Pelosi said."[103]
2. Democrats are portrayed as "Protecting the Mueller investigation. . . . [They] will protect the investigation so truth can come to light."[104]
3. Speaking of the president's comments decrying recent abortion expansions through birth championed by Democrats,[105] "The infant would be delivered. The infant would be kept comfortable. The infant would be resuscitated if that's what the mother and the family desired. And then a discussion would ensue between the physicians and the mother."[106]
4. "Shame on the president for using the State of the Union to vilify people who have abortions and the providers who care for them."[107]
5. "Stacey Abrams showed the President what real leadership was last night. She was thoughtful, caring, whereas he was not."[108]

6. "Trump made no mention of North Korea" human rights abuses or other atrocities."[109]
7. "Trump did not mention any steps to counter the nation's gun violence."[110]
8. "Trump sought to place the health care of Americans on center stage during his State of the Union address last night. But as on other issues, his record is decidedly mixed."[111]

*Loyalty(Ingroup)/Betrayal*

The grounding in Loyalty(ingroup)/Betrayal was at the level of the nation for President Trump, and the press, although downplaying many of the president's references in this area, did relay some of his emphasis: "This is the time to rekindle the bonds of love and loyalty and memory that link us together as citizens, as neighbors, as patriots."[112] And, "'We meet tonight at a moment of unlimited potential,' he said at the outset, telling Congress that Americans hoped 'we will govern not as two parties, but as one nation.'"[113] Be this as it may, overwhelmingly the press acted to undercut the president's use of this moral foundation, mostly around the idea of unity, both in the House chamber and the nation at large. For examples:

1. The speech was doomed to fail because President Trump was speaking before a highly "divided Congress . . . appealing to lawmakers' sense of unity at a moment of deepening partisan spite."[114]
2. "On Tuesday, the president renewed calls for unity: 'The decision is ours to make.' Slightly past the midpoint of Trump's first term in office, it has become clear that the Trump era will likely not be remembered for such sentiments."[115]
3. And he "did not address his role in inflaming partisan divisions."[116]
4. Some went so far as to read the president's mind: "he believes his success will be determined by division instead of unity."[117]

So, it was reported in passing by some that the president had "delivered a message of bipartisan unity"[118] and that perhaps there was even a "brief moment of unity."[119] It was then reframed as follows: the "President's track record indicates the luster of unity is unlikely to last."[120] Having framed Trump's own policy initiatives as divisive and doomed to failure, the press was able to report that "Trump did make an apparently genuine effort to bring Americans together. He tried to combine key themes from his 2016 campaign into a patriotic creed behind which everyone could unite."[121] In essence, making the claim of unity ring hollow. Unity instead depended on bringing in nothing that could offend Democrats: "The speech veered between calls for unity and bipartisan cooperation and Republican red meat on abortion, immigration, taxes, deregulation and anticommunism."[122] And in the same vein, "Pelosi maintained an even countenance as Trump ran through both odes to partisan unity and red meat lines such as 'walls save lives' that were calibrated to needle Democrats."[123]

Of note is that all the disunity was the president's fault, that the "apparently unbridgeable ideological divides that hold Washington hostage and stifle a latent yearning for national unity"[124] were so because of him. And this because "Trump offered few signs of flexibility on the political disputes that tear at national unity."[125] Moreover, through the "White House spin about how the President meant to unify a divided nation, he sent a clear message: Compromise means everyone needs to line up behind him."[126] Further targeting the president, the press depicted Democrats as having "scorned the idea of unity from a president who has practiced the politics of division."[127] Reporting using Loyalty(ingroup) foundations overwhelmingly cast President Trump as outside the American Ingroup:

1. "Trump's address was 'political, divisive, calculating, even nasty at times.'"[128]
2. "you can't talk about comity and working together and give a speech that is so divisive."[129]
3. "His calls for unity were undermined by the most divisive agenda in modern history."[130]
4. "Separating families does not unify our nation."[131]
5. "Taking away people's health care does not unify us. Blocking access to the ballot box does not unify us. Shutting down the government does not unify us. Building walls does not unify us."[132]
6. "It seems every year the president wakes up and discovers the desire for unity on the morning of the State of the Union, then the president spends the other 364 days of the year dividing us, and sowing a state of disunion."[133]
7. "He is so disingenuous that when he starts talking about unity it is almost laughable."[134]
8. "It's hard to listen to a man with such a demonstrated inability to tell the truth—or even keep his word with members of either party—try to sell us on the idea that he's now ready for bipartisanship and unity, that he's poised to bring us together."[135]

*Fairness/Cheating*

There was little evidence of the foundation of Fairness/Cheating, although when present, it was mainly associated with the president's focus on "fairer drug pricing."[136] For instance: "Trump highlights health agenda with vow to lower 'unfair' drug prices."[137] NBC News actually provided a lengthy quote from this section of the address: "It is unacceptable that Americans pay vastly more than people in other countries for the exact same drugs. . . . This is wrong, this is unfair, and together we will stop it. I am asking the Congress to pass legislation that finally takes on the problem of global freeloading and delivers fairness and price transparency for American patients."[138] This brief focus on fairness was impinged upon by another focus on the shutdown, sometimes described as "'a stunt engineered by the president of the United States, one that defied every tenet of fairness and abandoned not just our people—but our values.'"[139] Thus, what fairness was ascribed to the president was undercut by press perceptions of fairness.

*Authority/Subversion*

This foundation was seen primarily in President Trump's confrontation with Socialist policies being supported or advanced by some Democrats in Congress. He was quoted as saying, "America was founded on liberty and independence—not government coercion, domination and control."[140] Also some minor mentions concerning illegal immigration with respect to border security: "'America is committed to ending illegal immigration and putting the ruthless coyotes, cartels, drug dealers and human traffickers out of business,' Trump said, framing border security as a 'moral issue.'"[141]

However, in similar vein with the others, this foundation's impact was minimized in reporting; for instance, when the press reported, "Trump says the state of the southern border is 'lawless,' threatening the security of all Americans,"[142] it would then, as shown in examples above, explain away or argue against it being "lawless." Keep in mind that in the Care/Harm area when "lawless" is mentioned, then that is also here in authority: "issued another dark warning about the dangers of illegal immigration at the 'lawless' southern border . . . ."[143]

Additional examples of the press foundational use are randomly scattering throughout the reporting.

1. A sense of "obstruction" of justice being used strongly by the press: "Robert Mueller finding impeachable offenses related to [Trump's] campaign's connections to Russia or obstruction of justice. . . ."[144]
2. And contentions that "Mr. Trump himself recognized their [the investigations] ascension with his plea for Democrats not to pursue investigations of his administration. There was zero chance of them complying with that request."[145]
3. "[L]awmakers [at State of the Union addresses are usually] uneasy about skipping the ovations for fear of being caught on camera not applauding some patriotic or uplifting moment and seeming disrespectful or

churlish. . . . But Democrats on Tuesday had no qualms at all about failing to applaud Donald Trump."[146]
4. And Nancy Pelosi being described matriarchically: "She's the mother of the country."[147]

*Sanctity(Purity)/Degradation*

Very little of this foundation existed in press reports. When found, it was within discussion about abortion stemming from the president's direct reference to it in his speech: "'Let us work together to build a culture that cherishes innocent life'. . . . 'Let us reaffirm a fundamental truth: all children—born and unborn—are made in the holy image of God,' he added."[148] For the press, though, the abortion discussion revolved around new laws in New York and those proposed in Virginia that were done to protect the "life" of the mother. Trump was thus depicted as "degrading" the sanctity of the mother.

## Press Summary

The news media framed five key themes and conveyed three moral foundations (with two minimally represented). In terms of frames, Unity and Division was the most prevalent and the strongest by far. President Trump was framed as insincere, unwilling to compromise with Democrats, and pushing only polarizing policies to intentionally create division. The partial government shutdown was traumatic and completely Trump's fault. Immigration reform for Trump is only about building a divisive physical wall. The framing of Illegal Immigration was overwhelmingly focused on a concrete wall, a physical barrier, and how ineffective it would be. Immigration reform for Trump was thus reduced to only being about building "the wall," with this framing making other Trump immigration concerns less salient. The Mueller Investigation was exclusive to the press and was framed as almost a noble Democrat goal with Trump threatening Democrats in the address. Moreover, Trump was depicted as confused about the role of Congress, with the entire situation similar to Nixon and Watergate. In terms of the minor themes, congressional Women (Democrats) were framed as defiant and celebrating success at Trump's expense. Abortion was framed as Democrats being supporting of women and Trump as wrong. Socialism was framed as a limited, nonissue, in that Democrats were not embracing Socialism, that only the "gang of four" were socialist.

In terms of moral foundations, the news media overwhelmingly stressed the Care/Harm foundation. Pervasive and strong, it resonated throughout the press response; this was followed by a considerably less strong presence of

Loyalty(ingroup)/Betrayal, which in turn was followed by an even weaker presence of Fairness/Cheating. Authority/Subversion and Sanctity/Degradation were almost nonexistent, and were present as a response to Trump's speech. In terms of the Care/Harm foundation, some of Trump's foundational assertions were relayed, but in such a way as to minimize the Care portion; in short, Trump was depicted as wrong in wanting to bring troops home from Syria, for instance. Although his Care foundation with regard to immigration was hesitatingly shared, it too, like the others, was minimized. The overwhelming response of the press was to minimize and undercut these claims. In the speech Trump might have conveyed a Care foundation, but after recontextualization by the press, it was not a Caring foundation conveyed, but rather a Harm foundation, with the president as harming America. Loyalty(ingroup)/Betrayal was at the level of the Nation for Trump, and the press did relay this to some degree; however, at almost every turn the press acted to undercut this foundation, primarily using the notion of unity/division to do so. Instead of focusing on Trump's calls for unity, the press focused on division, points of disagreement, and laid all this at the feet of the president. Trump was inflexible, not Democrats, and as such was betraying America. Of note is that as the press was so focused on division that the country did not feel the speech divisive at all. Many of the proposed policies that the press was decrying were actually popular with a majority of Americans; with only 8 percent viewing the speech as divisive, as mentioned earlier. The Fairness/Cheating foundation was minimally conveyed, and almost entirely by the notion of unfair drug prices that the president stressed he was attempting to fix. The press, although relaying this, undercut the moral weighting of the president by arguing against what Trump said, and by pushing the partial government shutdown as "unfair." Since the shutdown was blamed on Trump, the unfair nature was ascribed to him. Authority/Subversion was even less conveyed, and almost entirely the areas of Socialism and Illegal Immigration. The press undercut the moral weighting of the president by minimizing or arguing against what he said. The essential moral argument pushed was that the president lacked Authority and was betraying Americans. Sanctity/Degradation existed to paint Trump as appealing to hard-core pro-lifers and degrading the life of mothers. It was a minimally present in overall coverage, however.

## NOTES

1. Eugene E. White, "Presidential Rhetoric: The State of the Union Address," *The Quarterly Journal of Speech* 54, no. 1 (1968): 76.

2. Donald J. Trump, "Remarks by President Trump in State of the Union Address," The White House, February 5, 2019, https://www.whitehouse.gov/briefing

s-statements/remarks-president-trump-state-union-address-2/ and video at https://www.youtube.com/watch?v=w4FyVGtMa4s.

3. John Gage, "Trump's 2019 State of the Union Address Was the Longest since Clinton's in 2000," *Washington Examiner*, February 5, 2019, https://www.washingtonexaminer.com/news/trumps-2019-state-of-the-union-address-was-the-longest-since-clintons-in-2000.

4. https://www.presidency.ucsb.edu/documents/presidential-documents-archive-guidebook/annual-messages-congress-the-state-the-union-3.

5. Anthony Salvanto, Jennifer De Pinto and Fred Backus, "Most Viewers Approved of Trump's Second State of the Union Address," CBS News, February 6, 2019, https://www.cbsnews.com/news/state-of-the-union-2019-most-viewers-approved-of-trumpssotu-address-cbs-news-poll/.

6. Salvanto, De Pinto and Backus, "Most Viewers Approved of Trump's Second State of the Union Address."

7. Kristinn Taylor, "POLL STUNNERS: Both CBS and CNN Polls: 76 Percent of Viewers Approve President Trump's State of the Union Speech; CBS: 72 Percent Approve His Immigration Ideas," *The Gateway Pundit*, February 5, 2019, https://www.thegatewaypundit.com/2019/02/poll-stunner-76-percent-of-viewers-approve-president-trumps-state-of-the-union-speech-72-percent-approve-his-immigration-ideas/; Ian Schwartz, "CNN Instant Poll: 76% of Viewers Approved of Trump State of the Union," *Real Clear Politics*, February 5, 2019, https://www.realclearpolitics.com/video/2019/02/05/cnn_instant_poll_76_of_viewers_approved_of_trump_state_of_the_union.html#!.

8. https://usmca.com/.

9. A total of forty-one articles were reported following President Trump's speech.

10. Matthew Dowd, "In State of the Union Address, Trump Bookends Bipartisanship Around a Core of Raw Division: ANALYSIS," ABC News, February 6, 2019, https://abcnews.go.com/Politics/state-union-address-trump-bookends-bipartisanship-coreraw/story?id=60883173.

11. "Most Important Problem," *Gallup*, https://news.gallup.com/poll/1675/Most-Important-Problem.aspx. Accessed October 25, 2019.

12. Stephen Collinson, "Trump Call for Compromise Is Only on His Own Terms," CNN News, February 6, 2019, https://www.cnn.com/2019/02/06/politics/donald-trump-state-of-the-unionaddress/index.html.

13. Philip Rucker and Toluse Olornnipa, "In Dissonant State of the Union Speech, Trump Seeks Unity while Depicting Ruin," *The Washington Post,* February 6, 2019, WPCOM00020190206ef26001b9 obtained from factiva.com.

14. Philip Bump, "Trump's State of the Union Speech Drew the One Parallel to Richard Nixon that it Shouldn't Have," *The Washington Post*, February 6, 2019, WPCOM00020190206ef26002xl obtained from factiva.com.

15. Collinson, "Trump Call for Compromise Is Only on His Own Terms."

16. Peter Baker, "Trump Asks for Unity, But Presses Hard Line on Immigration," *The New York Times*, February 5, 2019, NYTFEED020190205ef25008c2 obtained from factiva.com.

17. Dowd, "In State of the Union Address, Trump Bookends Bipartisanship Around a Core of Raw Division."

18. Kevin Liptak and Jeremy Diamond, "Trump Calls for Rejection of 'Politics of Revenge' in Speech that Jabs Democrats," CNN News, February 6, 2019, https://www.cnn.com/2019/02/05/politics/state-of-the-union-address/index.html.

19. David A. Fahenthold and Felicia Sonmez, "In State of the Union, Trump Plans to Urge Bipartisan Cooperation in a Sharply Divided Congress," *The Washington Post*, February 6, 2019, WP00000020190206ef2600016 obtained from factiva.com.

20. Anne Gearan and Josh Dawsey, "Trump Debuts His Case for Reelection in State of the Union Address," *The Washington Post*, February 6, 2019, WPCOM00020190206ef26002s1 obtained from factiva.com.

21. "Daily Presidential Tracking Poll," Rasmussen, http://www.rasmussenreports.com/public_content/politics/trump_administration/prez_track_oct24. Accessed October 25, 2019.

22. Lauren Egan, "Top 10 Highlights from Trump's State of the Union," NBC News, February 5, 2019, https://www.nbcnews.com/politics/white-house/top-10-highlights-trump-s-state-union-n968031.

23. Alex Seitz-Wald, "Trump Slams 'ridiculous partisan investigations' in State of the Union Address," NBC News, February 6, 2019, https://www.nbcnews.com/politics/donald-trump/trump-call-national-unity-state-union-address-n967746.

24. Liptak and Diamond, "Trump Calls for Rejection of 'Politics of Revenge' in Speech that Jabs Democrats."

25. Collinson, "Trump Call for Compromise is Only on His Own Terms."

26. Carl Hulse, "State of the Union Speech Puts Democratic Resurgence on Full Display," *The New York Times*, February 6, 2019, NYTFEED020190206ef260058x obtained from factiva.com.

27. Philip Bump, "Trump's Celebration of Women During the State of the Union Wasn't Quite as Lofty as It Seemed," *The Washington Post*, February 6, 2019, WPCOM00020190206ef2600cf9 obtained from factiva.com.

28. Trump's actual comments were: "There could be no greater contrast to the beautiful image of a mother holding her infant child than the chilling displays our nation saw in recent days. Lawmakers in New York cheered with delight upon the passage of legislation that would allow a baby to be ripped from the mother's womb moments from birth. These are living, feeling, beautiful babies who will never get the chance to share their love and their dreams with the world. And then, we had the case of the Governor of Virginia where he stated he would execute a baby after birth. To defend the dignity of every person, I am asking Congress to pass legislation to prohibit the late-term abortion of children who can feel pain in the mother's womb. (Applause.) Let us work together to build a culture that cherishes innocent life. (Applause.) And let us reaffirm a fundamental truth: All children—born and unborn—are made in the holy image of God."

29. Megan Keneally, "7 Memorable Lines from the State of the Union," ABC News, February 5, 2019, https://abcnews.go.com/Politics/memorable-lines-state-union/story?id=60872709.

30. Megan Keneally, "Explaining Trump's Talk of 'late-term abortions' During the State of the Union," ABC News, February 5, 2019, https://abcnews.go.com/Politics/memorable-lines-state-union/story?id=60872709.

31. Camilo Montoya-Galvez, "Citing Northam's Comments, Trump Urges Late-Term Abortion Ban During State of the Union," CBS News, February 5, 2019, https://www.cbsnews.com/news/state-of-the-union-late-term-abortion-pushed-by-trumpciting-gov-ralph-northams-comments/.

32. Frank Miles, "Trump Calls out Pro-Choice Abortion Bills During State of the Union," FOX News, February 5, 2019, https://www.foxnews.com/politics/to-rapturous-applause-at-sotu-trumpasks- congress-to-prohibit-late-term-abortion.

33. Liptak and Diamond, "Trump Calls for Rejection of 'Politics of Revenge' in Speech that Jabs Democrats."

34. "VA Governor on Abortion," Youtube.com, accessed January 30, 2020, https://www.youtube.com/watch?v=SkTopSKo1xs.

35. Liptak and Diamond, "Trump Calls for Rejection of 'Politics of Revenge' in Speech that Jabs Democrats."

36. "State of the Union Fact Check: What Trump Got Right and Wrong," *The New York Times*, February 5, 2019, NYTFEED020190206ef26000xd obtained from factiva.com.

37. Keneally, "7 Memorable Lines from the State of the Union."

38. Gregg Re, "Democrats Unmoved by Trump's State of the Union Bid to Break Gridlock on Border Security," FOX News, February 6, 2019, https://www.foxnews.com/politics/democratsunmoved-by-trumps-state-of-the-union-bid-to-break-gridlock-on-border-security.

39. Cheyenne Haslett, "Rep. Alexandria Ocasio-Cortez welcomes Trump's 'socialism' Jab, says He's 'scared,'" ABC News, February 6, 2019, https://abcnews.go.com/Politics/rep-alexandria-ocasiocortez-welcomes-trumps-socialism-jab/story?id=60893775.

40. Baker, "Trump Asks for Unity, But Presses Hard Line on Immigration."

41. Matt Mackowiak, "The Squad Is a Real Threat – To Democrats," *The Washington Times*, July 17, 2019, https://www.washingtontimes.com/news/2019/jul/17/the-squad-is-a-real-threat-to-democrats/.

42. Gearan and Dawsey, "Trump Debuts His Case for Reelection in State of the Union Address."

43. Seitz-Wald, "Trump Slams 'ridiculous partisan investigations' in State of the Union Address."

44. Ibid.

45. Stephen Collinson, "Trump's Call for Compromise is Only on His Own Terms," CNN News, February 6, 2019, https://www.cnn.com/2019/02/06/politics/donald-trump-state-of-the-unionaddress/index.html.

46. Baker, "Trump Asks for Unity, But Presses Hard Line on Immigration."

47. Ibid.

48. Gearan and Dawsey, "Trump Debuts His Case for Reelection in State of the Union Address."

49. Rucker and Olornnipa, "In Dissonant State of the Union Speech, Trump Seeks Unity while Depicting Ruin."

50. Hulse, "State of the Union Speech Puts Democratic Resurgence on Full Display."

51. Collinson, "Trump Call for Compromise is Only on His Own Terms."

52. Liptak and Diamond, "Trump Calls for Rejection of 'Politics of Revenge' in Speech that Jabs Democrats."

53. Marisa Fernandez, "Government Shutdown to Continue through Christmas," *Axios.com*, December 22, 2018, https://www.axios.com/mitch-mcconnell-up-to-democrats-shutdown-deal-with-trump--04f41d88-2a97-4b54-8d28-468d17f81fd6.html.

54. Cheyenne Haslett, "State of the Union 2019: President Donald Trump Calls for Unity, Renews Pledge to Build Wall," ABC News, February 6, 2019, https://abcnews.go.com/Politics/donaldtrump-address-nation-2nd-state-union/story?id=60785409.

55. Baker, "Trump Asks for Unity, But Presses Hard Line on Immigration."

56. Seitz-Wald, "Trump Slams 'ridiculous partisan investigations' in State of the Union Address."

57. Liptak and Diamond, "Trump Calls for Rejection of 'Politics of Revenge' in Speech that Jabs Democrats."

58. Suzanne Gamboa, "Xavier Becerra Blasts Trump's Wall in Spanish-language Rebuttal," NBC News, February 6, 2019, https://www.nbcnews.com/news/latino/xavier-becerra-blasts-trump-s-wall-spanish-language-rebuttal-n967986.

59. Seitz-Wald, "Trump Slams 'ridiculous partisan investigations' in State of the Union Address."

60. Baker, "Trump Asks for Unity, But Presses Hard Line on Immigration."

61. Rucker and Olornnipa, "In Dissonant State of the Union speech, Trump Seeks Unity while Depicting Ruin."

62. Collinson, "Trump's Call for Compromise is Only on His Own Terms."

63. Liptak and Diamond, "Trump Calls for Rejection of 'Politics of Revenge' in Speech that Jabs Democrats."

64. Ibid.

65. Collinson, "Trump's Call for Compromise is Only on His Own Terms."

66. Dowd, "In State of the Union Address, Trump Bookends Bipartisanship Around a Core of Raw Division."

67. Liptak and Diamond, "Trump Calls for Rejection of 'Politics of Revenge' in Speech that Jabs Democrats."

68. Seitz-Wald, "Trump Slams 'ridiculous partisan investigations' in State of the Union Address."

69. Keneally, "7 Memorable Lines from the State of the Union."

70. Rick Klein, "Trump Seeks to Upend Trumpism – if Only for a Night," ABC News, February 5, 2019, https://abcnews.go.com/Politics/trump-seeks-upend-trumpism-nightanalysis/story?id=60873521.

71. Haslett, "State of the Union 2019."

72. Rucker and Olornnipa, "In Dissonant State of the Union speech, Trump Seeks Unity while Depicting Ruin."

73. Ibid.

74. Alex Pappas, "State of the Union: Trump Decries 'Ridiculous' Investigations, 'Revenge' Politics in Unity Appeal," FOX News, February 5, 2019, https://www.foxnews.com/politics/presidenttrump-delivers-state-of-the-union-address.

75. Brooke Singman, "Trump Argues Border Wall in State of the Union, Says Tolerance for illegal Immigration is 'Cruel,'" FOX News, February 5, 2019, https://www.foxnews.com/politics/trump-urges- border-wall-in-state-of-the-union-says-tolerance-for-illegal-immigration-is-cruel.

76. Aaron Blake, "Five Key Takeaways, from the Border Wall to a Bipartisan Applause Line," *The Washington Post*, February 6, 2019, WP00000020190206ef2600009 obtained from factiva.com.

77. Karma Allen, "Lawmakers Slam Trump Over 'Ridiculous Partisan Investigations' Comment During State of the Union," ABC News, February 5, 2019, https://abcnews.go.com/Politics/lawmakers-slam-trump-ridiculous-partisan-investigationscomment-state/story?id=60870333.

78. Allen, "Lawmakers Slam Trump Over 'Ridiculous Partisan Investigations' Comment During State of the Union."

79. Bump, "Trump's State of the Union Speech Drew the One Parallel to Richard Nixon that it Shouldn't Have."

80. Collinson, "Trump's Call for Compromise is Only on His Own Terms."

81. Allen, "Lawmakers Slam Trump Over 'Ridiculous Partisan Investigations' Comment During State of the Union."

82. Egan, "Lauren Egan, "Top 10 Highlights from Trump's State of the Union."

83. Hulse, "State of the Union Speech Puts Democratic Resurgence on Full Display."

84. Ibid.

85. Klein, "Trump Seeks to Upend Trumpism – if Only for a Night"; Rucker and Olornnipa, "In Dissonant State of the Union speech, Trump Seeks Unity while Depicting Ruin"; Seitz-Wald, "Trump Slams 'ridiculous partisan investigations' in State of the Union Address"; Pappas, "State of the Union"; Collinson, "Trump's Call for Compromise is Only on His Own Terms"; Liptak and Diamond, "Trump Calls for Rejection of 'Politics of Revenge' in Speech that Jabs Democrats"; Allen, "Lawmakers Slam Trump Over 'Ridiculous Partisan Investigations' Comment During State of the Union"; Keneally, "7 Memorable Lines from the State of the Union."

86. Montoya-Galvez, "Citing Northam's Comments, Trump Urges Late-Term Abortion Ban During State of the Union"; Pappas, "State of the Union."; Miles, "Trump Calls out Pro-Choice Abortion Bills During State of the Union."

87. Seitz-Wald, "Trump Slams 'ridiculous partisan investigations' in State of the Union Address"; Brooke Singman, "Trump, in State of the Union Address, Announces Second Kim Summit Date," FOX News, February 5, 2019, https://www.foxnews.com/politics/trump-toannounce-new-kim-summit-during-state-of-the-union-address.

88. Seitz-Wald, "Trump Slams 'ridiculous partisan investigations' in State of the Union Address"; Singman, "Trump, in State of the Union Address, Announces Second Kim Summit Date."

89. Rucker and Olornnipa, "In Dissonant State of the Union speech, Trump Seeks Unity while Depicting Ruin"; Keneally, "7 Memorable Lines from the State of the Union."

90. Conor Finnegan, "Trump's Claims of US Success in Afghanistan Ring Hollow Amid Taliban Talks, Reality on Ground," ABC News, February 6, 2019, https://abcnews.go.com/Politics/trumpsclaims-us-success-afghanistan-ring-hollow-amid/story?id=60885154; Liptak and Diamond, "Trump Calls for Rejection of 'Politics of Revenge' in Speech that Jabs Democrats."

91. Liptak and Diamond, "Trump Calls for Rejection of 'Politics of Revenge' in Speech that Jabs Democrats."

92. Rucker and Olornnipa, "In Dissonant State of the Union speech, Trump Seeks Unity while Depicting Ruin."

93. Singman, "Trump Argues Border Wall in State of the Union, Says Tolerance for Illegal Immigration is 'Cruel.'"

94. Re, "Democrats Unmoved by Trump's State of the Union Bid to break Gridlock on Border Security."

95. See, for instance, Klein, "Trump Seeks to Upend Trumpism – if Only for a Night." Rucker and Olornnipa, "In Dissonant State of the Union speech, Trump Seeks Unity while Depicting Ruin." Seitz-Wald, "Trump Slams 'ridiculous partisan investigations' in State of the Union Address"; Pappas, "State of the Union"; Liptak and Diamond, "Trump Calls for Rejection of 'Politics of Revenge' in Speech that Jabs Democrats."

96. Klein, "Trump Seeks to Upend Trumpism – if Only for a Night."

97. Ibid.

98. Rucker and Olornnipa, "In Dissonant State of the Union speech, Trump Seeks Unity while Depicting Ruin."

99. Re, "Democrats Unmoved by Trump's State of the Union Bid to break Gridlock on Border Security."

100. Jane C. Timm and Carrie Dann, "State of the Union Fact Check: What's True and False in Trump's Address," NBC News, February 6, 2019, https://www.nbcnews.com/politics/politics-news/state-union-fact-check-what-s-true-what-s-false-n967326.

101. Baker, "Trump Asks for Unity, But Presses Hard Line on Immigration."

102. Ibid.

103. Hulse, "State of the Union Speech Puts Democratic Resurgence on Full Display."

104. Allen, "Lawmakers Slam Trump Over 'Ridiculous Partisan Investigations' Comment During State of the Union."

105. Liptak and Diamond, "Trump Calls for Rejection of 'Politics of Revenge' in Speech that Jabs Democrats."

106. "VA Governor on Abortion."

107. Julie Rovner, "Trump Highlights Health Agenda with Wow to Lower 'unfair' Drug Prices," NBC News, February 5, 2019, https://www.nbcnews.com/health/health-news/trump-highlights-health-agenda-vow-lower-unfair-drug-prices-n968281.

108. Devan Cole, "Schumer: Trump's Address was 'Political, Divisive, Calculating, Even Nasty at Times,'" CNN News, February 6, 2019, ttps://www.cnn.com/2019/02/06/politics/chuckschumer-trump-state-of-the-union-cnntv/index.html.

109. Rucker and Olornnipa, "In Dissonant State of the Union Speech, Trump Seeks Unity while Depicting Ruin."

110. Ibid.

111. Paige Winfield Cunningham, "The Health 202: Trump places health care at center stage in State of Union address," *The Washington Post*, February 6, 2019, WPCOM00020190206ef26006y1 obtained from factiva.com.

112. Klein, "Trump Seeks to Upend Trumpism – if Only for a Night."

113. Fahenthold and Sonmez, "In State of the Union, Trump Plans to Urge Bipartisan Cooperation in a Sharply Divided Congress."

114. Liptak and Diamond, "Trump Calls for Rejection of 'Politics of Revenge' in Speech that Jabs Democrats."

115. Klein, "Trump Seeks to Upend Trumpism – if Only for a Night."

116. Liptak and Diamond, "Trump Calls for Rejection of 'Politics of Revenge' in Speech that Jabs Democrats."

117. Dowd, "In State of the Union Address, Trump Bookends Bipartisanship Around a Core of Raw Division."

118. Ibid.

119. Haslett, "State of the Union 2019" and Keneally, "7 Memorable Lines from the State of the Union."

120. Liptak and Diamond, "Trump Calls for Rejection of 'Politics of Revenge' in Speech that Jabs Democrats."

121. Collinson, "Trump's Call for Compromise is Only on His Own Terms."

122. Gearan and Dawsey, "Trump Debuts His Case for Reelection in State of the Union Address."

123. Mike DeBonis, "Sharing the State of the Union Spotlight, Pelosi Softly Makes Her Own Statement," *The Washington Post*, February 6, 2019, WPCOM00020190205ef250099n obtained from factiva.com.

124. Collinson, "Trump's Call for Compromise is Only on His Own Terms."

125. Ibid.

126. Ibid.

127. Baker, "Trump Asks for Unity, but Presses Hard Line on Immigration."

128. Devan Cole, "Schumer: Trump's Address was 'Political, Divisive, Calculating, Even Nasty at Times,'" CNN News, February 6, 2019, ttps://www.cnn.com/2019/02/06/politics/chuckschumer-trump-state-of-the-union-cnntv/index.html.

129. Cole, "Schumer."

130. Pappas, "State of the Union."

131. Re, "Democrats Unmoved by Trump's State of the Union Bid to break Gridlock on Border Security."

132. Ibid.

133. Ibid.

134. Hulse, "State of the Union Speech Puts Democratic Resurgence on Full Display."

135. Ibid.

136. Liptak and Diamond, "Trump Calls for Rejection of 'Politics of Revenge' in Speech that Jabs Democrats."

137. Julie Rovner, "Trump Highlights Health Agenda with Vow to Lower 'unfair' Drug Prices," NBC News, February 5, 2019, https://www.nbcnews.com/health/health-news/trump-highlights-health-agenda-vow-lower-unfair-drug-prices-n968281.

138. Rovner, "Trump Highlights Health Agenda with Vow to Lower 'unfair' Drug Prices."

139. Klein, "Trump Seeks to Upend Trumpism – if Only for a Night"; Rucker and Olornnipa, "In Dissonant State of the Union speech, Trump Seeks Unity while Depicting Ruin."

140. Keneally, "7 Memorable Lines from the State of the Union.". See also, Gearan and Dawsey, "Trump Debuts His Case for Reelection in State of the Union Address." Pappas, "State of the Union"; Haslett, "Rep. Alexandria Ocasio-Cortez welcomes Trump's 'socialism' Jab, says He's 'scared'".

141. Liptak and Diamond, "Trump Calls for Rejection of 'Politics of Revenge' in Speech that Jabs Democrats."

142. Timm and Dann, "State of the Union Fact Check."

143. David Nakamura, "Immigration Agenda Is Emphasized, But No Talk of a National Emergency," *The Washington Post*, February 6, 2019, WP00000020190206ef260003f obtained from factiva.com.

144. Jonathan Allen, "On Trump's Big Applause Line, the Sound of Silence Was Stunning," NBC News, February 6, 2019, https://www.nbcnews.com/politics/white-house/trump-s-big-state-union-applause-line-sound-silence-was-n968136

145. Hulse, "State of the Union Speech Puts Democratic Resurgence on Full Display."

146. Ibid.

147. DeBonis, "Sharing the State of the Union Spotlight, Pelosi Softly Makes Her Own Statement."

148. Montoya-Galvez, "Citing Northam's Comments, Trump Urges Late-Term Abortion Ban During State of the Union." See, too, Rovner, "Trump Highlights Health Agenda with Vow to Lower 'unfair' Drug Prices."

*Chapter 7*

# Immigration Reform

Anyone who even marginally follows politics knows that immigration has been a contentious issue throughout both Trump's candidacy and presidency. It began in earnest with his initial campaign announcement on June 16, 2015: "They're [Mexico] sending people that have lots of problems, and they're bringing those problems with [them]. They're bringing drugs, they're bringing crime, they're rapists . . ." and most in the mainstream news media (MSM) stopped listening and starting reporting there. The rest of that ignored paragraph, like parts of the speech before, went like this: "and some, I assume are good people, but I speak to border guards and they tell us what we're getting. And it only makes common sense. They're sending us not the right people. It's coming from more than Mexico. It's coming from all over South and Latin America, and it's coming probably . . . from the Middle East."[1] The MSM, Democrat opponents, and left-leaning Twittersphere became fixated on "They're bringing drugs, they're bringing crime, they're rapists," and accusations of Trump's "racism" and "xenophobia" from those quarters have strongly continued unabated since.[2]

President Trump's initial attempts to modify border crossings, place a temporary ban on visa entries from terrorist compromised countries, and to build his promised wall were all met with extremely negative MSM coverage and also oppositional legal actions, much of which went initially against the Trump administration in lower courts only to end up at the Supreme Court where the Trump administration has prevailed about two-thirds of the time.[3] Regardless of the outcomes, immigration issues, even when echoing or extending those of the Obama administration, have become a lightening rod for criticism and negative press coverage of Trump and his administration. And yet, immigration is a well-known problem, one in desperate need of reform, an issue that no presidential administration since Johnson's in 1965 has addressed with any real success.

## PRESIDENT TRUMP'S SPEECH

On May 16, 2019, President Trump announced through a formal speech his plan for comprehensive *legal* immigration reform.[4] Trump framed the overall plan as a "fair, modern, and lawful system of immigration," stressing that "it's about time" that such an overhaul is made. For President Trump, the plan "proposal fulfills our sacred duty to those living here today, while ensuring America remains a welcoming country to immigrants joining us tomorrow. And we want immigrants coming in. We cherish the open door that we want to create for our country, but a big proportion of those immigrants must come in through merit and skill." Ultimately, for the Trump administration, the plan is "just common sense," and it is pushed as "pro-American, pro-immigrant, and pro-worker." Importantly, with the nationwide abundance of talk about "illegal immigration," including his own, Trump only uses that term once in his speech.

### Framing

There are four main themes in the president's speech, each distinctively framed: Legal Immigration, Purpose of the Plan, Physical Infrastructure, and Legal Issues.

*Legal Immigration: Framing Merit*

This was the heart of the speech, and President Trump frames the present system of legal immigration simply: it "is totally dysfunctional. . . . America's last major overhaul of our legal admissions policy was 54 years ago." In its place he wishes to see something "fair, transparent, and promot[ing] equality and opportunity for all." Importantly, the "plan makes no change to the number of green cards allocated each year. But instead of admitting people through random chance, we will establish simple, universal criteria for admission to the United States. No matter where in the world you're born, no matter who your relatives are, if you want to become an American citizen, it will be clear exactly what standard we ask you to achieve." Trump feels "merit" is the key, and thus the new plan.

Highlighting broken features of current law, the president offers this educational component: "66 percent of legal immigrants come here on the basis of random chance. They're admitted solely because they have a relative in the United States. And it doesn't really matter who that relative is. Another 21 percent of immigrants are issued either by random lottery, or because they are fortunate enough to be selected for humanitarian relief." He frames this as a problem, one fundamentally at odds with certain American values: "Random selection is contrary to American values and blocks out many qualified potential immigrants from around the world who have much to contribute." Ultimately, his plan is designed to "create a clear path for top talent," and this is linked with other Western countries such as Canada.

The randomness of the current admission system brings in those with or without skill sets, and that these "senseless rules of the current system" prevent the US government from giving preference to highly desirable vocations: "We're not able to give preference to a doctor, a researcher, a student who graduated number one in his class from the finest colleges in the world." Instead, "the annual green card flow is mostly low-wage and low-skilled. Newcomers compete for jobs against the most vulnerable Americans and put pressure on our social safety net and generous welfare programs." This policy has counterproductive results, and even though wages "are rising . . . our current immigration system works at cross-purposes, placing downward pressure on wages for the working class, which is what we don't want to do." Continuing an educational component, the president states that only "12 percent of legal immigrants are selected based on skill or based on merit. In countries like Canada, Australia, and New Zealand—and others—that number is closer to 60 and even 70 and 75 percent, in some cases."

To make necessary changes, then, the plan seeks to "increase the proportion of highly skilled immigration from 12 percent to 57 percent," and the president would like to see that "go higher." Stressing again the standardized nature of this plan, he adds, "This will bring us in line with other countries and make us globally competitive." The plan does not do away with family preferences, only truncates them, so spouses and children are still prioritized: "They go right to the front of the line . . . where they should be."

Certainly, the president must contend with the characterization from some quarters (Democrats, the press, etc.) that he is anti-immigrant. So, making a link with recent immigrants, and perhaps speaking to allegations of his anti-immigrant stance, Trump adds, "The millions of legal immigrants who have come to America over the past half century are now cherished members of our national family. [It is] in their interest, and their children's interest, to adopt a green card system that promotes a rising standard of living for all of our citizens."

## Purpose of the Plan

Presidential initiatives are often bold, and Trump's plan here is no exception. The plan is put forth as one to "transform America's immigration system into the pride of our nation and the envy of the modern world." Even more aspirational is the plan's envisioned purpose of building upon America's "rich history of immigration, while strengthening the bonds of citizenship that bind us together as a national family." To contextualize the political situation, and single out Congressional Democrats, Trump states, "Democrats are proposing open borders, lower wages, and, frankly, lawless chaos. We are proposing an immigration plan that puts the jobs, wages, and safety of American workers first." As part of contextualizing this policy initiative, the speech taps into a "time" element when it characterizes the administration's policy as "our strong, fair, and pro-America immigration policy. It's time to restore our national unity and reaffirm our national purpose. It is time to rebuild our country for all Americans." It then calls for unifying around a common purpose: "Together, we will create an immigration system to make America safer, and stronger, and greater than ever before." Ultimately, the plan is designed to "promote integration, assimilation, and national unity," while promoting a culture that "respects, and even strengthens, our culture, our traditions, and our values."

*Physical Infrastructure: Focus on Security Through Technology*

President Trump does seek common ground on border security, offering that "everyone agrees that the physical infrastructure on the border and the ports of entry [are] gravely underfunded and woefully inadequate." Pointing out current practices, he continues, stating that crossing points "scan only a small fraction of the vehicles, goods, and all of the other things coming across, including people. And, sadly, the drugs pour across our border." Alleviating such problems comes through infrastructure change, notably, investing in "technology to better scan everything coming through [and] curbing the flow of drugs and contraband, while speeding up legal trade and commerce." This will in part by accomplished by setting up a "permanent and self-sustaining border security trust fund."

Part of this infrastructure update and expansion includes continuing construction of the walls already on the border; however, "the wall," is positioned not as part of this particular plan, but of something already in process: "Importantly, we're already building the wall, and we should have close to 400 miles built by the end of next year, and probably even more than that. It's going up very rapidly." In this sense, the wall is not included as a solution to all problems, but rather a small component of the actions addressing a litany of problems at the border, and a solution already in the process of being enacted.

## Legal Issues: Framing Incentives

The president relies on expert testimony of sorts to focus on removal of incentives for smuggling women and children. He states that law enforcement personnel see the smuggling, but that the American people do not hear about it. Stating that current "law and federal court rulings encourage criminal organizations to smuggle children across the border," the president shares that the "tragic result is that 65 percent of all border-crossers this year were either minors or adults traveling with minors." Addressing this issue, and addressing a policy of family separation started with the Obama administration but made contentious under his own administration, the new plan "will change the law to stop the flood of child smuggling and to humanely reunite unaccompanied children with their families back home—and rapidly."

Specifically addressing concerns of false asylum claims, he adds that "legitimate asylum seekers are being displaced by those lodging frivolous claims . . . to gain admission into our country," and then shows how this harms more than just those honestly seeking asylum in that those abusing it are "also strain[ing] our public school systems, our hospitals, and local shelters, using funds that we should, and that have to, go to elderly veterans, at-risk youth, Americans in poverty, and those in genuine need of protection. We're using the funds that should be going to them. And that shouldn't happen." Asking for support for the plan, the president specifies that the plan "expedites relief for legitimate asylum seekers by screening out the meritless claims" and also "closes loopholes in federal law to make clear that gang members and criminals are inadmissible."

## Moral Foundations

President Trump's speech touches upon all five moral foundations, but not with equal emphasis. Overwhelmingly, we find Loyalty(ingroup)/Betrayal as the primary foundation in this speech. This is followed by Care/Harm, Fairness/Cheating, Sanctity/Degradation, and Authority/Subversion in decreasing order of presence.

### Loyalty(Ingroup)/Betrayal

The strongest and most pervasive moral foundation was that of Loyalty(ingroup)/Betrayal. The president spoke of creating a "fair, modern, and lawful system of immigration," one that would be the "pride of our nation," in addition to "strengthening the bonds of citizenship that bind us together as a national family"; the plan would capitalize on the fact that "we have forged one people and one nation under God." The plan was characterized as "pro-immigrant," one that "stops illegal immigration." Further heightening the link with loyalty/ingroups was the idea that the plan, although acting to stop unlimited chain migration, would still "prioritize the immediate family of new Americans—spouses and children." The stress on family was repeated by the president's plan in that new immigrant citizens are now "cherished members of our national family."

Part of the plan's name even stressed Ingroup Loyalty, "the Build America visa." The main idea was to "promote integration, assimilation, and national unity, [thus] future immigrants will be required to learn English and to pass a civics exam prior to admission." "We give them a history, a heritage, a home, and a future of limitless possibilities and potential." It was characterized as a "pro-America immigration policy," one that restores "our national unity and reaffirm our national purpose."

## Care/Harm

After Loyalty(ingroup)/Betrayal, the next most intense foundation was Care/Harm. Of note is that it was evenly split between just those two poles, with the president making half of his case for the Harm the present system is doing and the other half relying on how the new system would exhibit Caring qualities. In terms of Harm, the "Democrats are proposing open borders, lower wages, and . . . lawless chaos." There are problems at the border, including drugs and human trafficking. Additionally, rampant asylum abuse strains the entire system, as does the widespread instances of illegal immigration. Trump points out that "foreign workers are coming in and they're taking the jobs that would normally go to American workers."

In terms of Care, the new plan would put "the jobs, wages, and safety of American workers first" and "fully secures the border" while it also "protects American wages." Thus, it puts "security and wages first," through a "merit-based, high-security plan." The idea is to make the border "100 percent operationally secure"; "humanely reunite unaccompanied children with their families back home" while also "affording protection to those fleeing government persecutions"—all of this within a context of keeping out dangerous felons, gang members, and so on. According to the plan, the current policy is not obtaining the best and brightest from around world, whereas the new plan would, and is also in the interest of new immigrant citizens: "it is . . . in their interest, and their children's interest, to adopt a green card system that promotes a rising standard of living for all of our citizens."

## Fairness/Cheating

The main negative expressed in this foundation is that the random selection of the current policy is "inherently unfair." It "discriminate[s] against brilliance." Moreover, those who immigrate illegally are essentially line breaking, cheating; thus, another inherently unfair practice. Cheating is also implied by those gaming the present system through which "legitimate asylum seekers are being displaced by those lodging frivolous claims." The new policy will "create a fair, modern, and lawful system of immigration." For Trump, "The system will finally be fair, transparent, and promote equality and opportunity for all."

Part of the inherent Fairness is based on the idea that it will be "merit-based" not based on familial connections and line jumping. The plan will "establish simple, universal criteria for admission to the United States. Ultimately, the administration characterizes it as a "fair, and pro-America immigration policy."

## Sanctity/Degradation

Although in only a few instances, the new policy is firmly placed within the tradition of linking government actions with a higher purpose, a higher duty than to one's political party. Referring to both the founding of the nation and to legal immigrants, Trump states that "we have forged one people and one nation under God." And importantly, the plan is characterized in such a way that it enlarges its purpose: "Our proposal fulfills our sacred duty to those living here today."

## Authority/Subversion

This foundation, although present, was minimally touched upon: "we pledge allegiance to the same, great American flag" and the policy is one that "strengthens, our culture, our traditions, and our values." Although minimally touched upon, its presence in such a short speech does act to underpin the policy proposed, particularly with the focus on *legal* immigration.

## Trump Summary

The Trump speech framed seven key themes and conveyed on all five moral foundations. In terms of frames, Legal Immigration was dominant. The present system was characterized as old and broken, and entry relied primarily on luck of the draw and who you knew. The old system, because of its randomness, did not represent well American values. New system would be merit and skill based, and thus fairer to low-income Americans and current legal immigrants. The Purpose of the Plan was framed as an update to the legal immigration system, one that would focus on a common purpose, strengthen bonds of citizenship, and promote American unity. Framing of the Physical Infrastructure had to do with sharing potential points of bipartisanship, as well as stressing that this was more than the continuation of adding on to existing walls, but also the investment in security through technological innovations. Finally, Legal Issues were framed to accentuate the immediate need to change the laws so they no longer facilitated child and human smuggling. Moreover, false asylum claims were overwhelming the system, and Americans needed protection from criminals and abusers of the system.

Of the three moral foundations, Loyalty(ingroup)/Betrayal was the strongest and most pervasive. Strengthening "the bonds of citizenship that bind us together as a national family" through the creation of a new system of immigration that promotes national unity was stressed. Thus, the new system is pro-immigrant (Loyalty) and anti-illegal immigrant (Betrayal). The plan acts to protect immediate family members, and provides history, heritage, and a home. The Care/Harm foundation was evenly split, with the present system being harmful to immigrants, to citizens, and to national unity; the new system would care for legal immigrants, citizens, and promote national unity. The Fairness/Cheating foundation stressed both aspects of this foundation. Those coming in illegally, or making false asylum claims are cheating; the present system's randomness of selection is inherently unfair. Eliminating these issues, and focusing on merit-based immigration is fair. The Sanctity/Degradation foundation supports Trump's linking immigration reform to One Nation Under God, so it becomes a "sacred" duty. Finally, Authority/Subversion involved pledging allegiance to the Flag, and working to strengthening traditions and values.

## PRESS RESPONSE

Although a contentious issue, the overall press response was restrained in terms of sheer numbers.[5] The main themes expressed in the news stories are, in order of strength: Criticism of Plan Specifics, The 2020 Election, and What's Missing From the Plan.

### Framing

*Criticisms of Plan Specifics*

This was by far the most powerful frame in the press response, with the actual coverage about the specifics of the Trump administration's plan ranging from rather detailed to almost nothing. For instance, one article only mentioned the specifics of the plan in a quote by a Tea Party activist: "Ending the visa lottery system and increasing merit-based immigration practices are two good steps in the effort to realign America's immigration system with our own national priorities, but they're not nearly enough."[6] A more detailed article stated that the proposal would "create a system that favors applicants who are highly skilled, well-educated and speak English, as well as have potential employment over family-based immigration."[7] Some important contextualizing information was provided in this article as well. Sharing White House estimates, this article conveyed that "12 percent of people who obtain green cards and citizenship do so based on 'employment and skill,' while 66 percent enter via family-based connections and 22 percent through humanitarian visas and the diversity lottery. Under the new proposal, employment and skill would increase to 57 percent, 33 percent for family-based and 10 percent for everything else."[8] Finally, the newly created visa program is mentioned: "The merit-based system proposal is centered around what would be called the 'Build America' visa. It recognizes three categories: extraordinary talent, professional and specialized vocations, and exceptional students."[9]

However, the above are the exceptions, with the majority of articles contextualizing specifics within a frame of criticism. Both *The Washington Post* and *The New York Times*, for instance, erroneously stated that the plan would eliminate spouses and children of immigrants from being allowed into the country.[10] For instance, *The New York Times* wrote: "Democrats and immigration advocates have long opposed many of the proposals outlined by Mr. Trump, like scaling back the family-based immigration system, which allows immigrants to bring their spouses and children to live with them, and . . ."[11] Although true that family-based migration would be cut (from roughly 66 percent currently to about 33 percent), this is primarily targeted toward eliminating chain migration. The parent category would be curtailed, but not entirely eliminated, and spouses and children are prioritized. On this point *The Washington Post* wrote, "Because Trump does not intend to increase the number of green cards issued per year, that would mean that the parent category would be significantly cut if not eliminated."[12] *The New York Times* quoted those particularly opposed to the president's plan as saying, "It was no surprise that Trump is seeking to devastate family reunifications. 'That is the consistent theme of this administration. . . . Yet, Melania [Trump] has benefited from the immigration system; his in-laws are here because of the immigration system. He demonizes immigrants when he is benefiting and profiting from undocumented workers at his golf club.'"[13]

In particular, with the plan put into a context of the 2020 election (discussed below) instead of into a context of a starting point of immigration reform, the criticisms of the press are better understood. For instance, "But as the details trickled out, so did the questions. How would the administration address the massive influx of refugees at the border? What would happen to young immigrants living in the U.S. since childhood known as 'DREAmers' as well as millions more who have spent decades working in this country? And while Trump's plan called to improve border security in general, was the president ready to let go of that 'big, beautiful wall' he promised on the campaign?"[14]

The most frequently quoted source for criticism of the proposals came from House Speaker Nancy Pelosi. The Speaker was relayed repeatedly as objecting "to the use of the word 'merit' when it comes to immigration selection, calling it 'condescending.' 'Are they saying family is without merit? Are they saying most of the people who have ever come to the United States in the history of our country are without merit because they don't have an engineering degree?'"[15] She continues, "This dead-on-arrival plan is not a remotely serious proposal."[16]

Quotes from numerous critics were provided, conveying a sense of widespread criticism, even as the plan itself fell safely into the majority opinion of Americans:

1. "Maria Teresa Kumar, president and CEO of Voto Latino, said the plan is 'an illusion' that gives Trump space to 'own the airwaves' on immigration while side-stepping serious problems. 'We have created the cruelest modern-day policy against children,' she said of the situation at the border. 'There is no urgency in this plan.'"[17]
2. The proposed civics test was described as "at best unnecessary and could screen out some very skilled, ambitious immigrants who are ready to be productive in America, whatever the test says. . . ."[18]
3. And since it did not address DREAMers, it was "a nonstarter with Democrats in Congress."[19]
4. Left-leaning Amnesty International was quoted as calling the plan "an outrageous attempt to shut doors to everyone but the most wealthy and privileged individuals, circumventing human rights and legal obligations toward asylum-seekers."
5. The discredited Southern Poverty Law Center[20] was quoted as calling the plan "profoundly anti-American" and said the "English-language requirement is deeply at odds with our nation's values and diversity."[21]
6. For *The New York Times*, the plan was about "bashing Democrats as advocates of 'open boarders, lower wages and, frankly, lawless chaos. . . .'"[22]
7. *The New York Times* also made the argument that since you cannot send illegal unaccompanied children back because they left poor conditions, that the plan is essentially immoral and you might as well allow the parents of the children into the country.[23]

## 2020 Election

This frame intertwined with the other frames, providing important context for understanding, from the press's point of view, the new immigration policy. Although a year and a half away, the press strongly framed all coverage of the event, even the other frames, as an election issue. Speaking of the plan, the press asks, "Can it pass before the 2020 presidential election?" Injecting this goal into the mix, the press questioned President Trump on the issues, to which he was relayed as saying, "If for some reason Democrats don't go along with his plan, it will pass after Democrats [*sic*] win back the House in 2020, teeing up another reason for the president's supporters to come out to the polls next November."[24] Another example shows the strength of this framing: "The president also framed the immigration debate in terms of his reelection campaign, threatening that if Democrats refused to support what he called his 'merit-based, high-security plan,' he would pass it 'immediately after the election, when we take back the House, keep the Senate and, of course, hold the presidency.'"[25]

NBC News devoted an entire article to frame the policy announcement as an attempt to "play for the middle . . . with [a] legal immigration focus."[26] They, along with other news sources, suggested that the president was "choosing a thin slice of popular turf on which to make his stand. It's a rare Trump play for the middle. Ultimately, Trump's new plan is mostly a change in his rhetorical focus — from illegal immigration to overhauling the nation's legal immigration system."[27] Although the plan was specifically developed to stress areas of potential bipartisanship, the press presented it as an either/or consideration for the 2020 election: Trump must either deal with both illegal and legal immigration issues at the same time or deal with nothing. The plan had been placed into a context of "too narrow," with the press following this by quoting Democrats responding that it was not comprehensive enough: "And that's why Democrats rushed Thursday to put a wider lens on his overall policies."[28] This Democrat-led effort was presented as dangerous to Trump's policy priorities, since "there may be some risk for Trump in his omissions, as activists on both sides of the immigration debate called him out for not prioritizing matters they see as crises."[29] Thus, no starting point, and the middle ground is dangerous.

CNN was perhaps the most pointed in placing a partisan interpretation on the policy proposal, writing that Trump was hoping "for political victories to showcase to voters in the 2020 election. The President is a shrewd political operator. It's always possible that he's deluding himself—but not likely. So the most plausible interpretation . . . is that it's trying to maximize the political capital he can wring out of each initiative — a sure sign that an election is just 18 months away and approaching fast."[30] And, even as it seems likely, without evidence *The New York Times* speculated, "Mr. Trump's latest immigration proposal was drafted by [advisors] who spent months working on a plan that would double as a central plank of Mr. Trump's 2020 campaign."[31] Offering no support, *The Washington Post* simply quoted an immigration rights activist who "dismissed Trump's plan as a campaign ploy."[32]

## What's Missing

Closely linked with the Criticisms of Plan Specifics frame was inclusion of the idea that the plan was deficient because it did not contain items that the media thought it should; in short, a What's Missing frame. This frame intentionally omits the idea pushed by the administration that the plan was a starting point for discussion where it thought there might be opportunities for bipartisanship. The media pointed out that although the "plan does try to curb illegal immigration by building more wall and modernizing ports of entry, it does not tackle the issue of undocumented immigrants already in the United States."[33] Additionally, and importantly pointed out by most of the media outlets, "It does not discuss what to do with temporary workers and it does not handle finding a pathway to citizenship for the so-called 'DREAMers' or those temporarily covered by Deferred Action for Childhood Arrivals, DACA, an ongoing priority for Democrats and swing-state Republicans."[34] The assumption being that a pathway for citizenship must be found.

Others pointed out that it "avoids hot-button issues like the growing backlog of asylum-seekers and the status of so-called Dreamers and is almost certainly dead on arrival in Congress."[35] A few news organizations mentioned concerns of nonleft-leaning activists: "There may be some risk for Trump in his omissions, as activists on both sides of the immigration debate called him out for not prioritizing matters they see as crises—such as the surge of migrants to the U.S.-Mexico border on the political right and the undetermined status of the so-called DREAMers on the left."[36] However, it was the concerns of Democrats and liberal activists that were highlighted as making the plan untenable, summed up in this statement by House Speaker Nancy Pelosi, mentioned above: "This dead-on-arrival plan is not a remotely serious proposal."[37] This was in large part ascribed to the fact that "Trump's plan doesn't address millions of undocumented immigrants who are currently in the country, including the so-called DREAMers who were brought to the U.S. as children, or the treatment of minors and their families at the U.S.-Mexico border."[38] This type of criticism repeated itself often, just in slightly different phrasing: "Trump's plan does not address the status of immigrants brought to the U.S. illegally as children and thus is a nonstarter with Democrats in Congress."[39] It was thus, "dead-on-arrival."[40] The media went so far as to cherry-pick a quote from Democrat Senator Kamala Harris, who asserted that the plan "was rooted in an alternative reality that does not exist. 'I will tell you that I found the announcement today to be shortsighted. I found it to be an indication of an intention to not be relevant for the largest of number of people.'"[41]

The DREAMers were particularly focused upon: CNN quoted Democrat Senate Minority Leader Schumer as saying that a "plan that did not address protections for the so-called Dreamers, the roughly 700,000 young, undocumented immigrants brought to the United States as children or the 11 million undocumented immigrants currently living in the United States was a nonstarter. 'It ain't happening,' he said."[42] *The Washington Post* asserted that the plan "sidesteps some major components of the nation's immigration system that can be far more complex and controversial to resolve, such as the fate of the estimated 11 million immigrants without legal status and visas for temporary, low-skilled workers issues that have divided the Republican Party and pit the business community against labor unions."[43]

## Moral Foundations

In part due to the topic of the coverage—immigration—the news media's largest moral foundation was Loyalty(ingroup)/Betrayal, followed by relatively coequal uses of Authority/Subversion, Care/Harm, and, finally, minimal use of Fairness/Cheating.

### *Loyalty(Ingroup)/Betrayal*

Although most pronounced for both the Trump administration and the news media, the moral foundation the press relayed was decidedly negative. Some sense of the Trump administration foundation was provided, though, yet generally in a weakened sense, with no single sense of Ingroup Loyalty relayed: "'Our proposal is pro-America, pro-immigrant and pro-worker.'"[44] Additionally, the plan would "unify families,"[45] and allow in those "who will love and respect our country."[46] Minimally reported was Trump's hope that the "measures . . . would reinforce American values [and create] an immigration system that respects and even strengthens our culture, our traditions and our values."[47] Left out of the reporting was that the White House stressed that "What we tried to do is pick the places where we can unite."[48]

For the news media, there was a betrayal of the Ingroup. President Trump's record of immigration was relayed negatively, in that he allowed "lengthy detention of families at the border."[49] Through quotes his shift from chain migration to merit-based migration was depicted as an attack on the "family": "Are they saying family is without merit?"[50] For the press, "Trump's proposal would create a system that favors applicants who are highly skilled, well-educated and speak English, as well as have potential employment over family-based immigration."[51] In this sense, it would attack families since it would "cut deeply into family-based [chain] migration."[52] Because of this, "What the president is proposing is a xenophobic, anti-immigrant agenda that if applied to previous generations would have barred millions of European and Asian immigrants from contributing to our country."[53] This type of foundational contextualization continued throughout the coverage:

1. "Trump is seeking to devastate family reunifications."[54]
2. He is "gutting our asylum and refugee protections."[55]
3. The plan is "virulently antiimmigrant."[56]
4. It is a "'political document that is antiimmigration reform . . .' [it simply repackages] 'the same partisan, radical antiimmigrant policies . . .'"[57]
5. This "proposal to restrict family immigration undermines American values."[58]
6. "Democrats and immigration advocates have long opposed many of the proposals outlined by Mr. Trump, like scaling back the family-based immigration system, which allows immigrants to bring their spouses and children to live with them."[59]

Keep in mind that the proposed plan prioritized spouses and children.

They also attempted to downplay the president's concern with community safety, in that although he claims that "undocumented immigrants has caused a spike in crime, recent studies have shown no link between communities with increased undocumented immigrant populations and crime."[60] Too, the MSM use of "undocumented migrants"[61] or "undocumented immigrants" functions as repudiation of the president's use of "illegal immigrant," and thus acts to counter his term's link to a positive conception of Loyalty(ingroup)/Betrayal, whereas the media's use attempts to shift the notion from nation to global and nation to immigrant expanded family. This shift also involves the foundation of Authority/Subversion.

*Authority/Subversion*

The administration was depicted as stressing that the plan "is designed to become law,"[62] and differentiated between illegal and legal immigration. The plan was designed to "create a 'fair, modern and lawful system of immigration.'"[63] However, much stress was placed on the absence of policy initiatives dealing with illegal immigration, as such the administration being unable "legally to detain families" past twenty days.[64] The new plan "would by law allow"[65] longer detentions. Trump's assertion that if not passed, "illegal immigration and the crisis at our border will remain the issue at the forefront of the 2020 election" was partially conveyed.[66] However, little stressed was the president's moral assertion that "Democrats are proposing open borders, lower wages and frankly, lawless chaos."[67]

The press did relay to some extent the tension between illegal and legal, but almost exclusively in the context of dealing with the group known as DREAMers: the "plan does not address the status of immigrants brought to the U.S. illegally as children and thus is a nonstarter with Democrats in Congress."[68] Within this context the administration's change of focus "from illegal immigration to overhauling the nation's legal immigration system"[69] was noted, but to highlight its noncomprehensive nature, thus ensuring its "non-starter" status. Additionally, some criticism was brought in asserting the president was overstepping or abusing his authority: the plan was a "despicable abdication of moral authority,"[70] and his contemplation of using the "Insurrection Act, an arcane law that allows the president to employ the military to combat lawlessness or rebellion, to remove illegal immigrants, was another example of the same abuse."[71]

## Care/Harm

The moral underpinning of Care was conveyed by numerous quotes from the president. Thus, the plan, according to the president, "puts the jobs, wages and safety of American workers first,"[72] "fully secures the border," and "establishes a new legal immigration system that protects American wages.'"[73] Additionally, the White House considered it a "merit based, high-security plan."[74] Minimally reported by the MSM was the presidential conception that "putting in place measures to only allow high-qualified people to enter will help build a skilled workforce while not threatening Americans with blue-collar jobs"[75] and the importance of "protecting wages, attracting talent and unifying families."[76]

In contrast, the news media's conception of Care involved attempting to deflate President Trump's claims: Although the president claims that "undocumented immigrants has caused a spike in crime, recent studies have shown no link between communities with increased undocumented immigrant populations and crime."[77] Additionally, they acted to show the president as Harming people:

1. "His plans . . . would simply prolong his war on immigrants."[78]
2. "We have created the cruelest modern-day policy against children."[79]
3. "It could be a barrier to very productive immigrants becoming a part of American Society."[80]

## Fairness/Cheating

Although strongly asserted by President Trump, the press only lightly reported the administration position that "his proposal would create a 'fair, modern and lawful system of immigration'"[81] The single most quoted line was some form of the president's "we discriminate against brilliance."[82] The press highlighted instead what it considered the unfair (or cheating) nature of the proposal:

1. "President Trump's proposed immigration plan is . . . outrageous . . . circumventing human rights and legal obligations toward asylum-seekers."[83]
2. The plan is "profoundly anti-American."[84]
3. President Trump "demonizes immigrants when he is benefiting and profiting from undocumented workers at his golf club."[85]

**Press Summary**

The news media framed four key themes and conveyed four moral foundations. In terms of frames, Criticism of Plan Specifics was the dominant frame. Here we have the press opposing the plan, even to the point of inaccurately characterizing it. So, for instance, the press stated, erroneously, that immediate family members will be denied entry, complained that the plan, which focuses on legal immigration, did not address illegal immigrations, omitted that the plan was a place to start negotiations, intoned that the president should not persist in wanting a wall, pushed the use of "merit" as a consideration as demeaning, and asserted that criticism of the plan was widespread. In terms of the 2020 Election frame, the press stressed that the plan was only an election ploy and not a serious proposal. Thus, the plan as a starting point was ignored in favor of imposition of a 2020 frame. Thus, in terms of what is missing from the speech, the context of a "starting point," stressed by Trump, is lost. So, either no context is provided for understanding the speech and subsequent criticisms, or it was put into the context of the upcoming 2020 election. In terms of the What's Missing frame, the list was strongly pushed: doesn't address "undocumented migrants" in the United States already; doesn't find pathway to citizenship for "DREAMers"; doesn't address DACA; complained that a citizenship pathway was not found for all; did not fix asylum backlog.

In terms of moral foundations, the MSM overwhelmingly stressed the Loyalty(ingroup)/Betrayal foundation at the level of both the family and the world. The family unit was paramount, but only immigrant families, not those composed of US citizens; Loyalty to the United States did not exist. Trump's focus on merit was relayed as a Betrayal of the family, even as the plan specifically called for keeping the basic family unit of parents and children together. Authority/Subversion conveyed the president's shift in focus from illegal to legal immigration concerns, but also with excluding the legal status of DREAMers. The president was depicted as misusing or ignoring his Authority. The president's conception of Care/Harm was conveyed, and through his quotes elements of Caring for the nation and legal immigrants existed in press reports. However, building a skilled workforce, protecting wages, and unifying families were essentially ignored. The press foundational aspects acted to counter Trump's claims, actually arguing against his notion of Care as something unnecessary or even harmful for illegal immigrants, for families, and for children. Fairness/Cheating was relayed not through Trump's explanation of how the new system would be fair and eliminate "cheating," but rather through the press's conception of how it would be unfair to both legal and illegal immigrants.

## NOTES

1. "Donald Trump Announcement of Candidacy," *Trump Tower*, New York, NY, June 16, 2015 http://www.p2016.org/trump/trump061615sp.html.

2. Even to the point of some quarters now falsely stating that President Trump is "exterminating" Latinos. https://www.foxnews.com/opinion/tucker-carlson-a-sincere-message-to-washington-and-our-cable-news-colleagues-please-calm-down.

3. There are no exact figures here, and depending on what types of cases, the percentage can rise or fall. I've found it to be around two-thirds, and according to *The New York Times*, "On average, presidents win in the Supreme Court about two-thirds of the time. The Obama administration won just 50.5 percent of its cases." Adam Liptak, "Why Obama Struggled at Court, and Trump May Strain to Do Better," *The New York Times*, January 23, 2017, https://www.nytimes.com/2017/01/23/us/politics/obama-supreme-court-win-rate-trump.html.

4. Donald J. Trump, "Remarks by President Trump on Modernizing Our Immigration System for a Stronger America," *White House*, May 16, 2019, https://www.whitehouse.gov/briefings-statements/remarks-president-trump-modernizing-immigration-system-stronger-america/.

5. There were fourteen hard news/analysis articles specifically about the speech, although if opinion pieces were to be included, the numbers swelled considerably.

6. Jonathan Allen, "Trump Plays for the Middle – and 2020 – with Legal-Immigration Focus," NBC News, May 16, 2019, https://www.nbcnews.com/politics/white-house/trump-plays-middle-2020-legal-immigration-focus-n1006671.

7. Daniella Silva, "Trump's Plan for Civics Test For Legal Entrants Could Keep Out Highly Skilled Immigrants, Experts Say," NBC News, May 17, 2019, https://www.nbcnews.com/news/usnews/trump-s-plan-civics-test-legal-entrants-could-keep-out-n1006656.

8. Silva, "Trump's Plan for Civics Test For Legal Entrants Could Keep Out Highly Skilled Immigrants, Experts Say."

9. Ibid.

10. Colby Itkowitz, "Melania Trump's Parents Would Have Struggled to Come to the U.S. Under Trump's Immigration Plan," *The Washington Post*, May 19, 2019, WPCOM00020190517ef5h002jp obtained from factiva.com.

11. Anne Karni and Glenn Thursh, "Cool Reception for a Plan on Immigration," *The New York Times*, May 17, 2019, NYTF000020190517ef5h00042 obtained from factiva.com.

12. Colby Itkowitz, "Melania Trump's Parents Would Have Struggled to Come to the U.S. Under Trump's Immigration Plan."

13. Ibid.

14. Anne Flaherty, "Trump's Immigration Plan Fails to Address Key Parts of Debate: Analysis," ABC News, May 16, 2019, https://abcnews.go.com/Politics/trumps-immigration-plan-fails-addresskey-parts-debate/story?id=63061225.

15. Ibid.

16. Allen, "Trump Plays for the Middle – and 2020 – with Legal-Immigration Focus."

17. Ibid.

18. Silva, "Trump's Plan for Civics Test For Legal Entrants Could Keep Out Highly Skilled Immigrants, Experts Say."

19. Ibid.

20. Marc A. Thiessen, "The Southern Poverty Law Center Has Lost All Credibility," *The Washington Post*, June 22, 2018, https://www.washingtonpost.com/opinions/the-southern-poverty-law-center-has-lost-all-credibility/2018/06/21/22ab7d60-756d-11e8-9780-b1dd6a09b549_story.html and Jessica Prol Smith, "The Southern Poverty Law Center Is a Hate-Based Scam That Nearly Caused Me to be Murdered," *USA Today*, August 17, 2019, https://www.usatoday.com/story/opinion/2019/08/17/southern-poverty-law-center-hate-groups-scam-column/2022301001/.

21. Cahterine E. Shoichet, "What 'Merit-Based' Immigration Means, and Why Trump Keeps Saying He Wants It," CNN News, May 16, 2019, https://www.cnn.com/2019/05/16/politics/merit-basedimmigration-explainer/index.html.

22. Karni and Thursh, "Cool Reception for a Plan on Immigration."

23. Philip Bump, "Trump Is Now Claiming That a Surge in Children at the Border Is a Function of Smuggling," *The Washington Post*, May 16, 2019, WPCOM00020190516ef5g00f1p obtained from factiva.com.

24. Kathryn Watson, "Trump Announces Proposal to Overhaul U.S. Legal Immigration Policy," CBS News, May 16, 2019, https://www.cbsnews.com/news/trump-immigration-proposalannouncement-white-house-rose-garden-watch-live-stream-today-2019-05-16-live-updates/.

25. Karni and Thursh, "Cool Reception for a Plan on Immigration."

26. Allen, "Trump Plays for the Middle – and 2020 – with Legal-Immigration Focus."

27. Ibid.

28. Ibid.

29. Ibid.

30. Stephen Collinson, "Trump Offers Deals Where Only He Can Win," CNN News, May 17, 2019, https://www.cnn.com/2019/05/17/politics/donald-trump-immigration-middle-eastiran/index.html.

31. Karni and Thursh, "Cool Reception for a Plan on Immigration."

32. Itkowitz, "Melania Trump's Parents Would Have Struggled to Come to the U.S. Under Trump's Immigration Plan."

33. Meredith McGraw, "President Trump Unveils New Immigration Plan," ABC News, May 16, 2019, https://abcnews.go.com/Politics/president-trump-unveil-immigration-plan-speechthursday/story?id=63056289.

34. McGraw, "President Trump Unveils New Immigration Plan."

35. Adam Edelman, "Trump Immigration Plan: Give Me Your Doctors, Your Researchers, Your Top Graduate Masses Yearning to Breathe Free," NBC News, May 16, 2019, https://www.nbcnews.com/politics/immigration/trump-says-new-immigration-proposal-putswages-safety-americans-first-n1006556.

36. Allen, "Trump Plays for the Middle – and 2020 – with Legal-Immigration Focus."

37. Ibid.

38. Ibid.

39. Silva, "Trump's Plan for Civics Test For Legal Entrants Could Keep Out Highly Skilled Immigrants, Experts Say."

40. Collinson, "Trump Offers Deals Where Only He Can Win."

41. Ibid.

42. Karni and Thursh, "Cool Reception for a Plan on Immigration."

43. Seung Min Kim, Josh Dawsey, and David Nakamura, "Trump Outlines Migration Overhaul," *The Washington Post*, May 17, 2019, WP00000020190517ef5h00013 obtained from factiva.com.

44. McGraw, "President Trump Unveils New Immigration Plan." See also, Kim, Dawsey, and Nakamura, "Trump Outlines Migration Overhaul"; Edelman, "Trump Immigration Plan."; Watson, "Trump Announces Proposal to Overhaul U.S. Legal Immigration Policy."

45. McGraw, "President Trump Unveils New Immigration Plan."

46. Shoichet, "What 'Merit-Based' Immigration Means, and Why Trump Keeps Saying He Wants It."

47. Edelman, "Trump Immigration Plan."

48. McGraw, "President Trump Unveils New Immigration Plan."

49. Flaherty, "Trump's Immigration Plan Fails to Address Key Parts of Debate."

50. McGraw, "President Trump Unveils New Immigration Plan." and Kim, Dawsey, and Nakamura, "Trump Outlines Migration Overhaul."

51. Silva, "Trump's Plan for Civics Test For Legal Entrants Could Keep Out Highly Skilled Immigrants, Experts Say."

52. Ibid.

53. Allen, "Trump Plays for the Middle – and 2020 – with Legal-Immigration Focus."

54. Itkowitz, "Melania Trump's Parents Would Have Struggled to Come to the U.S. Under Trump's Immigration Plan."
55. Karni and Thursh, "Cool Reception for a Plan on Immigration."
56. Ibid.
57. Ibid.
58. Itkowitz, "Melania Trump's Parents Would Have Struggled to Come to the U.S. Under Trump's Immigration Plan."
59. Karni and Thursh, "Cool Reception for a Plan on Immigration."
60. McGraw, "President Trump Unveils New Immigration Plan."
61. Flaherty, "Trump's Immigration Plan Fails to Address Key Parts of Debate."
62. Ibid.
63. Edelman, "Trump Immigration Plan."
64. Flaherty, "Trump's Immigration Plan Fails to Address Key Parts of Debate."
65. Ibid.
66. Allen, "Trump Plays for the Middle – and 2020 – with Legal-Immigration Focus."
67. Kim, Dawsey, and Nakamura, "Trump Outlines Migration Overhaul."
68. Silva, "Trump's Plan for Civics Test For Legal Entrants Could Keep Out Highly Skilled Immigrants, Experts Say."
69. Allen, "Trump Plays for the Middle – and 2020 – with Legal-Immigration Focus."
70. Kim, Dawsey, and Nakamura, "Trump Outlines Migration Overhaul."
71. Ibid.
72. McGraw, "President Trump Unveils New Immigration Plan." See also, Kim, Dawsey, and Nakamura, "Trump Outlines Migration Overhaul."
73. McGraw, "President Trump Unveils New Immigration Plan."
74. Allen, "Trump Plays for the Middle – and 2020 – with Legal-Immigration Focus."
75. Edelman, "Trump Immigration Plan."
76. Karni and Thursh, "Cool Reception for a Plan on Immigration."
77. McGraw, "President Trump Unveils New Immigration Plan."
78. Collinson, "Trump Offers Deals Where Only He Can Win."
79. Allen, "Trump Plays for the Middle – and 2020 – with Legal-Immigration Focus."
80. Silva, "Trump's Plan for Civics Test For Legal Entrants Could Keep Out Highly Skilled Immigrants, Experts Say."
81. Edelman, "Trump Immigration Plan." See also, Watson, "Trump Announces Proposal to Overhaul U.S. Legal Immigration Policy."
82. McGraw, "President Trump Unveils New Immigration Plan."; Karni and Thursh, "Cool Reception for a Plan on Immigration"; Edelman, "Trump Immigration Plan."; Watson, "Trump Announces Proposal to Overhaul U.S. Legal Immigration Policy."
83. Cahterine E. Shoichet, "What 'Merit-Based' Immigration Means, and Why Trump Keeps Saying He Wants It."

84. Shoichet, "What 'Merit-Based' Immigration Means, and Why Trump Keeps Saying He Wants It."

85. Itkowitz, "Melania Trump's Parents Would Have Struggled to Come to the U.S. Under Trump's Immigration Plan."

*Chapter 8*

# Concluding Thoughts on Framing, Moral Foundations, the Press, and the American Republic

That President Trump believes the mainstream news media tries to harm him is no secret. He makes his views well known through repeated public statements on the issue, "tweeting," for instance, "The FAKE NEWS media (failing @nytimes, @NBCNews, @ABC, @CBS, @CNN) is not my enemy, it is the enemy of the American People!"[1] All presidents have privately complained, with research data showing Republican presidents have more to complain about than their Democrat peers, yet Trump is the first to single out the press for such public and severe denunciations.[2] As we saw in chapter 2, Trump has received extensive and overwhelmingly negative press coverage, and this antagonistic relationship continues with, for instance, his ordering Federal agencies in October 2019 to cancel subscriptions to *The Washington Post* and *The New York Times*.[3]

But are such presidential characterizations and actions warranted? Certainly the Trump administration thinks so, with, for instance, then White House chief strategist Steve Bannon reportedly saying on February 15, 2017, this about mainstream media (MSM) journalists in a presidential press line: "the opposition party, all lined up."[4] Some in the MSM think there are problems as well, although usually such acknowledgments come from *outside* the MSM. For example, Piers Morgan, no friend of the Trump administration, stated that it is "a largely liberal media that's lost all sense of impartiality over Trump and just rants hysterically about him 24/7 because (a) it makes them feel good and (b) it makes them big money."[5] There is also evidence that some news organizations are intentionally skewing the news to negatively impact the president. For instance, serious allegations have emerged that CNN president and CEO Jeffrey Zucker is "carrying out [a] 'personal vendetta' against Trump" and that the network has "anti-GOP bias."[6] And with MSM coverage of the fall 2019 House impeachment inquiry reaching a 96 percent–negative coverage of Trump,[7] one could see how the president and Bannon feel the way they do, or why Trump "tweeted" this following the report of the negative coverage: "There has never been a time in the history of our Country that the Media was so Fraudulent, Fake, or Corrupt!"[8] He is not alone in his assessment, either. Almost three in four Americans agree with some of his charges, with 72 percent saying that traditional news outlets knowingly report fake or misleading news.[9] Yet, how does this perception of negative coverage manifest itself in our case studies? To answer this, let us turn to answering the questions posed in chapters 2 and 3. In the pages that follow, we look first at the results of the framing portion of our case studies, then turn to the moral foundations portion, with this followed by general observations of news media bias discovered through the case studies. The chapter concludes with some general observations about news media ethics and how biased reportorial practices impact the American Republic.

## FRAMING

Researchers in news framing have long known that the news media framing process begins "in the universe of shared culture and on the basis of socially defined roles."[10] Thus, the liberal world in which journalists live is the incubation ground for their reportorial output, which clearly showed in how they framed the speeches given by the president. In this section, I provide a table of the frames of the president and the frames of the news media for each case study and summarize the differences, concluding this section with observations about the framing process.

### Framing and National Security

Clearly seen in table 8.1 is the almost total disjunction between what the president said and what the news media reported. In only one theme was there overlap—Present American Actions: America First. Although both the president and the news media framed this theme, here again the frames could not be more different, with the president highlighting his idea of putting the good of the American people before all others, and the press expressing confusion about its meaning and disparaging the concept. Only in the small area related to trade, "America First, but not alone," did elements of the frame overlap. In all other areas, the important themes and their framing by the president were not conveyed, with the news media instead pushing its own agenda.

The response of the news media here also demonstrates the power of already-established frames. At the time of the National Security speech, the Mueller investigation was in full swing, and the press was reporting on it

**Table 8.1  National Security**

| Themes | President's Frame | MSM Frame |
|---|---|---|
| Past actions of American leaders | Leaders of both parties hurt the people with bad policies | N/A |
| Present American actions: America First | Americans' interests should come first in all policy decisions foreign and domestic<br>America First, but not alone | Confusion about meaning: campaign slogan, doctrine, strategy, ideology, etc.<br>Not defined<br>Selfish concept<br>America First, but not alone |
| National security strategy | Five fundamental truths; four pillars; focus on national interest, not global | N/A |
| Border security | Secure nation: border, cyber<br>Stop terrorist threats | N/A |
| Economic security | Highlight economic vitality: cut taxes and regulations<br>Necessary for national security | N/A |
| National defense | Invest in military; peace through strength | N/A |
| American influence | Advance interests and values globally but starts at home | N/A |
| Speech versus document | N/A | Trump tone and document tone different; Trump soft on Russia, document not<br>Domestic campaign speech<br>Speech about Trump, not document—Trump wrong |
| Cyber warfare | N/A | Document and Trump not specifically call out Russia for interference in 2016 election<br>Trump wrong for this; lacks credibility |
| Revisionist powers | N/A | Russia and China focused on exclusively, but only for election meddling and unfair trade, respectively<br>Implied not as bad a threat as Trump says |
| Putin/Trump/2016 election | N/A | Trump not focus enough on Russia election interference<br>Russia extremely important, Trump diminishes this |

*Source*: Author.

152                           Chapter 8

every day. The idea of a then potential Trump/Russian election collusion was continually reported, and we see here its injection into reporting about Trump's speech. Overall, Trump was framed as not being hard enough on Russia for election meddling, and essentially giving a campaign speech.

## Framing and the Economy

Clearly seen in table 8.2 is the total disjunction between what the president said and what the news media reported. Although certainly elements of the president's speech were conveyed, the important themes and the framing of those themes were not. The news media instead focused on its priorities, notably attacking the president for his use of America First and for "selling" America. Trump's patriotic-style nationalism was met with the news media's embrace of globalism. They also spent a good deal of effort in particular to call out a minor moment, really a sentence only, when Trump responded to a question by sharing his surprise at how "mean" the press could be. Their intentional misframing of this brief exchange was pushed seemingly to hurt Trump.

## Framing and the State of the Union

Clearly seen in table 8.3 is the almost total disjunction between what the president said and what the news media reported. Overlap existed in only one theme—Illegal Immigration. This theme was framed differently by Trump and the news media, with the president framing it as an urgent moral issue and the press essentially saying there was no real urgency, that things were not as bad as the president said, and implying that the problem was Trump wanting a wall. The lack of thematic overlap is surprising for a State of the Union Address, given that the president sets, according to past studies, the focus for news coverage by the topics he chooses to discuss. Not so here. The press introduced five new themes for coverage, each either downplaying what the president said or disparaging him or his policies. Of particular note is that the president made a concerted effort to offer bipartisan moments in his discussion of the facts (yes, there were a few exceptions), the press framed the speech overwhelmingly as divisive, even in the face of National polling that found a plurality of Americans believing the exact opposite.

## Framing and Immigration

Clearly seen in table 8.4 is the total disjunction between what the president said and what the news media reported. Although Trump framed this

Table 8.2  Economy

| Themes | President's Frame | MSM Frame |
|---|---|---|
| Reforms/results | Tax and regulation cuts excellent for trade<br>Economy roaring back to life<br>Focus on fair trade for all | N/A |
| New competitive model | America First is not America alone<br>Independent nations should put their people first, trading as equals; this is healthy | N/A |
| American people | A nation's people come first<br>Purpose of reform to improve lives of Americans<br>America First<br>Invest in the people | N/A |
| Dangers in the world | That which can derail prosperity: terrorism, rogue nations, revisionist powers (Russia, China)<br>Unfair trade practices<br>Must be common security with all paying fair share | N/A |
| America First | N/A | Undefined<br>Confusion as to status (policy, slogan, agenda, etc.)<br>Wrong because it promotes nationalism<br>Globalism is good; nationalism/populism bad.<br>Trump was "selling" America, so downplayed anti-globalism. |
| Populism/globalism | N/A | Trump assertion only |
| "Open for business" | N/A | Trump is being a "salesman" |
| Trade | N/A | Trade must be fair<br>End predatory practices |
| Attacking the press | N/A | Attacked the press<br>Negatively received |

Source: Author.

Table 8.3  State of the Union

| Themes | President's Frame | MSM Frame |
|---|---|---|
| Framing of facts | Mainly nonpartisan statistics and accomplishments, some Republican alone<br>Future policies are potential bipartisan areas | N/A |
| Illegal immigration | Expansive, urgent, moral issue<br>Cruel if allowed to continue<br>Stop illegal; reform and protect legal immigration<br>"Wall" is metonym for "smart wall" and other reforms | No real problem<br>Trump wants ineffective "concrete wall" only |
| The economy | Positive growth now and into future<br>China a danger to economy; takes advantage of America and must be stopped now<br>Replace old, bad trade deals with better new ones | N/A |
| National security | Strong military = American security<br>Security means freedom, not socialism<br>Too long in the Middle East; bring troops home soon<br>Confront totalitarianism and hate | N/A |
| Healthcare | Fighting for lower costs<br>Americans should not fund world's healthcare<br>Definitely bipartisan issue | N/A |
| Call for collective action | Have come together before, can do so now | N/A |
| Unity and division | N/A | Trump insincere, uncompromising<br>Pushing polarizing policies to intentionally create division<br>Partial government shutdown was traumatic, completely Trump's fault<br>Immigration reform = building divisive physical wall |
| Mueller investigation | N/A | Noble Democrat goal<br>Trump threatening democrats<br>Trump confused about congressional role<br>Similar to Nixon and Watergate |
| Congressional Democrat women (minor) | N/A | Defiant<br>Celebrating at Trump's expense |
| Abortion (minor) | N/A | Democrats support women<br>Trump is wrong |
| Socialism (minor) | N/A | Socialism a nonissue<br>Only the "gang of four" are socialist |

Source: Author.

## Table 8.4 Immigration

| Themes | President's Frame | MSM Frame |
|---|---|---|
| Legal immigration | System old and broken, relies primarily on luck<br>Old system ≠ American values<br>New rules must be merit (skills) based, have uniform standards<br>Old system unfair to low-income Americans and current legal immigrants | N/A |
| Purpose of plan | Update legal immigration system<br>Focus on common purpose<br>Strengthen citizenship bonds, promote unity | N/A |
| Physical infrastructure | Can be bipartisan<br>Security through technology<br>Continue expanding existing walls | N/A |
| Legal issues | Present laws facilitate child human trafficking, so must stop<br>False asylum claims overwhelming system<br>Protect from criminals and abusers | N/A |
| Criticism of plan specifics | N/A | Immediate family will be denied (false)<br>Nothing about illegal immigration<br>Nothing about it being a place to begin (omission)<br>Should not keep wall<br>Using "merit" condescending<br>Widespread criticism |
| 2020 election | N/A | An election ploy<br>Not a serious proposal |
| What's missing | N/A | Doesn't address "undocumented migrants" in the United States already<br>Doesn't find pathway to citizenship for DREAMers<br>Doesn't address DACA<br>A citizenship pathway must be found for all<br>Doesn't fix asylum backlog |

*Source:* Author.

156                                    Chapter 8

proposal as a starting point for bipartisan negotiations, intentionally avoiding initially the controversial issues, the news media reframed it to present a highly contentious plan set up as an election ploy.

**Framing Summary**

1. The news media clearly failed to relate both the same themes and framing of those themes by the president. If news consumers had no firsthand knowledge of the speeches or policy proposals they would have come away with an entirely different understanding of the president's efforts and the proposed policy than was actually presented by the president.
2. The news media introduced new themes and framed those themes to advance their own beliefs and political goals. Although it is a mark of good reporting to bring in other points of view, and to provide context, such was not the case here. Each of the frames of the news media worked to treat the president, not as a source of news, but as a political opponent, with the news media actively helping the political opposition of the president.
3. The prior frames and assumptions of the news media do carry over into new events, coloring the way new themes are framed. This makes it exceedingly difficult for anyone to introduce new materials or proposals; it certainly includes those who share press opposed points of view, but would also make it difficult for reporters to offer new frame-breaking revelations. In this manner, journalists come into any given presidential speech with a priori assumptions that guide their interpretations and framing. Minimal evidence is given since the press already has the "correct" answers.

The relationship between frames and moral foundations will be discussed in the summary section below.

## MORAL FOUNDATIONS

In this section, we look at comparisons between the moral foundations used by President Trump and those used by the news media when reporting on him. Table 8.5 compares the foundations used.

**Table 8.5  National Security**

| Moral Foundations: Trump | Moral Foundations : MSM |
|---|---|
| 1. Loyalty(ingroup)/Betrayal | 1. Care/Harm |
| 2. Fairness/Cheating | 2. Fairness/Cheating |
| 3. Care/Harm | 3. Loyalty(ingroup)/Betrayal |

*Source*: Author.

## Trump Moral Foundations and National Security

National security is a subject matter naturally inclined to elicit portions of discourse grounded in Loyalty(ingroup)/Betrayal cues. Even so, the deeply moral basis of much of the president's speech was linked expansively to this foundation. Part of this was due to Trump's reasoning that the nation and the people were one; it was the people that made the nation, not the other way around. As a people, they infuse America with greatness. Betrayal of this relationship and its moral aspect comes from politicians of both parties who put themselves before the people, and from illegal immigrants who, as part of the Outgroup, violate the security and role of the Ingroup (both citizens and legal immigrants working toward Ingroup status). There are other threats to the Ingroup, and the Trump administration's policies are designed to protect and privilege this group. This vision of America goes further, in that Trump projects "a vision of strong, sovereign, and independent nations," not America alone. For Trump, the new National Security document is to protect American interests first; to weaken it by putting other nations coequal with the United States would be a form of Betrayal. All of this involves advancing policies that build a cohesive nation.

The Fairness/Cheating foundation resonated throughout Trump's speech as well, although to a lesser degree. America has worked for justice around the world, and Trump also wants justice for America through fair dealings from other nations in terms of fair, mutually beneficial trade, and more support from nations America protects (paying their fair share). It was unfair of American politicians to have "the people" (the Ingroup) support other nations while hurting at home (unfair). With "fair" trade now being part of national security, Trump elevated the importance of this moral foundation, as well as Loyalty above, in America's international policy making.

Working for peace, and for security, grounds the speech in the Care/Harm foundation, although this was not the primary motivating foundation at all. This foundation is best summed by the president's insistence that a primary task of his administration is to protect America from those who "attack our nation or threaten our society," and that his goal is to "preserve peace through strength." So that which directly "harms" Americans—bad trade deals, security threats, illegal immigration—must be confronted, and the threat neutralized.

## News Media Moral Foundations and National Security

Just as Loyalty(ingroup)/Betrayal was overwhelmingly present in Trump's discourse, Care/Harm was so present in the press response. The press did relay some of Trump's foundation of Care/Harm, such as "protecting the homeland and American people," and the general idea of defending the people." Some of what Trump relayed in terms of potential Harm to the American people was also conveyed, but here we see a recontextualization by the press. Trump was actually linked with Harming the country due to not listing climate change in the document; moreover, threats, what Trump depicted as Harm to America, were frequently downplayed or denied by the press response. In short, although Trump's linkages with this moral foundation were conveyed, they were filtered through and thus minimized by the press advancing its own interpretation of Trump Harming the Nation.

Fairness and Cheating were relayed primarily through Trump's comments about fair trade being necessary for security, and these accurately reflected his emphasis. However, fairness in terms of dealing with allies, defense, was often characterized as being "unfair."

Loyalty(ingroup)/Betrayal, although nuanced and expansive in the speech, was linked almost exclusively to Trump's America First policy, and so made to seem confused, thus diminishing its Trump-originated moral impact. Additionally, there was a mélange of press assertions based in this foundation that acted to contradict what the president was attempting to convey (see table 8.5).

## Trump Moral Foundations and the Economy

For Trump, the Fairness/Cheating foundation ran fairly strong throughout his speech, most notably attached to the ideas of fair trade and business opportunities. Both sides of this foundation were evident, with other countries cheating America, as well as politicians and business leaders being unfair to Americans due to selfishness and the imposition of unfair regulations. Fairness requires all laws to be fairly enforced, so no more turning a blind eye to piratical trade practices of other nations.

Harm is minimally stressed through bad political decisions and predatory business practices, but the foundational aspect of Care is pervasively relayed through highlighting Trump's new economic policies that "advance

**Table 8.6 Economy**

| Moral Foundations: Trump | Moral Foundations : MSM |
|---|---|
| 1. Fairness/Cheating | 1. Loyalty(ingroup)/Betrayal |
| 2. Care/Harm | 2. Care/Harm |
| 3. Loyalty(ingroup)/Betrayal | 3. Fairness/Cheating |
| 4. Authority/Subversion | |

*Source*: Author.

prosperity, security, and peace." These policies are good for more than Americans only, and help other peoples of the world as well, thus Caring for them. Care is also stressed through security, with the goal of "every child [to] grow up free from violence, poverty, and fear."

Loyalty(ingroup)/Betrayal is interanimated with the previous two foundations, and is linked strongly, not with the world, but with the American people. That is not to say that Trump did not show concern for the world, but that the American people come first for him, and his policies are designed to better enhance their standard of living. In short, "helping every American find their path to the American Dream." His policy of America First was both explained and highlighted here. For the president, "A nation's greatness is the sum of its citizens."

Authority is linked strongly, albeit briefly, with the people, not with top-down authoritarianism. A large part of the stress of this foundation is on Subversion, in that past leaders had Subverted the interests and will of the people through "state-led economic planning." Loyalty to the people is the role of a leader, not the other way around.

## News Media Moral Foundations and the Economy

The press exhibited almost a reverse order from the Trump speech, with Loyalty(ingroup)/Betrayal taking up the lion's share of its moral elements. Through his language used around the phrase "America First," the president was depicted as a nationalist. However, this nationalistic support was recharacterized away from Loyalty to the American people to Betrayal of the global. Any movement by Trump to work with other nations was depicted hypocritically in light of his past stress on America, and thus as only an opportunistic ploy rather than genuine effort to reach out. Furthermore, they depicted Trump as Betrayer, demeaning what they called his "faux populism." Even as the news media relayed some of the positive aspects of Trump's tax cuts, it depicted them as a Betrayal of the global as well. Since the press Ingroup included illegal immigrants, it highlighted this issue in coverage also depicting the president as a Betrayer.

Mitigating against Harm was somewhat conveyed by the press, with Trump's call for more cooperative trade and working internationally to combat terrorism and harmful trade practices being mentioned. However, this was unusual, with the overall reporting acting to minimize any caring component to the Trump rhetoric, and at times to actually assert that Trump Harms America.

Through conveying the president's own words, his foundation of Fairness/Cheating did make it into press coverage; however, these were often recontextualized to stress what the press felt were inequalities. Interestingly, there was a sense of not equality of opportunity, but equality of outcome that was used to determine what was fair (see table 8.6).

## TRUMP MORAL FOUNDATIONS AND THE STATE OF THE UNION

Overwhelmingly the president stressed the Loyalty(ingroup)/Betrayal foundation, integrating these moral touchstones within the sharing of policy and also helping to contextualize other moral foundations in the sense of infusing them with purpose. The people are the purpose, they are America, and this foundation is squarely focused on America as the basic loyalty unit. Jobs, fair trade, diminishment of illegal immigration, military security, and so on, are all advanced grounded in this foundation. In particular, Trump differentiates between legal and illegal immigration policies, with legal immigration as advancing ingroup participation, whereas illegal immigration and its supporters would be Betraying the American ideal. Almost all groundings in this foundation were positive in the speech, with the president expressing a desire to help achieve "America's destiny [as] one nation."

The Care/Harm foundation, although found throughout the speech, was a lesser presence than Loyalty(ingroup)/Betrayal, and consisted of clearly delineated divisions between Care aspects and Harm aspects. Americans had been and were being Harmed by policies of both parties, and the president's new policies were designed to provide Care for the people. Many of the president's policies, such as reduction of illegal immigration, have their roots in the Harm portion of this foundation in that, without change, Americans would continue to be hurt. Thus, those who do nothing to stop these policies, were actually Harming America, and in the case of illegal immigration, being cruel. Trump projected Care, in that his policies were meant to protect the people from damaging policies.

Table 8.7 State of the Union

| Moral Foundations: Trump | Moral Foundations : MSM |
| --- | --- |
| 1. Loyalty(ingroup)/Betrayal | 1. Care/Harm |
| 2. Care/Harm | 2. Loyalty(ingroup)/Betrayal |
| 3. Fairness/Cheating | 3. Fairness/Cheating |
| 4. Sanctity/Degradation | 4. Authority/Subversion (minor) |
| 5. Authority/Subversion | 5. Sanctity/Degradation (minor) |

Source: Author.

Not quite as strong as Care/Harm, but also found throughout the speech, Fairness/Cheating is linked with most of the president's policies. For the president, "things" that needed fixing in the country were grounded in a sense of being "unfair" to the people, so they must be addressed. Illegal immigration in particular was linked to this foundation; it is unfair to legal immigrants and American citizens, so must be stopped. The same existed for unfair trade practices, with "global freeloading," as well as other actions that hurt the American people.

The Sanctity/Degradation was minimally present, but enough to suggest certain of the president's polices being grounded in it. There is a certain sanctity associated with actions taken to protect the innocent lives taken by abortion. It is found in other places in the speech, particularly with innocent lives lost through illegal immigration and the sadism of human traffickers.

The Authority/Subversion foundation was minimally present, but did resonate in areas such as the lawless southern border and the idea that immigrants needed to come into the United States legally.

## News Media Moral Foundations and the State of the Union

The Care/Harm foundation was overwhelmingly stressed and was strong and pervasive. Some of Trump's foundational Care/Harm assertions were relayed, yet were presented so as to minimize the Care portion. As an example, Trump was depicted as wrong in wanting to bring troops home from the Middle East—he would "Harm" America. His Care/Harm foundation with regard to immigration was hesitatingly shared, but like other policies through which this foundation resonated, it was minimized, with the press relaying not the president's foundations, but their own interpretations. The overwhelming response of the press was to minimize and undercut the president's moral foundations. For instance, he might have conveyed a Care foundation, but after recontextualization by the press, it was not a caring foundation conveyed, but a Harm foundation, with the president depicted as harming America. By not conveying the president's sense of Care, the public was presented with only the press's interpretation of harm. Democrats were made to seem to Care; the president was made to seem to Harm.

Loyalty(ingroup)/Betrayal, a considerably less strong presence than Care/Harm, was at the level of the Nation for Trump, and the press did relay this to some degree. The press used the notion of unity/division to undercut and redirect the president's use of the Loyalty(ingroup)/Betrayal foundation at every turn, however. Sweeping aside Trump's calls for unity, the press focused instead on division, points of disagreement, and laid all this at the feet of the president. Trump was inflexible, not Democrats, and as such was betraying America. Of note is that as the press was so focused on division that the country did not feel it divisive at all, and that may of the proposed policies that the press was decrying were actually popular with a majority of Americans.

The Fairness/Cheating foundation was an even weaker presence than Loyalty(ingroup)/Betrayal, and was minimally conveyed. This took the form almost entirely through description of unfair drug prices that the president stressed he was attempting to fix. The press, although relaying this, undercut the moral weighting of the president by arguing against what Trump said, and by pushing the partial government shutdown as "unfair," and laying the blame for this, not on bipartisan disagreement, but at the president's feet alone. In so doing, the little of President Trump's foundation of Fairness that made it into press coverage was greatly undercut.

Authority/Subversion was even less conveyed than Fair/Cheating, and was centered around the president's brief remarks on Socialism and also on the topic of illegal immigration. Although some presidential quotes were provided, the press undercut the moral weighting of the statements through later minimization of what he said. At its essence, the press pushed a moral assertion that the president lacked Authority and was Betraying Americans through his policies and ignorance.

Sanctity/Degradation was almost nonexistent, and where it did appear was used to cast Trump as appealing to hard core pro-lifers and "degrading the life of mothers" (see table 8.7).

## Trump Moral Foundations and Immigration

Loyalty(ingroup)/Betrayal was the strongest and most pervasive of the foundations. The link with immigration was about "family," so strengthening "the bonds of citizenship that bind us together as a national family." This is to be accomplished by the creation of a new system of legal immigration that would promote national unity. It was pro-legal immigrant, thus working to bring legal immigrants more into the Ingroup. Thus, the new system is

**Table 8.8 Immigration**

| Moral Foundations: Trump | Moral Foundations : MSM |
|---|---|
| 1. Loyalty(ingroup)/Betrayal | 1. Loyalty(ingroup)/Betrayal |
| 2. Care/Harm | 2. Authority/Subversion |
| 3. Fairness/Cheating | 3. Care/Harm |
| 4. Sanctity/Degradation | 4. Fairness/Cheating |
| 5. Authority/Subversion | |

Source: Author.

pro-immigrant (Loyalty) and anti-illegal immigrant (Betrayal). The plan acts to protect immediate family members and provides history, heritage, and a home. It is, according to Trump, to promote integration, assimilation, and national unity.

The Care/Harm foundation was evenly split, with the present system being Harmful to immigrants, to citizens, and to national unity; in short, the system as it is now, and by extension those who supported it, is Harming the Nation. The proposed new system would Care for legal immigrants, citizens, and promote national unity; it would put "the jobs, wages, and safety of American workers first," and thus Care for citizens here and now.

The Fairness/Cheating foundation was limited in application even as it stressed both elements. Those coming in illegally, or making false asylum claims, are Cheating; the present system's randomness of selection is inherently unfair. Eliminating these issues, and focusing on merit-based immigration is Fair. By being merit-based and applying universal criteria for entrance, the new plan stressed Fairness.

The Sanctity/Degradation foundation bypasses partisan party concerns and focuses instead on Trump's linking immigration reform to One Nation Under God, so it becomes a "sacred" duty. For Trump, the "proposal fulfills our sacred duty to those living here today."

The Authority/Subversion foundation was almost invisible, but did involve pledging allegiance to the Flag, and working to strengthening traditions and values, in that the proposed policy was designed to "strengthens, our culture, our traditions, and our values."

## News Media Moral Foundations and Immigration

Loyalty(ingroup)/Betrayal was strongly stressed by the press at the level of both the family and the world. Although Trump's position was relayed, it was generally in a weakened sense, with no single sense of Loyalty(ingroup) stressed. The family unit was paramount, but only immigrant families, not those composed of US citizens; Loyalty to the United States did not exist for the press. Thus, Trump's detentions at the border of families was a Betrayal, as was his overall immigration stance. Trump's focus on merit was relayed as a Betrayal of the family, even as the plan specifically called for keeping the basic family unit of parents and children together. Community safety was a nonissue for the press; thus, Trump's Loyalty to legal immigrants and citizens was minimized. Additionally, the press focus on *undocumented* immigrants functioned as a repudiation of the president's concern with *illegal* immigration. The press saw being Loyal to the global as important, with Trump's focus on the nation as a Betrayal; and as Trump focused on legal immigrant families, the press depicted him as Betraying illegal immigrant families.

Authority/Subversion conveyed the president's shift in focus from illegal to legal immigration concerns, but was subsumed into the press focus on the legal status of DREAMers who the president did not address. The president was depicted as misusing or ignoring his Authority, both through his polices and by ignoring other problems areas of illegal immigration.

The president's conception of Care/Harm was conveyed, although his focus on the new plan's protections (Care) that would in particular help build a skilled workforce while not threatening Americans with blue-collar jobs was essentially ignored. Thus, a significant portion of the president's Care foundation was omitted; so, building a skilled workforce, protecting wages, and unifying families were essentially ignored. The press foundational aspects acted to counter Trump's claims, actually arguing against his notion of Care as something unnecessary or even Harmful for illegal immigrants, for families, and for children. The president was, at best, shown to be trying to hurt immigrants, at worse, as being at war with them.

Although strongly stressed by Trump, Fairness/Cheating was relayed not through Trump's explanation of how the new system would be Fair to legal immigrants and Americans, and eliminate "cheating," but rather through the press's conception of how it would be *unfair* to both legal and illegal immigrants (see table 8.8).

## Moral Foundations Summary

Of note is that even as President Trump is accused of being an authoritarian leader by both the news media and political opponents, the moral foundations in his speeches simply belie that categorization, especially given his minimal reliance on the foundation of Authority. Instead the foundation that resonates most pervasively throughout his speeches is Loyalty(ingroup)/Betrayal, with a focus on the American people and putting "America First." If anything, there is a populist/nationalist/patriotic streak in his leadership style as presented in the speeches.

Brian J. Bowe found that the Care/Harm and Fairness/Cheating foundations dominate public discourse as expressed through the news media.[11] This correlates well with the news media's liberal/progressive identity, resulting in primary moral filters being through the two above foundations. Conservatives can get in, but are generally stripped down to and judged through these two major foundations, and as Bowe found, liberals dominate here. Trump in particular was harmed by this in that even when he relayed the foundation of Care, the press twisted it into Harm; thus, even as he grounded appeals in the news media (liberal) primary moral foundation, he was shut out. If extended to conservatives in general, one will most likely find their foundations reduced so that the negative is stressed, even if they state the positive. Scott Clifford and Jennifer Jerit also found Harm and Fairness appeals to dominate public debate, writing that in "spite of the strong relationship between the Purity foundation and stem cell attitudes at the individual level, Purity language was surprisingly uncommon in the debate. This finding has important implications for the rhetorical landscape in the United States. If partisan political actors invoke only the most widely endorsed foundations, elite rhetoric may come to be dominated by Harm and Fairness appeals."[12] Viewed in light of our present study, it might not be so much partisans relying only in these appeals, but the press allowing only certain appeals through. Thus, other than liberal arguments are disadvantaged in the present news media journalistic milieu. This was certainly the case with Trump.

This result is particularly important in terms of our study. Recall the Model of Intuitive Morality and Exemplars (MIME), discussed in chapter 2, which stressed that moral themes are embedded within a wide variety of media content. MIME theory supports the idea that "over time, consistent exposure to messages emphasizing the superiority of one moral foundation over another will increase the salience of that foundation among audiences and maintain its salience in the face of other influences. . . . Furthermore, the MIME holds that insulation from value inconsistent messages will foster polarized values within ideological groups and reduce openness to divergent views."[13] This works two ways here. First, in terms of journalists who are insulated in a liberal confirmation bias bubble, we can see that without exposure to a viewpoint diverse and inclusive work environment, they simply parrot the correct political and moral views of the group. They reinforce their own thinking, allowing almost all political discourse to be filtered through their Care/Harm and Fairness/Betrayal foundations. Second, the readers of these publications have public discussion of political issues reduced and judged primarily at the level of these two discourses, something clearly seen with the reporting on Trump. This diminishes and demeans the entire Democratic process, especially since it privileges such a small percentage of the population (recall graph 3.2: Moral Foundation Population Distribution).

## LIMITATIONS OF MORAL FOUNDATION THEORY

1. Framing theory asserts that frames provide moral assessments. My findings in this study do not support that assertion. Instead, moral foundations as potentially expressed within the framing of each theme in news coverage simply do not provide enough substance. *The frames do not give rise to the*

*moral foundations but rather the presence of the moral foundations gives moral substance to frames as they are developed and found throughout news coverage.* Certainly frames can highlight some moral foundations over others, but it is more likely that it is a combination of the moral foundations of the originating source mingled with journalists' moral assessment followed by the framing of an issue or event that gives rise to a moral foundation presence in a particular news discourse. Simply put, *frames do not fuel moral foundations, moral foundations fuel frames.*

2. Moral Foundation Theory strongly posits that we have an "intuitive (and often emotion-filled) response" to moral stimuli, after which "slow reasoning is used primarily (post hoc) to find reasons to confirm and justify one's own intuitive reaction to the situation and to recruit/persuade others why they ought to join us in our judgment."[14] To the degree that this is true, we can make certain assumptions about this process as applied to journalists. We do know that journalists, overwhelmingly liberal, have a liberal moral register, and react in a liberal manner, privileging liberal moral foundations. They feel a particular way, and then, as evidenced in the articles analyzed for this study, move to support that judgment cognitively, and this is facilitated through confirmation bias, and so on.

The four case studies presented here demonstrated that at almost every turn the press contradicted, minimized, and disparaged Trump's expressed moral foundations. So, even when Trump used Care/Harm or Fairness/Cheating, the press twisted it into the opposite meaning. When Trump expressed Care, the press turned it to Harm, for instance. Clearly, there was political bias operating here. Additionally, *as very liberal, their moral palettes privilege a liberal expression of Care/Harm, followed by Fairness/Cheating, with the other foundations being minimized*, thus Trump's expressions were not presented within his own moral underpinnings, but through the judgmental eye of the news media's liberal understanding of these moral foundations.

It seems reasonable to assume that since moral foundations are innate and often first felt as an emotional response to a trigger, that a journalist would respond in that way as well: exposure to liberal ideas brings equanimity and confirmation; exposure to conservative moral concerns bring disgust and ill ease. After this innate feeling, the journalist has several possibilities for a cognitive response. For instance, a journalist may feel unease at a conservative expression reflecting the moral foundation of Loyalty. That journalist could respond with Loyalty(ingroup)/Betrayal rationalizations, in a sense, presenting the opposite of what the original person presented (Trump brings in Loyalty, the journalist brings in Betrayal); or, respond using a different foundation, using the primary available pallets selections to that person (Trump brings in Loyalty, the journalist brings in Care/Harm). Or, as so often happened in our case studies, President Trump offers a Care foundation, the press responded by twisting it to Harm.

Thus, we have varying degrees of journalistic bias operating here. One, journalists could be so entwined with their own liberally understood moral foundations that they are unconsciously judging Trump, and reporting in such a way that his moral foundations are inadequately expressed. Two, journalists could be intentionally arguing against Trump, treating him not as a source of news, but as a political opponent. As will be discussed below, whichever type prevails in a journalist, norms of objective reportorial practices are violated, and an ever stronger case for newsroom viewpoint diversity is made.

3. As an initial foray into using Moral Foundations Theory (MFT) to discover the political positioning of journalists and its relationship to framing, I linked my analysis primarily to the key words MFT researchers have used as indicative of moral foundations within a text. I looked also for how statements *functioned* as moral expressions, an important element of a rhetorical case study. It quickly became apparent that moral foundations also exist independently of the specific words within the coding indices used by MFT researchers. For instance, consider this quote: "'The infant would be delivered. The infant would be kept comfortable. The infant would be resuscitated if that's what the mother and the family desired. And then a discussion would ensue between the physicians and the mother,' Northam said."[15] Within the context of the article flow, this statement is clearly an example of the journalist inserting a quote linked with moral foundation of Care/Harm, yet no indicator words linking it with Care/Harm are present. Some additional examples:

--Authority/Subversion: "Rep. Elijah Cummings . . . said . . . that Trump is mixed up about Congress' role. 'The president seems to believe that because Congress must legislate, we should not investigate,' Cummings said in a statement. 'Of course, the Constitution requires us to do both. That is exactly how it works.'"[16]

--Authority/Subversion: "Representative Lloyd Doggett . . . spoke for many of his colleagues when he called it 'totally outrageous' for the president to use his nationally televised speech to try to undermine the special counsel's investigation into Russian interference in the 2016 election and multiple inquiries that Democrats are now beginning into the Trump administration."[17]

--Loyalty(ingroup)/Betrayal: "Stacey Abrams. . . gave her party's response. She highlighted her hardscrabble upbringing and values of cooperation and camaraderie, saying, 'We do not succeed alone' and promising 'a better America.'"[18]

--Care/Harm: "'I am asking the Congress to pass legislation to prohibit the late term abortion of children who can feel pain in the mother's womb,' the president said."[19]

*These are a few examples of the very type of expression of moral foundations that would be missed by researchers limiting their analysis to word counts and content analyses.* Additionally, the political speeches analyzed for this study, and in particular the press articles, exhibited noticeably few of the wide variety of terms in the coding indices used by MFT researchers. Part of this could be the nature of the speeches of policy, another could be that the average news story is written between a sixth and an eighth grade reading level, as were a random sample of the articles used for this analysis, so more nuanced descriptions or advanced words are missing. This would be another reason to augment existing social scientific counting with rhetorical understandings of news texts.

## FOUR FORMS OF BIAS

Those who study news discourse have long been aware that journalists inject political bias into the news. For example, Thomas Patterson and Wolfgang Donsbach wrote in 1996 that, particularly in the United States, "partisanship can and does intrude on news decisions, even among journalists who are conscientiously committed to a code of strict neutrality. [And this] partisan bias occurs at measurable levels throughout the news systems of Western Democracies. As we have seen . . . journalists' opinions affect the interpretation of facts, and fairness leans to the left."[20] Aside from the biased reporting uncovered from the framing and moral foundations analysis summarized above, other forms of biased reported were rampant in the hard news articles used in this research project. There are four common means whereby journalists can inject bias into news stories while purporting to remain objective, and all four were found here: labeling, sandwiching, lopsided use of sources, and bias by omission.[21]

### Labeling

The process of labeling is intrinsic to our day-to-day communication practices and, of course, to news production practices. Every time we use a descriptive adjective, we are engaged in some sort of labeling; these "are words that describe nouns. Specifically, adjectives describe the action, state, or quality" to which nouns refer.[22] For news stories, when done correctly, and without favoritism and bias, this can help readers/viewers more precisely navigate the world in which they live. When done perniciously, or uncritically (as in when caught up in groupthink), it becomes a partisan tool for the advancement of the press's political causes. Labeling is at its core a press "practice of describing its sources or those persons upon whom it is reporting. Some researchers have found these terms used in such a way as to provide a positive association with pro-press sources [and positions] and negative associations with anti-press [sources and] positions."[23] Usually, this takes the form of describing most Republicans as "conservative," or other labels to denote even further right positions—hard right, ultra-conservative, and so on—to make them seem out of the mainstream. Democrats and liberals are usually not labeled as "liberal"—or hard left, or ultraliberal, progressive, and so on—except in rare instances, and sometimes they are labeled to make them appear *less* liberal than they are. For example, a recent analysis found that *The New York Times* was labeling liberal Democratic presidential primary candidates in such a way to make them appear less liberal, calling, for instance, candidate Pete Buttigieg a "centrist."[24] Buttigieg supports, among other progressive efforts, the New Green Deal, decriminalizing illegal border crossings, and eliminating the Electoral College, which places him squarely on far left terra firma. But not to the *Times*.

Part of this labeling process is inherent in the political nature of the journalists themselves. Even as they are progressive and left, they do not necessarily see themselves as such. They see themselves not as extreme, but as moderate, unbiased, and in the possession of the truth. Accordingly, those with whom they agree are viewed favorably, in a similar light, and those with whom they disagree need labeling for clarification. So, as an example, why tag hard-left writer Gore Vidal as such? He is, after all, within the mainstream of the groupthink of the press; however, Senator Ted Cruz is not, so is readily labeled a "conservative" and as "tacking even further to the right."[25]

These labels overwhelmingly single out political opponents of the press to label as conservatives, with little to no labeling of liberals as such. One analysis found that by a 20-to-1 margin that ABC, CBS, and NBC "apply ideological labels to Republicans over Democratic presidential candidates."[26] But they can also be used to help those with whom the press agrees or to downplay some negative aspect. Sometimes this takes the form of misleading descriptions, as when *The New York Times* intentionally labeled a major Democratic donor, Ed Buck, as a "small-time Democratic donor," after it was revealed that two men died in his home and that the FBI alleged that he had exchanged drugs and money for sexual favors, citing at least eleven victims.[27] Or when the MSM refuses to identify the political party of high-ranking Democrats when they are accused of wrongdoing, as happened in the 2019 Jeffrey Epstein sex scandal.[28] Or when the MSM labels a mainstream conservative pro-life, pro-religious freedom group a "hate group." But why call them a hate group? "Because the Southern Poverty Law Center, a far-left, anti-Christian hate group, lists them as an extremist/hate group."[29] And yet, the discredited SPLC is not mentioned as left-leaning or progressive, or as ethically challenged, or as a potential hate group that has inspired domestic terrorism.[30] Such omissions, and labels, serve to push audience thinking in a particular, press-guided direction.

We find these ubiquitous and well-documented labeling practices within the four case studies in this book as well. Speaking of Trump's immigration plan, NBC News wrote that "some *Democratic* officials hammered Trump for wanting to make it harder for refugees and legal immigrants' family members to come to the U.S. 'What the president is proposing is a *xenophobic, anti-immigrant* agenda that if applied to previous generations would have barred millions of European and Asian immigrants from contributing to our country,' [said] Rep. Linda Sanchez, D-Calif." And after setting up Trump's plan labeled in such despicable terms, the *Times* bring in "Kay Cole James, president of the *conservative* Heritage Foundation, [who] called it "a step in the right direction.""[31] In this case, good Democrats versus bad conservatives and Trump.

Here are other examples taken from the various press coverage of President Trump analyzed in our study here. Labeling works to bias in more ways than just using derivations of the word "conservative" or "liberal." It also pushes our thinking in a particular direction, asking us to accept the characterizations offered by the press.

1. "The Trump administration has repeatedly touted *so-called* merit-based or points-based systems, such as in Canada and Australia."[32]
2. "Mr. Trump's latest immigration proposal was drafted by Jared Kushner, *his son-in-law* and senior adviser, and Mr. Miller, who spent months working on a plan that would double as a central plank of Mr. Trump's 2020 campaign."[33]
3. "The [immigration] proposal—drafted by the president's *son-in-law* Jared Kushner and backed by immigration *hardliner* Stephen Miller. . . ."[34]
4. Calls left-leaning organizations nonpartisan but somewhat conservative organizations conservative or right-leaning: "the *nonpartisan* Migration Policy Institute" and "the *right-leaning* Heritage Foundation. . . ."[35]
5. With regard to abortion, "More *conservative* states have been pushing for *so-called* 'heartbeat' bills. . . " but those states expanding abortion availability are not labeled as liberal or progressive.[36]
6. Here are just a few of the other terms used to describe President Trump and his policies: "searing," "awkward," "disrupter."[37] Engaging in "Braggadocia"[38] "touting," "boasting," "racist," "liar."[39]

Rarely did the press label anyone or any organization left leaning or progressive, except Fox News, which on occasion, though not consistently, would so label both liberal and conservatives: the president "condemning recent *liberal* efforts in Virginia and New York to change abortion laws."[40]

## Sandwiching

This reportorial practice involves the placement of something in between two other items of a different nature, so one element of a story "sandwiched" in between two other elements. As mentioned in chapter 2, there is a "fairness and balance" bias inherent within the American press, so the press often thinks that it is being "fair" by presenting "both sides" of an issue. However, even though the "other side" is often presented in a story, the way that a reporter places the sides can change their meaning or interpretation. Often this takes the form of journalists placing explanation or support for whatever "side" of the issue they disagree with in between complimentary points of view, and these views tend to agree with the position espoused by the journalists. So, whatever positions journalists dislike are made to seem weaker than those they support. This is often accomplished by journalists writing a summation of the story (with or without quotes) that supports a point of view (side 1) and then presentation of the other point of view (side 2), and then quotes supporting the journalists' point of view (side 1). Although on its face balanced (since "both" sides are presented), in practice the story is biased toward one side.

Consider, for example, this example from a story written in response to Trump's immigration speech. Presented in the order the statements appeared in the story, one can clearly see the sandwiching and which "side" comes out more favorably:

*(Side 1—Press):* "'[the proposed policy] could be a barrier to very productive immigrants becoming a part of American society,' one expert said."
*(Side 1—Press):* "President . . . Trump announced a sweeping immigration proposal Thursday that would alter the way legal immigrants are allowed into the U.S. The plan includes a civics test, a measure that experts said was highly unusual and could exclude high-skilled applicants from entering the country."
*(Side 1—Press):* "This test is at best unnecessary and could screen out some very skilled, ambitious immigrants who are ready to be productive in America, whatever the test says. . . ."
*(Side 1—Press):* "It could be a barrier to very productive immigrants becoming a part of American society. . . ."
*(Side 2—Trump):* "Trump's proposal would create a system that favors applicants who are highly skilled, well-educated and speak English, as well as have potential employment over family-based immigration."

172                              Chapter 8

*(Side 2—Trump):* "The White House estimates 12 percent of people who obtain green cards and citizenship do so based on 'employment and skill,' while 66 percent enter via family-based connections and 22 percent through humanitarian visas and the diversity lottery. Under the new proposal, employment and skill would increase to 57 percent, 33 percent for family-based and 10 percent for everything else."

*(Side 2—Trump):* "The merit-based system proposal is centered around what would be called the 'Build America' visa. It recognizes three categories: extraordinary talent, professional and specialized vocations, and exceptional students. The U.S. grants about 1.1 million green cards a year. . . . The administration has said the number would not change, just the composition."

*(Side 1—Press):* "But [critics] said that would depend on what the points system would look like. 'How many people would meet the new point criteria and how many of those want to come to the U.S.?' 'They may or may not be able to keep the numbers the same.'"

*(Side 2—Trump):* "The Trump administration has repeatedly touted so-called merit-based or points-based systems, such as in Canada and Australia."

*(Side 1—Press):* "'Family-based migration was already bringing in educated, highly skilled people. . . . In fact, the current inflow of family-based and diversity lottery immigrants are better educated than the average American. . . .' 'It's a myth that you either let in high-skilled immigrants or we get low-skilled, poorly educated family-based immigrants. . . .'"

*(Side 1—Press):* "[Critics] added that the Canadian system awards points to immigrants for having family ties in the country. 'They admit more family relatives than the United States on a per capita basis. . . .'"[41]

## Lopsided Use of Sources

The press may also support one position or politician over another by the way it uses sources in a story, in particular because sources can be used to support one position over another. This can also take the form of citing no sources at all except anonymous sources, or unnamed "experts" for which readers must simply take the word of the journalist that a source was actually consulted, that the source actually did say what was quoted, and that the source is actually credible. Some journalists use the phrase, "experts say," or perhaps "most people believe," or "research suggests" as ways of supporting the press generated narrative as well. Finally, one may look at the simple number of pro-press (liberal) position individuals being quoted versus the number of anti-press (conservative) position individuals being quoted. In most cases, journalists appear to find it easier to locate and quote those who agree with their position than they do those who do not.

Looking only at named sources linked to actual quotes in our present case studies, we find the following use of sources in the news articles. Those

Table 8.9  Type of Source

|  | National Security | Economy | SOTU | Immigration | TOTAL |
|---|---|---|---|---|---|
| Support president | 4 | 10 | 13 | 3 | 30 |
| Oppose president | 15 | 10 | 70 | 20 | 115 |
| Neutral | 12 | 11 | 31 | 12 | 56 |

Source: Author.

sources which shared both a positive and a negative statement were counted as neutral (see table 8.9).

As can be seen, oppositional (negative) sources clearly outnumber both neutral explanations and supporting quotes. Keep in mind that the oppositional quotes fall in line with the general tone and framing of the press report. Additionally, in the one instance where there seems to be a balance, concerning Trump's speech at DAVOS, the context in which the supportive quotes occurred minimize their supporting nature. *The Washington Post* provides a good example of the context in which these quotes occurred: "Trump wins over global elites at Davos. All it took was a $1.5 trillion tax cut."[42] In short, the press frames the quoted positive comments of global elites concerning Trump's policies as mercenary in nature.

## Omission of Oppositional Information

Frames can be supported by information that is left out.[43] We know that frames both increase and decrease the saliency of certain information, but they also make it easier for those writing stories to leave out contradictory information that does not "fit" in the frame the journalist is constructing. This can be both intentional and unintentional. This "reinforcement of existing attitudes through omission is far from the trivial effect that many scholars imply. Holding support under adverse new conditions is a crucial goal in politics, not just winning over new supporters. So one way the media wield influence is by omitting or de-emphasizing information, by excluding data about an altered reality that might otherwise disrupt existing support."[44] For instance, Reuters and AFP recently *deleted* stories immediately after they discovered that the high numbers they had reported were from the Obama administration "caging" children at the Mexican border and not the Trump administration.[45] This type of bias is especially difficult for news audiences to detect since such detection presupposes knowledge of the omitted information. The Trump administration is the one "caging" children, at least according the MSM, but when "a UN study claimed the United States had some 100,000 children in migrant-related detention [cages]," its reporting would have cast light on the exceptionally high numbers of children detained under the Obama administration policies, something that did not fit within the press defined narrative on this issue. This is why supplementing MSM news reports with alternative, nonmainstream sources of news is so important. There were a *multitude* of examples of bias by omission within the coverage of President Trump's speeches, of which I share nine instances here to provide examples of how omissions act to frame.

Within the State of the Union, for example, there was a major disjunction between the positive level of reception from those who watched it and the framing of news media. Except for a brief mention by CBS of its own poll, news reports left out polls showing majority of viewers thinking it was not divisive, even though a major action of the press was to frame it as extremely divisive.

Although briefly, President Trump did strongly describe Socialism in his State of the Union address, and there was some mention of this in the press. ABC listed this as one of seven "Memorable Lines" from the address: "Here, in the United States, we are alarmed by new calls to adopt socialism in our country. America was founded on liberty and independence—not government coercion, domination and control. We are born free, and we will stay free. Tonight, we renew our resolve that America will never be a socialist country."[46] What was not mentioned by almost all who reported on this was that while Republicans stood and cheered wildly, almost all Democrats remained largely silent and impassive; few joined Republicans in applause, and even fewer stood. The closest that any article came to mentioning any of this important information was from Fox News, which stated, "And the House Speaker applauded briefly when Trump asserted that the U.S. would never become a socialist country, even as many Democrats remained expressionless."[47] This is an extremely important moment since it was the first time the term "socialism" is used in a State of the Union Address. The MSM minimizes this monumental laying down of the gauntlet, as well as how the major political parties reacted.

The press made much ado about the mention of abortion in the State of the Union, and laid out a case to oppose Trump's depictions of abortion practices:

> The CDC reported in 2015 that 1.3 percent of abortions took place at or after the 21st week of a pregnancy, and [an OB-GYN] said that fewer than 1 percent of abortions happen after 24 weeks of a pregnancy. "In terms of second trimester terminations, there are often cases where serious anomalies are not detected in the fetus until the second trimester. There are also cases in which the life or medical condition of the woman is at serious risk if the pregnancy were to continue," [an ABC News medical correspondent] said.[48]

The second trimester begins at week 13, and the third trimester begins at week 27 or 28 depending on source; regardless, the above article (and the others which mention this) ignores abortions in almost all of the second trimester (around 9 percent), referring to late second-trimester pregnancies and actually using figures that include the third.[49] Aside from misrepresenting the numbers, left out of the discussion is that about 98.3 percent of abortions in the United States are elective; thus, not for cases of rape, 0.3 percent; cases of incest, 0.03 percent; cases of risk to maternal life, 0.1 percent; cases of risk to maternal health, 0.8 percent; or cases of fetal health issues, 0.5 percent.[50] Another way of looking at this is that the very reasons being given for allowing late-term abortions—"health" of fetus and/or mother—are not as pronounced as the press would lead one to believe.[51] Additionally, important contextualizing information for understanding Trump's remarks vis-à-vis Virginia and New York state was left out by all press sources covered in this study:

> Pro-life critics of the law are pointing out that the exception for health, which is not restricted to a physical definition and can be interpreted to cover psychological and emotional health, subject only to the medical judgment of the abortion provider, is broad enough to cover basically any possible late-term abortion. Insofar as the goal of the law was to guarantee access to abortion and remove restrictions on it, this is part and parcel of that goal. The new law does not contain any meaningful restriction that is likely to ever prevent an abortion.[52]

These figures and issues are complicated, and Americans need all facts to make informed choices.

Immigration is another area that the press failed to provide a full palette of factual information. For example, CNN all but called Trump a liar here: "Without evidence, Trump accused Mexican cities of bussing undocumented immigrants to the southern US border."[53] Yet there were international papers, some even providing pictures, that clearly showed that migrants were taking large busses at times.[54]

On immigration reform, the press framed the new policy in such a way as to change what was being proposed: "Democrats and immigration advocates have long opposed many of the proposals outlined by Mr. Trump, like scaling back the family-based immigration system, which allows immigrants to bring their spouses and children to live with them, and replacing it with a merit-based system."[55] Such framing makes it appear that spouses and children will not be allowed in, when Trump actually stated, "we prioritize the immediate family of new Americans—spouses and children. The loved ones you choose to build a life with, we prioritize. And we have to do that. They go right to the front of the line. Right to the front of the line, where they should be."[56] Although some news outlets shared Trump's statement, many did not.

Whereas others focused almost exclusively on "the wall," leaving out important elements of Trump's overall immigration proposal, Fox News, by no means completely friendly to the president in our case studies, brings in contextualizing information, whereas others left it out. In short, you have "a wall" for consideration or this:

> Trump outlined his administration's "common-sense proposal" to end the "crisis" on the southern border, which has been sent to Congress, and which he said includes "humanitarian assistance, more law enforcement, drug detection," a way to close "loopholes that enable child smuggling," and "plans for a new physical barrier or wall."" Which would be a "smart, strategic, see-through steel barrier—not just a simple concrete wall," he explained.[57]

The press tried to minimize the impact of some of Trump's immigration comments, such as illegal immigrant violence, or that "countless Americans are murdered by criminal illegal aliens." For example,

> The president . . . sought to paint undocumented immigrants who cross the southern border, often seeking asylum, as an invading force prone to violent crime. . . . Illegal border crossings are down significantly from their historic peaks, and some research indicates that undocumented immigrants commit crimes at lower rates than U.S. citizens do. Still, Trump has claimed that only a border wall would be effective in keeping out the migrants, many of whom are families with children.[58]

Although the actual numbers are contested by opposing politics groups, ranging from highs and lows, according to the Government Accounting Office, there were over 52,000 arrests of illegal aliens for homicide between 2006 and 2016, with an average of 12 murders committed a day, which rounds up to around 44,000 murders committed during that period.[59] Of note is that 77 percent of Federal prison incarcerations of illegal aliens are from Mexico. These figures are routinely left out of press reports.

Again on immigration, the press omits important contextualizing information. For example, this NBC News story speaks to refugees:

> While the U.S. has historically resettled more refugees than the rest of the world, that number has steadily declined under the Trump administration. Meanwhile, Canada and Australia have been leading in the number of refugees admitted per capita. [A pro-immigration activist] said through his research he has compared the U.S., Canadian and Australian systems and found "the big differences are Canada and Australia admit significantly more people relative to the population. They're more generous in admitting immigrants as part of their population," he said.[60]

However, important contextualizing information is left out. Since the journalist is discussing "per capita," it is crucial that we know relative populations, yet the journalists pointedly leaves this out. Canada's population for 2019 was around 37.5 million; Australia's only 25 million.[61] Knowing this, readers could make a better judgment about American policy.

Concerning National security and Trump's goal of having NATO allies pay their fair share (2 percent of a member's GDP), the press made it seem as if they already were or that President Obama was the one responsible for the increase:

> The secretary general of the military alliance, Jens Stoltenberg, said in July that five countries contributed at least 2 percent of their G.D.P. in 2016. He said he expected Romania to reach the benchmark this year, and Latvia and Lithuania to do so next year. It is conceivable that Mr. Trump ushered along the process, but efforts to address the disparity predated his complaints. He exaggerated when he said foreign countries were not sharing the "cost of defending them."[62]

Routinely left out of reports is that there are twenty-nine member states; an important bit of information to know. So only five of twenty-nine (including the United States) are paying "their fair share." Additionally, Americans need to know that the United States alone pays more for the common defense than all other NATO member states combined, and approximately 22 percent of NATO's direct budget.[63] NATO member states agreeing to pay what they promised to pay is a major step forward, and by 2019, after Trump's pressure, we see seven of twenty-nine meeting their 2 percent goal, with almost all other members increasing their share toward that goal.[64] A major accomplishment for any president, but one minimized by the press through omission.

Certainly, journalists have to make editing decision about what to include and exclude from their stories. Yet overwhelmingly they find ways of including that which supports their point of view and omit that which could challenge their preferred narrative. Press bias by omission is a result of framing, moral foundations, and confirmation bias; it can be an intentional or unintentional action by reporters (constrained by their confirmation bias) so they leave out information that would diminish their own positions and that would help those with whom they disagree. So, this aspect of bias by omission could explain how journalists downplay or reframe both facts and moral foundations that support conservative points of view.

## UNETHICAL BEHAVIOR OF THE MAINSTREAM NEWS MEDIA

### Norms of Journalistic Ethics

The news media is, of course, free in America to report as it sees fit. Free speech is a cornerstone of the American Republic, and the press was knowingly quite partisan in the early days of our Republic. And that is the key, it *knowingly and publicly* embraced its partisanship; since that time, however, it has evolved to adopt a norm of reportorial objectivity that it has willingly enshrined in its various codes of ethics. In this section, we review some of the more applicable elements of the various ethical codes and then juxtapose them against the findings from our case studies.

Articles 1 and 4 of the American Society of Newspaper Editors (ASNE) statement of principles (in existence since 1922) are particularly noteworthy:

> ARTICLE I: The primary purpose of gathering and distributing news and opinion is to serve the general welfare by informing the people and enabling them to make judgments on the issues of the time.
>
> ARTICLE IV: Every effort must be made to assure that the news content is accurate, free from bias and in context, and that all sides are presented fairly. Significant errors of fact, as well as errors of omission, should be corrected promptly and prominently.[65]

The Society of Professional Journalists hold similar views:

> Public enlightenment is the forerunner of justice and the foundation of democracy. The duty of the journalist is to further those ends by seeking truth and providing a fair and comprehensive account of events and issues. Conscientious journalists from all media and specialties strive to serve the public with thoroughness and honesty. Journalists should be honest, fair and courageous in gathering, reporting and interpreting information. Journalists should: Test the accuracy of information from all sources and exercise care to avoid inadvertent error. Deliberate distortion is never permissible. Examine their own cultural values and avoid imposing those values on others.[66]

The Associated Press Managing Editors Code of Ethics states in part:

1. The good newspaper is fair, accurate, honest, responsible, independent and decent.
2. Truth is its guiding principle.
3. It avoids practices that would conflict with the ability to report and present news in a fair, accurate and unbiased manner.
4. The newspaper should serve as a constructive critic of all segments of society. It should reasonably reflect, in staffing and coverage, its diverse constituencies.
5. The newspaper should guard against inaccuracies, carelessness, bias or distortion through emphasis, omission or technological manipulation.
6. The newspaper should strive for impartial treatment of issues and dispassionate handling of controversial subjects.[67]

Individual papers have their own codes as well, reflecting the principles expressed above. For instance, *The New York Times* has an extensive handbook and asserts that it tells its "readers the complete, unvarnished truth as best we can learn it."[68] *The Washington Post* boasts that it adheres to its original 1935 principles of ethical conduct; three of those are of note for this study: "The first mission of a newspaper is to tell the truth as nearly as the truth can be ascertained. The newspaper shall tell ALL the truth so far as it can learn it, concerning the important affairs of America and the World. The newspaper shall not be the ally of any special interest, but shall be fair and free and wholesome in its outlook on public affairs and public men."[69]

*To summarize, America's mainstream news media voluntarily pledge to follow ethical reporting practices by providing the public with complete, accurate details, within an unbiased context, so that the people may make informed political judgments.* It is the responsibility of the Fourth Estate in our American Republic to provide citizens the objective information necessary to make informed choices. And this role is seen as *indispensable* to the proper function of a Constitutional Republic. The MSM analyzed for this study adheres to these standards. And yet, with the possible exception to some degree by Fox News, all the outlets in this study repeatedly, *intentionally and unintentionally*, violated tenants of these codes to which they ascribe.

It is difficult to prove intentionality based upon the results of this study alone, yet with journalists' self-admissions, the exposes (such as with CNN above), the absolutely jaw-dropping journalistic collusion demonstrated by like-minded liberal journalists in groups such as JournoList, Cabalist,[70] GameJournoPros,[71] JournoList 2,[72] and demonstrable anti-conservative reporting,[73] there is no room for doubt that it does exist. Suffice it to say that there is some degree of intentional action involved with the injection of biased reporting favoring progressive positions and politicians into what is characterized as objective news. This, in and of itself, is an appalling violation of the very norms of ethical conduct to which these journalists subscribe. Be that as it may, a more insidious bias, one less easily weeded out, is that injected into reporting through confirmation bias, which, while including some degree of intentionality, crosses well into the line of unconscious actions. We see both types in our case studies when reviewing the aggregate responses of the press.

## Framing and Bias

As seen from the framing portion of our study, the MSM failed to accurately relay the themes stressed by the president; instead, the MSM stressed its own counter themes, framed in a way that Trump was hurt and his Democrat critics were helped. In the limited times the president's themes were stressed, they were framed completely different than he had framed them. In short, had a citizen not listened to the speech first hand, that person would have an utterly warped, incomplete, inaccurate understanding of what the president had said about a particular issue or event. Out of the twenty-one themes covered and well framed by the president in his four speeches, the press relayed fully only two, and those presented considerably different frames than those expressed by the president. *Thus, major policy initiatives, context, tone, bipartisan overtures, were all contested and presented in a press determined manner, one lock step with the president's critics and the Democrats in Congress.*[74] This is simply an unconscionable deviation from reportorial honesty and ethical comportment.

As mentioned earlier, the news media introduced new themes and framed those themes to advance its own beliefs and political goals. Certainly we want a free press that brings in other points of view; *no* press should simply parrot what a president or any politician says. We do, however, expect fair, equitable, and impartial reporting, but such was not the case here. Instead, the press provided one side, ensconced in an incomplete context designed to bolster its own opinions. *Each of the frames of the news media worked to treat the president, not as a source of news, but as a political opponent, with the news media actively helping the political opposition of the president.* As such, the president was denied the opportunity to make his case to the American people.

## Moral Foundations and Bias

I am inclined to believe that the moral foundations aspect of this study reveals a more unconscious form of bias against the president, and more concretely demonstrates confirmation bias among journalists. We see in each case study that journalists' reporting overwhelmingly contested Trump's use of moral foundations. Yet consider the innate nature of moral foundations. Are journalists so enmeshed in their own moral-political world that they see only their own point of view, and instinctively argue against other moral positions? Apparently so, for when Trump used Care, journalists recast it has Harm; when Trump used Harm, journalists minimized it. When Trump used Fairness, journalists recast it as Cheating; when Trump used Cheating, journalists minimized it. When Trump used Loyalty(ingroup), journalists interpreted this through a liberal lens focusing on the global, and recast Loyalty as Betrayal; when Trump used Betrayal, journalists minimized it, or depicted Trump as the Betrayer. When Trump used Authority, which was unusual, journalists depicted it as a misuse of Authority. When Trump used Sanctity, journalists recast it as Degradation. When Trump used Degradation, journalists twisted it to Trump as the Degrader.

We have two possible types of journalistic bias operating here. One, journalists could be so entwined with their own liberally understood moral foundations that they are unconsciously judging Trump, and reporting in such a way that his moral foundations are inadequately expressed. Two, journalists could be intentionally arguing against Trump. Either way, the press is treating him not as a source of news, but as a political opponent, and norms of objective reportorial practice are violated, with an ever stronger case for newsroom viewpoint diversity being made. There is clear bias operating here, both innate and intentional.

## NEWS MEDIA BIAS AND THE FUTURE OF THE REPUBLIC: THE EFFECTS OF CONFIRMATION BIAS

Such wholesale partisan reporting has lasting and potentially disastrous consequences for the American Republic, for press failure to expose others to value inconsistent messages acts to further polarize values within ideological groups. The press bias operating today acts to severely circumscribe the information citizens receive about matters of import; moreover, when taking into consideration moral foundations, we can see the press acting (in keeping with their liberal nature) to privilege Care/Harm and Fairness/Cheating foundations, so much so that this disadvantaged not only the president but also conservatives in general in public debates through circumscribing their palette of foundations and how they are used.

Moral foundations are, of course, more unconscious in their expressions, demonstrating the need for viewpoint diversity among reporters. The mainstream news media is an exclusive club. Although as a group it speaks of the importance of diversity and inclusion, this in practice only applies to matters of race, not to ideological points of view.[75] Yet the news media states that it is important to describe events accurately and to provide "a representative picture of the constituent groups in society."[76] Yet by its own composition it is incapable of doing this.

Our case studies have clearly shown that the press has violated numerous tenants in the above ethical codes. Nurtured by its homogeneous political composition, the press engages in unethical and biased reportorial practices, and in so doing functions as an anti-Democratic institution, with journalists routinely undermining the very Democratic ideals they profess to uphold.[77] This is an especially pernicious practice in that journalists invoke objectivity while tainting the news with their personal political ideology. News organizations that wish to engage in partisan reporting are free to do so, but are ethically expected to announce it as such. And therein lies the quite serious problem with the MSM. They purport to be objective, clearly are not, thus they operate hypocritically and unethically.

Yet why would an institution willingly turn a blind eye to its complicity in damaging itself and the Republic in which it operates? Confirmation bias offers one answer to this. Aside from those actively plotting (as Journolist, Cabalist, etc. demonstrate), much of the bias operating simply results from being part of such an ideologically inbred group. Within this groupthink incubation chamber, it is easy to perpetuate liberal beliefs and attitudes, and these find their way into news; after all, *everybody* thinks this way. Moral psychologist Jonathan Haidt calls such a grouping of like-minded others a "tribal-moral community," and suggests that members are "united by 'sacred values' that hinder research and damage their credibility—and blind them to the hostile climate they've created for non-liberals."[78] With the rise of activist journalism, and now deliberate calls to "resist" Trump, we have intentional activism coupled with groupthink, which severely hinders the production of objective reporting.

Importantly to our purpose in this book, Moral foundation Theory provides evidence that moral reasoning is often used to support our "social agendas—to justify our own actions and to defend the teams to which we belong."[79] To the degree that this is true, we can see how the press would operate to protect its own narrow political identity. This tribal mentality, with its very exclusive and limited embrace of one portion of the ideological spectrum, was on full display, with the worldview of the press in some ways explaining the bias detected in our case studies. Recall the MIME discussed earlier. It posits that "consistent exposure to messages emphasizing the superiority of one moral foundation over another will increase the salience of that foundation among audiences and maintain its salience in the face of other influences. . . . Insulation from value inconsistent messages will foster polarized values within ideological groups and reduce openness to divergent views."[80] So, for those leaning left receiving the press message and for journalists themselves, this means a reinforcing of what they already believe as true. The press, in its confirmation bias bubble, continually reinforces its own values and presuppositions, making it increasingly easier to support one ideological point of view and denigrate or ignore others, and the like-minded audiences of those news reports, unless actively seeking out alternative sources of news, are exposed to the same process.

Herein lies a particular danger to the contemporary American Republic, though. Without question a free and vibrant press is necessary for the proper functioning of our Republic; our Democratic ideals will flourish only when citizens have free access to information generated by a free and impartial press operating in watchdog fashion. Yet without full access to the day's intelligence, without a vibrant clash of ideas, without trust in a news media to provide impartial descriptions of policies and events, the public, and our Republic, simply cannot function properly.

Survey evidence suggests that many Americans are aware of the press interference with the full functioning of our Republic, and the results are distressing. In 2005, Pew found that the public believed that the press "hurt democracy" (33 percent), "are politically biased" (60 percent), and "favor one side in politics" (72 percent).[81] And this perception has only grown worse. As pointed out by Gallup, Rasmussen, and others:

"Raw partisan shaping of political news has come back to haunt the mainstream press; American's trust in the news media is at an historic low."[82]

"Voters don't trust news media fact checking."[83]

"A majority of Americans believe it was the media, not the Russians, that [were] attempting to influence the 2016 election."[84]

A majority of voters believe the press was and is biased against Trump.[85]

"46 percent of voters believe that major news organizations make up stories about Trump."[86]

Voters "are mistrusting of polls themselves and feel that pollsters are out to stop the now elected president's agenda."[87]

Over two-thirds believe the news media publish "fake news."[88]

Seventy-two percent of Americans believe that "traditional major news sources report news they know to be fake, false, or purposely misleading."[89]

Only 17 to 23 percent of Americans rate journalists high or very high in ethical standards.[90]

There are, unfortunately, many more such surveys, all of which suggest the same disheartening conclusion: *the American mainstream news media, in terms of political reporting, is seen as partisan, unethical, and untrustworthy, and is contributing to an increasing sense of partisanship and distrust in American Institutions.* As Michael Goodwin wrote, "There is a national crisis of confidence in all media."[91] And the news media has only itself to blame. Loss of trust in any institution weakens that institution's ability to perform its job. In the case of the press, how can it function properly as a watchdog when so many distrust it?[92] This loss of trust is incredibly damaging to not only the press, but to our American Institutions in general and to our Constitutional Republic. Such mistrust in the very institution that is supposed to be a trusted, impartial source for information from which to make political decisions only leads to poor decision by voters and opens the way to authoritarian rule by one party.

Supporting one side of an issue or policy while weakening or deprecating the other presents an incomplete picture to the public; it is little better than propaganda. Moreover, such presentations circumvent Democratic processes, and moves clearly into an authoritarian realm. In a sense, our case studies here have the mainstream American news media willingly moving into collusion with one political party over another.[93] Although some may point out that our country began with a partisan press, which is true, there is a major difference between then and today's partisan press. During the early days of the Republic papers were diverse, with sometimes several in one city, and though partisan, were *openly* partisan, and collectively represented a wide range of views that were subsequently discussed among the citizens. Today's partisan press is a monolithic structure in both ideology and corporate ownership that sees itself as a branch of government, working to advance one set of policies over another, thus working to help one political party over another. The press is acting not to support a robust Constitutional Republic, but rather acting to advance its own partisan political beliefs over those of others. And this pushes it away from a libertarian or social responsibility model of the press squarely into an authoritarian one.[94]

Of note is how the reporting of the press in our four case studies was so closely aligned with what Democrat critics of Trump were saying. Democrat criticisms and policy ideas were never subjected to a critical reception, as were Trump's utterances. So striking was this that it appeared that the press had, consciously or not, subordinated itself to Democrat Party views, adopting *in practice* an authoritarian model of press functioning, meaning that the press voluntarily served the needs of the Democrat party, and would print little that would undermine that party's authority or standing, or that would give offense to the existing political values endorsed by that party. In a sense, *the press acted as an extension of the Democrat party, grounded in a liberal ideology.*[95] To the degree that this is true, and certainly echoing the criticisms of moderates and conservatives, "our national media now sees itself as part of the government, and as a consequence, the media's mission to hold institutions accountable has been dropped entirely in favor of relentless agenda-pushing."[96] Such an understanding goes a long way toward explaining mainstream news media hostility toward President Trump, his polices, and his supporters; perhaps it also explains how the White House can officially say that it is "Democrats and their media allies" pushing for impeachment,[97] and how Trump can so unabashedly and publicly call the mainstream news media the "enemy of the people," and accuse them of acting as "partners," with the Democrats.[98]

## THE NECESSITY OF VIEWPOINT DIVERSITY

Just how is the mainstream news media to extricate itself from the deplorable problem in which it exists? Taking no action will only find it continuing along the same Democracy-damaging path it has taken, pretending it would not have a problem if only news audiences were smarter, or understood the issues like journalists do. This path will surely lead to a continued diminution of its credibility and of the standing of the institution of journalism in American; ultimately, this will lead to more authoritarian government as the public's trust in journalists continues to wane, and journalistic practices fan the flames of division and partisanship. The MSM could also simply own up to being so biased, embrace its partisanship, and announce proudly to the world that it works to help those of like mind. At least then it will be honest and open, and Americans can choose sides accordingly. Or, and I think this the best option, if the mainstream news media is going to overcome its credibility problem, it needs to break free from its confirmation bias and regain the trust of the American people.

The last option is not an easy path to follow since it requires admitting that there is a problem in the first place. The press is reluctant to do this, and as the recent *New York Times* firing of Libertarian Quinn Norton and CNN's firing of Steve Cortez demonstrate, so strong is the confirmation bias that the press seems determined to purge itself of any thinking but leftist.[99] Moreover, instead of meeting research and accusations of bias spanning decades with open minds and self-scrutiny, journalists instead reply with adamant denials and obfuscation. There is some small hope, however, since there are some in the news media who see the problem and seek solutions. One obvious solution, and the one most likely to promote immediate results, is to encourage viewpoint diversity[100] within various press organizations and to drop the pretense that journalists know better than the population what policies are best for the country. Viewpoint diversity addresses problems such as "confirmation bias, motivated reasoning, tribalism, and the worship of sacred values,"[101] all of which describe the situation in which MSM journalists find themselves today. Journalists write about varying societal and political issues and events every day, and for those issues and events "that can be framed in multiple ways and that may trigger passions or partisan motivations—viewpoint diversity is essential."[102] Stated simply, viewpoint diversity acknowledges that "we need multiple perspectives to solve difficult problems. If everyone thinks the same way, biases go unchallenged and creativity stalls."[103] As Margaret Heffernan asserted in one of her TED Talks, "stepping out of our echo chambers and collaborating with those with whom we disagree is essential to successful businesses, organizations, and relationships."[104] Such successes were seen during the Gulf War when some journalists were embedded with US troops in combat. Their reporting was strikingly different in both content and tone than their nonembedded peers.[105] Even introductory journalism textbooks recognize the ethical need for journalists to maintain an "open-mindedness that seeks out and tries to comprehend various points of view, including those in conflict with those the reporter holds."[106]

In short, news rooms must burst the confirmation bias bubble by hiring those who are not liberal, and return to a notion of a press that serves the people instead of telling them how to think. In a free society, it is simply not the role of the press to effect partisan change, but to provide *complete, accurate details, within an unbiased context, so that the people may make informed political judgments*. Thomas Patterson has written that the

> news media cannot provide the guidance that citizens need. The function of news . . . is to signalize events. In carrying out this function properly, the press contributes to informed public opinion. However, politics is more a question of values than of information. To act on their interests, citizens must arrive at an understanding of the relationship of their values and those at stake in public policy. Political institutions are designed to help citizens make this connection. The press is not.[107]

With only around 20–25 percent of Americans identifying as liberal, the news media is in dire need of diversifying its ideological composition if it is really wanting to help with this Democratic process.

Given the evidence about the challenges of comingling of ideologically distinct, partisan minded coworkers, it would be a shotgun wedding of sorts. As Walter Lippman shared, "Since my moral system rests on my accepted version of the facts, he who denies my moral judgments or my version of the facts, is to me perverse, alien, dangerous."[108] So bringing those of *not* like mind into news rooms would surely be a difficult task. Additionally, some research suggests that "both liberals and conservatives were less willing to work with someone who held opposing perceptions. But liberals took a harder line against them. Across several different perceptual disputes, conservatives were on average 37 percent less likely to want to work with [others] when [they] saw the facts of the world differently. But liberals were 56 percent less likely."[109] Nevertheless, at its core, news media outlets need to hire those with ideological perspectives with which they disagree—this clearly means conservatives. For it is only within the newsroom crucible, with coworkers of differing political ideologies working together to produce an objective news report, that we can arrive at a fairer, more accurate, and Democracy-nourishing product for the American Republic.

## NOTES

1. "Inside Trump's Nixonian Strategy to Make the Media the Enemy," *MSNBC*, February 17, 2017. http://www.msnbc.com/the-last-word/watch/inside-Trump-s-nixonian-strategy-to-make-the-media-the-enemy-880058435528.

2. See, for instance, Thomas E. Patterson, "News Coverage of Donald Trump's First 100 Days," *Shorenstein Center*, May 18, 2017, https://shorensteincenter.org/news-coverage-donald-Trumps-first-100-days/; Danielle Kurtzleben, "Study: News Coverage Of Trump More Negative Than For Other Presidents," *NPR*, October 2, 2017, https://www.npr.org/2017/10/02/555092743/study-news-coverage-of-Trump-more-negative-than-for-other-presidents; and Jennifer Harper, "Unprecedented Hostility: Broadcast Coverage of President Trump Still 90% Negative, Says Study," *The Washington Times*, March 6, 2018, https://www.washingtontimes.com/news/2018/mar/6/Trump-coverage-still-90-negative-says-new-study/.

3. Joan E. Greve, "White House to Federal Agencies: Cancel New York Times and Washington Post Subscriptions," *The Guardian*, October 24, 2019, https://www.theguardian.com/us-news/2019/oct/24/white-house-Trump-new-york-times-washington-post.

4. Francesca Chambers, "Trump's Chief Strategist Steve Bannon Strolls by White House Reporters, Says It's 'the opposition party, all lined up,'" *DailyMail.com*, February 15, 2017, http://www.dailymail.co.uk/news/article-4229064/Bannon-trolls-White-House-reporters-opposition-party.html.

5. Piers Morgan, "Forget the Polls, Rampaging Trump's Going to Win Easily in 2020 Unless Democrat Ostriches Drag Their Heads Out of the Sand and Wake Up to Reality," *Daily Mail*, June 20, 2019, https://www.dailymail.co.uk/news/article-7163567/PIERS-MORGAN-Trumps-going-win-easily-2020-unless-Democrat-ostriches-drag-heads-sand.html.

6. Valerie Richardson, "CNN President Carrying Out 'personal vendetta' Against Trump, Employee Says in Undercover Sting," *The Washington Times*, October 14, 2019, https://www.washingtontimes.com/news/2019/oct/14/cnns-zucker-accused-by-staffer-of-personal-vendett/.

7. Rich Noyes, "Impeachment Frenzy: TV Networks Blast Trump With 96% Negative News," *NewsBusters*, November 12, 2019, https://www.newsbusters.org/blogs/nb/rich-noyes/2019/11/12/impeachment-frenzy-nets-aim-destroy-trump-96-negative-news.

8. Donald J. Trump, "There Has Never Been a Time in the History. . ." *Facebook*, November 12, 2019, https://www.facebook.com/pg/DonaldTrump/posts/.

9. Joe Concha, "Poll: 72 Percent Say Traditional Outlets 'report news they know to be fake, false, or purposely misleading,'" *The Hill*, June 27, 2018, https://thehill.com/homenews/media/394352-poll-72-percent-say-traditional-outlets-report-news-they-know-to-be-fake-false.

10. Zhongdong Pan and Gerald M. Kosicki, "Framing Analysis: An Approach to News Discourse," *Political Communication* 10 (1993): 55.

11. Brian J. Bowe, "Permitted to Build? Moral Foundations in Newspaper Framing of Mosque Construction Controversies," *Journalism & Mass Communication Quarterly* 95, no. 3 (2018): 782–810.

12. Scott Clifford and Jennifer Jerit, "How Words Do the Work of Politics: Moral Foundations Theory and the Debate Over Stem Cell Research," *The Journal of Politics* 75, no. 3, (2013): 669.

13. René Weber, J. Michael Mangus, Richard Huskey, Frederic R Hopp, Ori Amir, Reid Swanson, Andrew Gordon, Peter Khooshabeh, Lindsay Hahn and Ron Tamborini, "Extracting Latent Moral Information from Text Narratives: Relevance, Challenges, and Solutions," *Communication Methods and Measures* 12, no. 2–3 (2018): 119–139.

14. Paul R. Gladden and Anthony M. Cleator, "Slow Life History Strategy Predicts Six Moral Foundations," *EvoS Journal: The Journal of the Evolutionary Studies Consortium*, 9, Sp. Iss (2), (2018): 44.

15. Kevin Liptak and Jeremy Diamond, "Trump Calls for Rejection of 'Politics of Revenge' in Speech that Jabs Democrats," CNN News, February 6, 2019, https://www.cnn.com/2019/02/05/politics/state-of-the-union-address/index.html.

16. Jonathan Allen, "On Trump's Big Applause Line, the Sound of Silence Was Stunning," NBC News, February 6, 2019, https://www.nbcnews.com/politics/white-house/Trump-s-big-state-union-applause-line-sound-silence-was-n968136.

17. Carl Hulse, "State of the Union Speech Puts Democratic Resurgence on Full Display," *The New York Times*, February 6, 2019, NYTFEED020190206ef260058x obtained from factiva.com.

18. Philip Rucker and Toluse Olornnipa, "In Dissonant State of the Union Speech, Trump Seeks Unity While Depicting Ruin," *The Washington Post*, February 6, 2019, WPCOM00020190206ef26001b9 obtained from factiva.com.

19. Rucker and Olornnipa, "In Dissonant State of the Union Speech, Trump Seeks Unity While Depicting Ruin."

20. Thomas Patterson and Wolfgang Donsbach, "News Decisions: Journalists as Partisan Actors," *Political Communication* 13 (1996): 466.

21. These four modes and one additional mode of bias are found in Jim A. Kuypers, *Press Bias and Politics: How the Media Frame Controversial Issues* (Westport, CT: Praeger, 2002).

22. "List of Descriptive Adjectives: Simple, Compound, and Proper," *Your Dictionary*, https://grammar.yourdictionary.com/parts-of-speech/adjectives/List-of-Descriptive-Adjectives.html, accessed December 8, 2019.

23. Abe Aamidor, Jim A. Kuypers, and Susan Wiesinger, *Media Smackdown: Deconstructing the News and the Future of Journalism* (New York, Peter Lang Publishing, 2013), 149.

24. Clay Waters, "Really, NY Times? Buttigieg, Klobuchar 'Centrist,' WP's Rubin 'Conservative,'" *Newsbusters*, October 25, 2019, https://www.newsbusters.org/blogs/nb/clay-waters/2019/10/25/really-ny-times-buttigieg-klobuchar-centrist-wps-rubin-conservative. The *Times* is not alone; see also Julia Manchester, "Bloomberg Bets 2020 Campaign on Unprecedented Strategy," *The Hill*, November 27,

2019, https://thehill.com/homenews/campaign/472269-bloomberg-bets-2020-campaign-on-unprecedented-strategy.

25. "CBS Applies Multiple Ideological Tags to Ted Cruz But Refuses to Label Gore Vidal," *Media Research Center*, https://www.mrc.org/biasalerts/cbs-applies-multiple-ideological-tags-ted-cruz-refuses-label-gore-vidal, accessed November 1, 2019.

26. Rich Noyes, "By 20-to-1, Nets Apply Ideological Labels to Republicans Over Democratic Presidential Candidates," *Media Research Center*, https://www.newsbusters.org/blogs/nb/clay-waters/2019/10/25/really-ny-times-buttigieg-klobuchar-centrist-wps-rubin-conservative, accessed November 1, 2019.

27. Brian Flood, "New York Times Slammed as 'disgusting' for Downplaying Ed Buck as 'small time' Democratic Donor," FOX News, September 20, 2019, https://www.foxnews.com/media/new-york-times-slammed-as-disgusting-for-downplaying-ed-buck-as-small-time-democratic-donor.

28. Rich Noyes, "MISSING! Evening Newscasts Hide the (D) in Epstein-Linked Democrats," *NewsBusters*, August 13, 2019, https://www.newsbusters.org/blogs/nb/rich-noyes/2019/08/13/missing-evening-newscasts-hide-d-epstein-linked-democrats.

29. "Media Labels Mainstream Conservative Organization a Hate Group Based On Terrorist Inspiring Group's List," *RedState*, July 13, 2017, https://www.redstate.com/streiff/2017/07/13/media-labels-mainstream-conservative-organization-hate-group-based-terrorist-inspiring-groups-list/.

30. "Media Labels Mainstream Conservative Organization a Hate Group Based On Terrorist Inspiring Group's List"; Marc A. Thiessen, "The Southern Poverty Law Center Has Lost All Credibility," *The Washington Post, June 22, 2018*, "https://www.washingtonpost.com/opinions/the-southern-poverty-law-center-has-lost-all-credibility/2018/06/21/22ab7d60-756d-11e8-9780-b1dd6a09b549_story.html; "SPLC Honchos Sued for Racketeering," *WND*, January 16, 2019, https://www.wnd.com/2019/01/splc-sued-in-federal-court-as-hate-racket/; Tyler O'Neil, "5 Reasons the SPLC Is Profoundly Wrong About Two Notorious Christian 'Hate Groups,'" *PJ Media*, August 20, 2019, https://pjmedia.com/trending/5-reasons-the-splc-is-profoundly-wrong-about-two-notorious-christian-hate-groups/These are only a few examples of the push back on the actions of the SPLC.

31. Jonathan Allen, "Trump Plays for the Middle – and 2020 – with Legal-Immigration Focus," NBC News, May 16, 2019, https://www.nbcnews.com/politics/white-house/Trump-plays-middle-2020-legal-immigration-focus-n1006671. Italics mine.

32. Allen, "Trump Plays for the Middle – and 2020 – with Legal-Immigration Focus."

33. Anne Karni and Glenn Thursh, "Cool Reception for a Plan on Immigration," *The New York Times*, May 17, 2019. NYTF000020190517ef5h00042 obtained from factiva.com. ABC News, *NYT*, CNN, and *WP* all insist in labeling Kusher as son-in-law whenever he is mentioned. Italics mine.

34. Anne Flaherty, "Trump's Immigration Plan Fails to Address Key Parts of DebaTS: Analysis," ABC News, May 16, 2019, https://abcnews.go.com/Politic

s/Trumps-immigration-plan-fails-addresskey-parts-debate/story?id=63061225 Italics mine.

35. Flaherty, "Trump's Immigration Plan Fails to Address Key Parts of Debate." and Daniella Silva, "Trump's Plan for Civics Test For Legal Entrants Could Keep Out Highly Skilled Immigrants, Experts Say," NBC News, May 17, 2019, https://www.nbcnews.com/news/usnews/Trump-s-plan-civics-test-legal-entrants-could-keep-out-n1006656 Italics mine.

36. Megan Keneally, "Explaining Trump's Talk of 'Late-Term Abortions' During the State of the Union," ABC News, February 7, 2019, https://abcnews.go.com/Health/explaining-Trumps-talklate-term-abortions-state-union/story?id=60883835. Italics mine.

37. Stephen Collinson, "Trump Call for Compromise is Only on His Own Terms," CNN News, February 6, 2019, https://www.cnn.com/2019/02/06/politics/donald-Trump-state-of-the-unionaddress/index.html.

38. Rucker and Olornnipa, "In Dissonant State of the Union Speech, Trump Seeks Unity While Depicting Ruin."

39. Philip Bump, "Trump's State of the Union Speech Drew the One Parallel to Richard Nixon That It Shouldn't Have," *The Washington Post*, February 6, 2019, PCOM00020190206ef26002xl obtained from factiva.com. See also, Margaret Sullivan, "The Words Trump Uses, and the Words the Media Must Use in Response," *The Washington Post*, January 14, 2018, https://www.washingtonpost.com/lifestyle/style/the-words-Trump-uses-and-the-words-the-media-must-use-in-response/2018/01/14/089c8672-f7ae-11e7-a9e3-ab18ce41436a_story.html There are others, certainly. See Kuypers, *Press Bias and Politics* for additional examples beyond presidents. In almost all cases, labels work to hurt those persons and policies with whom the press disagrees and to help those whom the press agrees.

40. Frank Miles, "Trump Calls Out Pro-Choice Abortion Bills During State of the Union," FOX News, February 5, 2019, https://www.foxnews.com/politics/to-rapturous-applause-at-sotu-Trumpasks-congress-to-prohibit-late-term-abortion. Italics mine.

41. Silva, "Trump's Plan for Civics Test For Legal Entrants Could Keep Out Highly Skilled Immigrants, Experts Say."

42. Heather Long and Tory Newmyer, "Trump Wins Over Global Elites at Davos. All It Took Was a $1.5 Trillion Tax Cut," *The Washington Post*, January 25, 2018, https://www.washingtonpost.com/business/economy/Trump-wins-over-global-elites-at-davos-all-it-took-was-a-15-trillion-tax-cut/2018/01/25/3c688624-0201-11e8-8acf-ad2991367d9d_story.html?utm_term=.3254fa99e852.

43. Bias by omission is a well-known press characteristic. See the concluding chapter of Kuypers, *Press Bias and Politics*; Aamidor, Kuypers, and Wiesinger, *Media Smackdown*; and the Media Research Center (mrc.org) routinely publishes examples of MSM omissions.

44. Robert M. Entman, "How the Media Affect What People Think: An Information Processing Approach," *The Journal of Politics* 51, no. 2 (1989): 367.

45. Kyle Smith, "When the Villain Is Obama, Not Trump, News Suddenly Becomes Not Worth Reporting," *New York Post*, November 20, 2019, https://nypost.

com/2019/11/20/when-the-villain-is-obama-not-trump-news-suddenly-becomes-not-worth-reporting/.

46. Megan Keneally, "7 Memorable Lines from the State of the Union," ABC News, February 5, 2019, https://abcnews.go.com/Politics/memorable-lines-state-union/story?id=60872709.

47. Gregg Re, "Democrats Unmoved by Trump's State of the Union Bid to break Gridlock on Border Security," FOX News, February 6, 2019, https://www.foxnews.com/politics/democratsunmoved-by-Trumps-state-of-the-union-bid-to-break-gridlock-on-border-security.

48. Keneally, "Explaining Trump's Talk of 'Late-Term Abortions' During the State of the Union," ABC News, February 7, 2019, https://abcnews.go.com/Health/explaining-Trumps-talklate-term-abortions-state-union/story?id=60883835.

49. "Pregnancy: The Three Trimesters," *University of California San Francisco*, https://www.ucsfhealth.org/conditions/pregnancy/trimesters.html, accessed November 17, 2019.

50. Wm. Robert Johnston, "Reasons Given for Having Abortions in the United States," *Johnson Archives*, http://www.johnstonsarchive.net/policy/abortioN/Abreasons.html, accessed November 17, 2019.

51. Lawrence B. Finer, Lori F. Frohwirth, Lindsay A. Dauphinee, Susheela Singh and Ann M. Moore, "Reasons U.S. Women Have Abortions: Quantitative and Qualitative Perspectives," *Guttmacher Institute*, https://www.guttmacher.org/sites/default/files/pdfs/journals/3711005.pdf, accessed November 17, 2019. See also Carole Novielli, "In Just One Year, 100,000 Abortions Happened in 2nd and 3rd Trimesters," *Live Action*, July 18, 2018, https://www.liveaction.org/news/state-abortions-happening-later/.

52. Sam Sawyer, "Explainer: What New York's New Abortion Law Does and Doesn't Do," *America: The Jesuit Review*, January 30, 2019, https://www.America-magazine.org/rha2019.

53. Kevin Liptak and Jeremy Diamond, "Trump Calls for Rejection of 'Politics of Revenge' in Speech That Jabs Democrats," CNN News, February 6, 2019,https://www.cnn.com/2019/02/05/politics/state-of-the-union-address/index.html.

54. "5,000 Migrants Have Registered with Immigration in Just Four Days," *Mexico News Daily*, January 21, 2019, https://mexiconewsdaily.com/news/5000-migrants-have-registered-with-immigration/; Ashley Collman, "Mexico Announces It Is 'disbanding' Marching 'caravan' of Immigrants as Organizers Lash Out at 'bully' Trump and Vow to Continue Push Towards the U.S. Border," *Daily Mail*, April 3, 2018, https://www.dailymail.co.uk/news/article-5574353/Marching-caravan-immigrants-lash-bully-Trump.html; Ben Ashford, "EXCLUSIVE: 'We'll see you soon Mr. President!' Immigrants on the Sprawling Human Caravan Taunt Trump and Reveal That Despite the 'tough Mexican immigration laws' He Touted They Have Passes to Travel with NO Restrictions as They Move Toward the U.S.," *Daily Mail*, April 5, 2018, https://www.dailymail.co.uk/news/article-5582733/Well-soon-Mr-President-Immigrants-caravan-Mexico-taunt-Trump.html; "Immigrant Caravan Sets Up Camp Along the Mexican Border After US Officials Told Them the Crossing Was FULL, Meaning They Will Have to Wait Until It Re-Opens to Apply for Asylum,"

*Daily Mail*, April 29, 2018, https://www.dailymail.co.uk/news/article-5671809/Central-American-asylum-seekers-climb-Mexico-border-fence.html.

55. Karni and Thursh, "Cool Reception for a Plan on Immigration."

56. Donald J. Trump, "Remarks by President Trump on Modernizing Our Immigration System for a Stronger America," *White House*, May 16, 2019, https://www.whitehouse.gov/briefings-statements/remarks-president-Trump-modernizing-immigration-system-stronger-America/.

57. Brooke Singman, "Trump Argues Border Wall in State of the Union, Says Tolerance for illegal Immigration is 'Cruel,'" FOX News, February 5, 2019, https://www.foxnews.com/politics/Trumpurges- border-wall-in-state-of-the-union-says-tolerance-for-illegal-immigration-is-cruel.

58. Rucker and Olornnipa, "In Dissonant State of the Union Speech, Trump Seeks Unity While Depicting Ruin."

59. "Criminal Alien Statistics," *Government Accounting Office*, March 2011, https://www.gao.gov/assets/320/316959.pdf and "Criminal Alien Statistics," *Government Accounting Office*, July 2018, https://www.gao.gov/assets/700/693162.pdf. Numbers differentiate among murder, manslaughter, and homicide.

60. Silva, "Trump's Plan for Civics Test for Legal Entrants Could Keep Out Highly Skilled Immigrants, Experts Say."

61. "Australia Population," *Worldometers*, https://www.worldometers.info/world-populatioN/Australia-population/, accessed November 29, 2019.

62. Linda Qiu, "Trump Inaccurately Claims 'Firsts' in Defense Speech," *The New York Times*, December 18, 2017, NYTFEED020171219edcj000xd obtained from factiva.com.

63. Amanda Macias, "The US Spent $686 Billion on Defense Last Year—Here's How the Other NATO Countries Stack Up," *CNBC*, July 6, 2018, https://www.cnbc.com/2018/07/03/nato-spending-2017.html and Lucie Béraud-Sudreau and Nick Childs, "The US and Its NATO Allies: Costs and Value," *International Institute for Strategic Studies*, July 9, 2018, https://www.iiss.org/blogs/military-balance/2018/07/us-and-nato-allies-costs-and-value.

64. And President Trump continues this pressure even as of this book's writing: Harry J. Kazianis, "Harry Kazianis: NATO Should Die If Allies Won't Increase Defense Spending as Trump Wants," Fox News, December 4, 2019, https://www.foxnews.com/opinion/harry-kazianis-nato-should-die-if-allies-wont-increase-defense-spending-as-trump-wants.

65. American Society of Newspaper Editors Statement of Principles. "ASNE's Statement of Principles was originally adopted in 1922 as the 'Canons of Journalism.' The document was revised and renamed 'Statement of Principles' in 1975." The full document can be obtained at http://www.asne.org/kiosk/archive/principl.htm.

66. Code of Ethics, Society for Professional Journalists, http://spj.org/ethics/code.htm.

67. Numbers are mine. For the complete listing of the Associated Press's code of ethics, see http://www.asne.org/ideas/codes/apme.htm.

68. "Ethical Journalism: A Handbook of Values and Practices for the News and Editorial Departments," *The New York Times*, https://www.nytimes.com/editorial-standards/ethical-journalism.html, accessed November 17, 2019.

69. "Policies and Standards," *The Washington Post*, https://www.washingtonpost.com/news/ask-the-post/wp/2016/01/01/policies-and-standards/, accessed November 17, 2019.

70. Jeffrey Goldberg, "Meet the New Journolist, Smaller Than the Old Journolist," *Blog Post*, July 21, 2010, *The Atlantic*, https://www.theatlantic.com/national/archive/2010/07/meet-the-new-journolist-smaller-than-the-old-journolist/60159/.

71. Milo, "The E-mails That Prove Video Games Journalism Must be Reformed," *Breitbart*, September 18, 2014, https://www.breitbart.com/europe/2014/09/18/the-emails-that-prove-video-games-journalism-must-be-reformed/.

72. Charlie Nash, "'JournoList' 2 Revealed, Over 400 'Left-Of-Center' Members," *Breitbart*, June 28, 2018, https://www.breitbart.com/tech/2018/06/28/journolist-2-discovered-over-400-left-of-center-members/.

73. Evan Siegfried, "Media Bias Against Conservatives Is Real, and Part of the Reason no One Trusts the News Now," NBC News, July 29, 2018, https://www.nbcnews.com/think/opinion/media-bias-against-conservatives-real-part-reason-no-one-trusts-ncna895471; Sally Zelikovsky, "The Enemy of the People," *The American Spectator*, November 15, 2018, https://www.americanthinker.com/articles/2018/11/the_enemy_of_the_people.html; Kuypers, *Press Bias and Politics*, 214–216; Jim A. Kuypers, *Partisan Journalism: A History of Media Bias in the United States* (Lanham, MD: Rowman & Littlefield, 2014), esp. chapter 11.

74. Something most definitely noticed by both moderates and those who lean right politically. For example, see: Ryan Foley, "David Limbaugh to Levin: Media 'Completely Tied to the Democrats and Their Agenda,'" *NewsBusters*, October 29, 2019, https://www.newsbusters.org/blogs/nb/ryan-foley/2019/10/29/david-limbaugh-life-liberty-levin-media-completely-tied-democrats-and?fbclid=IwAR0HqzBEDTUioph27Ld-EtX0A8fIWl2ralIMnJ028wHrwryrqSaQbJjJj30.

75. Doris Truong, "American Newsrooms Should Employ More People of Color, Annual ASNE Survey Finds," *Poynter*, September 11, 2019, https://www.poynter.org/business-work/2019/american-newsrooms-should-employ-more-people-of-color-survey-finds/.

76. Fred S. Siebert, Theodore Peterson, and Wilbur Schramm, *Four Theories of the Press* (Urbana: University of Illinois Press, 1956), 87–89.

77. As mentioned in chapter 1, I have repeatedly found this to be true in other studies. For instance, in *Press Bias and Politics* I found press interference in the formulation of the American public's political knowledge so extreme that I wrote, "by its political composition and its biased reportorial practices, the press not only breaks its own code of ethics, it functions as an anti-democratic institution since it undermines the very democratic ideals it professes to uphold" (202). See also, Jim A. Kuypers, "News Media Framing of the Donald J. Trump and Hillary Clinton 2016 Presidential Nomination Acceptance Speeches: Terministic Screens and the Discovery of the Worldview and Bias of the Press," in Jim A. Kuypers, Ed. *The 2016 American*

*Presidential Campaign and the News Media: Implications for the American Republic and Democracy* (Lanham, MD: Lexington Books, 2018).

78. John Tierney, "Social Scientist Sees Bias Within," *The New York Times*, February 8, 2011: A1.

79. Jonathan Haidt, *The Righteous Mind: Why Good People are Divided by Politics and Religion* (New York City, NY: Pantheon Books, 2012), xiv.

80. Weber et al., "Extracting Latent Moral Information from Text Narratives, 119–139.

81. "Public More Critical of Press, But Goodwill Persists: Online Newspaper Readership Countering Print Losses," *The Pew Research Center for the People and the Press*, 26 June 2005. < http://people-press.org/reports/display.php3?ReportID=248>. Accessed 13 August 2006.

82. Benjamin Mullen, "Gallup: Trust in Media Is At All-Time Low," *Poynter*, September 14, 2016. http://www.poynter.org/2016/gallup-trust-in-media-is-at-all-time-low/430342/.

83. "Voters Don't Trust Media Fact-Checking," *Rasmussen Reports*, September 30, 2016. http://www.rasmussenreports.com/public_content/politics/general_politics/september_2016/voters_don_t_trust_media_fact_checking.

84. "Most Say Media, Not Russians, Tilting the Election," *Rasmussen Reports*, October 18, 2016. http://www.rasmussenreports.com/public_content/politics/general_politics/october_2016/most_say_media_not_russians_tilting_the_election.

85. Nolan D. Mccaskill, "Poll: Majority of Voters Believe Media Biased against Trump," *Politico.com*, October 19, 2016, http://politi.co/2el8Vgf. See also, John Lott, Jr., "The Media Just Can't Stop Lying About Trump," *The Hill*, June 16, 2018, https://thehill.com/opinion/campaign/393553-the-media-just-cant-stop-lying-about-Trump.

86. Chris Wallace, "The Media Is Giving Up Its Place in Our Democracy," *The Washington Post*, November 17, 2017, https://www.washingtonpost.com/opinions/trump-is-assaulting-our-free-press-but-he-also-has-a-point/2017/11/17/b3b8ec24-c8b2-11e7-b0cf-7689a9f2d84e_story.html.

87. "Voters Don't Trust Polls, See Anti-Trump Bias," *Rasumssen Reports*, May 5, 2017, http://www.rasmussenreports.com/public_content/politics/general_politics/may_2017/voters_don_t_trust_polls_see_anti_trump_bias.

88. Sharyl Attkisson, "Americans Don't Trust the Media, and for Good Reason," *The Hill*, August 18, 2018, https://thehill.com/blogs/pundits-blog/media/347091-Americans-dont-trust-the-media-and-for-good-reason.

89. John Concha, "Poll: 72 Percent Say Traditional Outlets 'report news they know to be fake, false, or purposely misleading,'" *The Hill*, June 27, 2018, https://thehill.com/homenews/media/394352-poll-72-percent-say-traditional-outlets-report-news-they-know-to-be-fake-false.

90. Melvin Mencher, *Melvin Mencher's News Reporting and Writing*, 12th ed. (New York City, NY: McGraw-Hill, 2011), 552 and Jim Norman, "Americans Rate Healthcare Providers High on Honesty, Ethics," *Gallup*, December 19, 2016, https://news.gallup.com/poll/200057/americans-rate-healthcare-providers-high-honesty-ethics.aspx.

91. Goodwin also wrote of the *Times's* role in this: "By ending the commitment to fairness and impartiality, [executive editor of The New York Times, Dean] Baquet is destroying the credibility of The New York Times. Standards made it the most trusted news organization in America and by trashing those standards, Baquet has turned the Times into a purely partisan outlet. It would be tragic enough if his actions had destroyed only the Times. But there is a national crisis of confidence in all media, and the Times no longer offers a solution. It is a major part of the problem." Michael Goodwin, "Goodwin: The New York Times' Long Descent from Credibility," *The New York Post,* November 30, 2019, https://nypost.com/2019/11/30/goodwin-the-new-york-times-long-descent-from-credibility/.

92. Steven D. Cooper addresses this issue in his excellent book, *Watching the Watchdog: Bloggers as the Fifth Estate* (Spokane, WA: Marquette Books, 2006).

93. I have noted this movement also in Kuypers, *Press Bias and Politics* and Kuypers, "News Media Framing of the Donald J. Trump and Hillary Clinton 2016 Presidential Nomination Acceptance Speeches."

94. Siebert, Peterson, and Schramm, *Four Theories of the Press.*

95. This is not unlike other studies showing a press worldview similar to Hillary Clinton. See Kuypers, "News Media Framing of the Donald J. Trump and Hillary Clinton 2016 Presidential Nomination Acceptance Speeches," 101–132. On this issue, David Harsanyi wrote that the MSM was now "an overtly partisan media, exemplified by CNN, which has dropped any pretense of fairness and become an organ of the Democratic Party." See, "CNN's Bias Is Now Beyond Laughable," *The New York Post*, January 16, 2020, https://nypost.com/2020/01/16/cnns-bias-is-now-beyond-laughable/.

96. John Nolte, "How the Political Media's Corruption Destroyed America's Most Crucial Institutions," *The Daily Wire*, November 7, 2016. http://www.dailywire.com/news/10555/how-political-medias-corruption-destroyed-americas-john-nolte#exit-modal.

97. White House, 1600 *Daily*, December 11, 2019, email correspondence with the author.

98. White House, "President Trump Holds a Press Conference," *YouTube.com*, January 22, 2020, (at 37mins, 46 sec), https://www.youtube.com/watch?v=tWZuQHLowmo.

99. John Tierney, "Journalists Against Free Speech," *FrontPage Magazine*, December 4, 2019, https://www.frontpagemag.com/fpm/2019/12/journalists-against-free-speech-john-tierney/ and Shelby Talcott, "CNN Forces Out Another One Of Its Pro-Trump Commentators," *Daily Caller*, January 21, 2020, https://dailycaller.com/2020/01/21/cnn-forces-out-pro-trump-commentator-steve-cortes/.

100. "Heterodox Academy: What Is Viewpoint Diversity?," *Heterodox Academy*, February 2, 2018, https://www.youtube.com/watch?v=3BklwqLBjI.

101. "Viewpoint Diversity in the Academy," *The Righteous Mind*, https://righteousmind.com/viewpoint-diversity/, accessed November 18, 2019.

102. Nick Phillips, "What are the Limits of Viewpoint Diversity?" *Heterodox Academy*, March 5, 2018, https://heterodoxacademy.org/thelimitsofviewpointdiversity/.

103. Phillips, "What are the Limits of Viewpoint Diversity?"

104. Margaret Heffernan, "Dare to Disagree," *TED.com*, margaret_heffernan_dare_to_disagree, accessed November 18, 2019.

105. Jim A. Kuypers and Stephen Cooper, "A Comparative Framing Analysis of Embedded and Behind-the-Lines Reporting on the 2003 Iraq War," *Qualitative Research Reports in Communication* 6, no. 1 (2005): 1–10.

106. Mencher, *Melvin Mencher's News Reporting and Writing*, 564.

107. Thomas Patterson, "The News Media: An Effective Political Actor?," *Political Communication* 14 (1997): 445.

108. Walter Lippman, *Public Opinion* (Digireads.com, 2011): 58.

109. Morgan Marietta, "Do Conservatives or Liberals Hold More Biased Perceptions?," *Psychology Today Blog*, May 24, 2019, https://www.psychologytoday.com/us/blog/inconvenient-facts/201905/do-conservatives-or-liberals-hold-more-biased-perceptions.

# Index

ABC News, 2, 92, 174; abortion and, 104; America First and, 77, 83; border wall and, 109; labeling and, 169; on revisionist powers, 52; socialism and, 105
ABCNews.go.com, 35
abortion, 100, 117, 170; late, 96, 112; Partial-Birth Abortion Ban Act, 11; *Roe v. Wade* and, 104; State of the Union address and, 104–5, 174–75; Trump and, 104–5, 112, 120n28
Abrams, Stacey, 113, 167
accountability journalism, 8
AFP. *See* Associated Foreign Press
African Americans, 70, 93, 100
agenda-setting, 7, 15
AIDS/HIV, 96, 108
America First: care/harm and, 58; competitive model and, 72; DAVOS and, 83; with economy and press response, 77–78; loyalty(ingroup)/ betrayal and, 60, 74; MSM and, 78; national security and framing of, 41–42, 47; press response and national security with, 55; with trade, healthy, 71
American influence, national security and framing of, 44

American people, economy and framing of, 72, 76
American Society of Newspaper Editors (ASNE), 178
Amnesty International, 136
Antifa members, 17
anti-globalism, 69, 71, 85
anti-Semitism, 96, 100
approval numbers: Obama with, 103; Trump with, 102–3
Asian Americans, 93
Asians, immigrants, 140, 170
ASNE. *See* American Society of Newspaper Editors
Associated Foreign Press (AFP), 173
Associated Press Managing Editors, 178
asylum seekers, 131, 133, 136, 138, 142
attacks: electromagnetic and cyber, 43; on press and economy, 81–82, 85–86
Australia, 129, 170, 172, 176, 177
authority/subversion, 44; binding dimensions and, 27; economy and moral foundations with, 75, 76; MFT and, 26; moral foundations and, 167; moral foundations and immigration reform with, 133, 140–41; moral foundations and journalistic bias with, 28–29; moral foundations and

State of the Union address with, 100–101, 116–17

bad news bias, 11–12
Bannon, Steve, 149, 150
Baquet, Dean, 195n91
Becerra, Xavier, 108
betrayal. *See* loyalty(ingroup)/betrayal
biases, 193n77; bad news, 11–12; coverage, 7; fairness and balance, 11, 171; four forms of, 168; Lehrer on, 8; liberal ideological and partisanship, 12; money, 9, 10; moral foundations and, 180–81; moral foundations and journalistic, 25–38; perceptual, 8–9; recency, 10–11; selective, 8; status quo, 8, 9, 11; theoretical, 7–8; visual, 9–10, 11. *See also* confirmation bias; journalistic bias, moral foundations and; news media bias
binding dimensions, 27
bin Laden, Osama, 33
Bissell family, 99
border security: family separation and, 131, 132, 173–74; national security and framing of, 43; with smuggling of women and children, 131
border wall, 43, 74, 94, 108–10, 113, 127, 130, 175
Bowe, Brian J., 33–34, 38n43, 164
Bowman, Nicholas, 33
Brinkley, Christie, 9, 11
Buck, Ed, 169
Bush, George W., 39, 92
*Bush's War* (Kuypers), 38n43
Buttigieg, Pete, 169

Cabalist, 179
Canada, 95, 129, 170, 172, 176–77
care/harm, 44; America First and, 58; individualizing dimensions and, 27; liberals and, 30, 33; MFT and, 26; moral foundations and, 168; moral foundations and economy with, 74, 83–84; moral foundations and immigration reform with, 132, 141; moral foundations and journalistic bias with, 27; moral foundations and national security with, 46–47, 56–59, 61; moral foundations and State of the Union address with, 98–99, 101–2, 112–14
Carter, Jimmy, 12
CBS News, 2, 92, 174; abortion and, 104; America First and, 55, 77; with attack on press, 81; labeling and, 169; politics section of, 32
CBSNews.go.com, 35
Charlottesville, 83
cheating. *See* fairness/cheating
children: DACA, 83, 136, 138–39, 141–43, 164; family immigration and, 135, 136; family separation and, 131, 132, 173–74; smuggling of, 131, 176
China: NSS document and, 49, 50, 53, 57; as revisionist power, 52–54, 61; Russia and, 39, 40; as threat, 60, 61; with trade, 59, 95
CIA, 51, 55, 59
Clifford, Scott, 165
climate change: Obama and, 39, 57, 59, 85; Paris Climate Accord and, 46; Trump and, 50, 55, 56–57, 59, 61, 82, 85, 158
Clinton, Bill, 69
Clinton, Hillary, 12, 13
CNN, 2, 9, 10, 92, 185; American First and, 77, 78; with attack on press, 81, 82; border wall and, 109; care/harm and, 57; on cyber warfare/social media and, 51; DACA and, 139; election (2020) and, 137; omission of oppositional information and, 175; on Putin/Trump/2016 elections, 54; with speeches of Trump and NSS document, 48, 49; women and, 104
CNN.com, 35
CNNe, 92

collective action: call for, 101; with State of the Union address, framing, 96–97
competitive model, economy and framing of, 71–72, 76
confirmation bias, 13, 25; as cognitive process, 14; concluding thoughts, 181–85; objectivity and, 182
conservative bias. *See* status quo (conservative) bias
conservatives: fairness/cheating and, 30; with journalist bias, 29–32, *30*, *31*; liberty/oppression and, 36n9; with MFT, 31–32; moral palettes, *31*; populations, 31
Cortez, Steve, 185
coverage bias, 7
crime, immigration and, 176
Crimea, 49
*Crooks and Liars* (blog), 18
Cruz, Ted, 169
Cummings, Elijah, 167
cyber attacks, electromagnetic and, 43
cyberterrorism, 43
cyber warfare/social media, 59; press response and national security with, 50–52, 61

DACA. *See* Deferred Action for Childhood Arrivals
dangers, economy and framing of, 72–73, 76
DAVOS. *See* World Economic Forum
Deferred Action for Childhood Arrivals (DACA, DREAMers), 83, 136, 138–39, 141–43, 164
degradation. *See* sanctity/degradation
Democratic Capitalism, 11
Denton, Robert E., 11
division, not unity, 106–8
Doggett, Lloyd, 167
Donsbach, Wolfgang, 168
DREAMers. *See* Deferred Action for Childhood Arrivals

drugs: illegal, 94, 127; prescription, 96, 98, 99, 100, 108, 116

economic security, 40, 47, 50, 53, 113; national and, 57, 58, 61, 74; national security and framing of, 43
economy: framing and, 70–73; moral foundations and, 73–75, 82–85; news media moral foundations and, 159–60; press response and, 77–82; press summary and, 85–86; recovery of, 42; with State of the Union address, framing, 94–95; with Trump, speeches of, 69–70; Trump moral foundations and, *158*, 158–59; Trump summary and, 75–76
economy, framing and: American people with, 72, 76; competitive model, 71–72, 76; concluding thoughts, 152, *153*; dangers and, 72–73, 76; reform/results with, 70–71, 75–76
economy, moral foundations and: authority/subversion and, 75, 76; care/harm and, 74, 83–84; fairness/cheating, 73–74, 84–85; loyalty(ingroup)/betrayal and, 74–75, 82–83, 86
economy, press response and: framing, 77–78; open for business, 79–80, 85; populism/globalism, 78–79, 85; with press attacked, 81–82, 85–86; trade, 80–81
efficiency/waste, 36n10
election (2020): frames, 142; immigration reform and, 135, 137–38, 140
elections (2016): press response and national security with Putin, Trump and, 54–55, 61; Russia with, 48, 49, 51, 61; Trump on, 45
electromagnetic attacks, cyber and, 43
Entman, Robert, 19
Epstein, Jeffrey, 169
ethics, journalistic code of, 177–79

eyerolling, 106

facts: with neutral frames, 1–2, 16; salience of, 19; State of the Union address and framing of, 92–93
fairness and balance bias, 11, 171
fairness/cheating, 44; conservatives and, 30; economy and moral foundations with, 73–74, 84–85; individualizing dimensions and, 27; liberals and, 30; MFT and, 26; moral foundations and immigration reform with, 133, 141–42; moral foundations and journalistic bias with, 27–28; moral foundations and national security with, 45–46, 47, 59–60, 61; moral foundations and State of the Union address with, 99–100, 102, 115–16; trade and, 59–60, 61, 73–74, 76, 86
fake news media, 81, 149, 183
families: immigration, 135, 136; separation, 131, 132, 173–74
Farnsworth, Stephen J., 3
first draft, of moral mind, 26–27
FOX BUSINESS, 92
FOXNC, 92
Fox News, 2, 9, 10, 92, 112, 174, 175, 179; abortion and, 104; America First and, 55; with bad news bias, 11–12; border wall and, 110; climate change and, 57; Latinos and, 143n2; NSS document and, 50, 53; on Putin/Trump/2016 elections, 54–55
FoxNews.com, 35
frames: comparisons, 17–18; defined, 1; election (2020), 142; facts with neutral, 1–2, 16; moral foundations, journalistic bias and comparing, 35; moral judgments and, 19; power of, 17
framing: with economy and press response, 77–78; of issues and events and news media bias, 5–24; of news, 15–20, *18*; with press response and national security, 48; State of the Union address, 92–97, 103–12; summary, 156. *See also* economy, framing and; immigration reform, framing; national security, framing and
framing theory, summary of findings, 3
freedom, 36, 59, 96, 97, 98; pluralism and individual, 21n17; religious, 170; security and, 101; social responsibility and, 7; Venezuela and, 95

Gallup, 12, 183
GameJournoPros, 179
"gang of four," 117
gate-keeping, 7
Georgia, 51, 53
global cooperation, 55
globalism. *See* populism/globalism, with economy and press response
Global Risk Report, 78
Goldwater-Nichols Department of Defense Reorganization Act (1986), 39
Goodwin, Michael, 183, 195n91
government shutdown, 107–9, 116–18, 162
Graham, Jesse, 29
groupthink, 13, 169, 182
Guaido, Juan, 95

Haidt, Jonathan, 26, 30, 36n9, 182
harm. *See* care/harm
Harris, Kamala, 138–39
healthcare, 92, 114, 115; costs, 99, 101; single payer, 16, 106; with State of the Union address, framing, 96
Heffernan, Margaret, 186
Heritage Foundation, 170
Hispanic Americans, 70, 93
HIV/AIDS, 96, 108
Homeland security, 43
honesty/deception, 36n10
*The Huffington Post* (newspaper), 18
human rights, 114, 136, 142

human traffickers, 94, 100
Hutchins Commission (1956), 7

ICE officers, 43, 98
Identity-Protective Cognition, 14
immigrants: Asian, 140, 170; asylum seekers, 131, 133, 136, 138, 142; population of undocumented, 139
immigration, 55; crime and, 176; DACA and, 83, 136, 138–39, 141–43, 164; families, 135, 136; ICE officers and, 43, 98; illegal, 45, 93–94, 100, 108–10; legal, 43, 94, 98, 101, 128–29, 133–34, 137, 140–43, 162, 164; news media moral foundations and, 163–64; Obama and, 7, 83; restrictions, 42; Trump moral foundations and, *162*, 162–63
immigration reform, 43; concluding thoughts, 152, *155*, 156; framing, 134–39; moral foundations and, 131–33, 139–42; press response and, 134; press summary, 142–43; with Trump, speeches of, 128; Trump summary and, 133–34
immigration reform, framing: election (2020) and, 135, 137–38, 140; incentives, 131; merit, 128–29; plan specifics, criticism of, 134–36; purpose of plan, 129–30; security through technology, 130; what's missing, 138–39
immigration reform, moral foundations and: authority/subversion, 133, 140–41; care/harm, 132, 141; fairness/cheating, 133, 141–42; loyalty(ingroup)/betrayal, 131–32, 139–40; sanctity/degradation, 133
impeachment, 149–50, 184
individualizing dimensions, 27
INF Treaty, 95
Iran, 99; ISIS, 47; with nuclear program, 42, 48; as rogue state, 40, 49, 72; terrorism and, 73, 98
ISIS, 83, 85, 95, 112

Islam, 33, 42, 43, 48, 52, 58n11
isolationism, 61, 77

Jena 6 incident, 17–18, *18*
Jerit, Jennifer, 165
jihadist terrorism, 40, 61
Johnson, Alice, 100
Johnson, Lyndon B., 8
journalism, accountability, 8
journalistic bias, moral foundations and: authority/subversion and, 28–29; care/harm and, 27; fairness/cheating and, 27–28; frames compared with, 35; journalists and, 32–35; loyalty(ingroup)/betrayal and, 28; with moral perceptions, conservative and liberal, 29–32, *30*, *31*; with moral values, priming of, 25–27; sanctity/degradation and, 29
journalistic ethics: norms of, 177–79; objectivity and, 178
journalistic objectivity, 5
journalists, with moral foundations and journalistic bias, 32–35
JournoList, 179
JournoList 2, 179

Kavanaugh, Brett, 7
Kinsley, Michael, 12
Ku Klux Klan, 16–17
Kumar, Maria Teresa, 136
Kushner, Jared, 170
Kuypers, Jim A., 38n43, 193n77

labeling, 168–71
languages: choices, 16; purity, 34
late night news comedy shows, 5
Latinos, 136, 143n2
Latvia, 177
leaders, past actions of American, 41, 47
Lehrer, Jim, 8
liberal ideological and partisanship bias, 12

"Liberal News Media Bias Has a Serious Effect," 14
liberals: care/harm and, 30, 33; fairness/cheating and, 30; liberty/oppression and, 36n9; with MFT, 31–32; moral palettes, *31*; populations, 31
liberty/oppression, 36nn9–10
Linguistic Inquiry and Word Count (LIWC) software, 38n43
Lippman, Walter, 186
Lithuania, 177
LIWC software. *See* Linguistic Inquiry and Word Count software
loyalty(ingroup)/betrayal: America First and, 60, 74; binding dimensions and, 27; MFT and, 26; moral foundations and, 167; moral foundations and economy with, 74–75, 82–83, 86; moral foundations and immigration reform with, 131–32, 139–40; moral foundations and journalistic bias with, 28; moral foundations and national security with, 44–45, 47, 60–61, 62; moral foundations and State of the Union address with, 97–98, 101, 102, 114–15

Maduro, Nicolás, 95, 99
mainstream media (MSM), 6; agenda-setting and, 15; America First and, 78; speeches of Trump and, 35; unethical behavior of, 177–79. *See also specific mainstream media outlets*
Markle, Meghan, 9
Marxism, 28
McGovern, George, 16
Mexico: border wall and, 43, 74, 94, 108–10, 113, 127, 130, 175; racism against, 127; the USMCA, 95
MFT. *See* Moral Foundations Theory
*Michelle Malkin* (blog), 18
Middle East, 41, 92, 95, 101, 127, 161
Migration Policy Institute, 170
Miller, Stephen, 170

MIME. *See* Model of Intuitive Morality and Exemplars
Model of Intuitive Morality and Exemplars (MIME), 32–33, 165, 182
money bias, 9, 10
moral emotion, 26
moral foundations: authority/subversion and, 167; biases and, 180–81; care/harm and, 168; concluding thoughts, 156, *156*; economy and, 73–75, 82–85; with framing in news media coverage, 1–3; immigration reform and, 131–33, 139–42; journalistic bias and, 25–38; loyalty(ingroup)/betrayal and, 167; national security and, 44–47, 56–61; other, 36nn9–10; State of the Union address and, 97–101, 112–17; summary, 164–65; summary of findings, 3. *See also* authority/subversion; care/harm; fairness/cheating; loyalty(ingroup)/betrayal; news media moral foundations; sanctity/degradation; Trump moral foundations
Moral Foundations Theory (MFT), 1, 2, 3, 6, 25; conservatives and liberals with, 31–32; limitations of, 165–68; moral reasoning and, 182; principles of, 26–27
moral intuitions, 27, 32
moral judgments, 19, 25, 33, 34, 186
moral mind, first draft of, 26–27
moral palettes, conservative and liberal, *31*
moral perceptions, moral foundations and journalistic bias with, 29–32, *30*, *31*
moral psychology, 3, 19, 25–26, 182
moral reasoning, 26–27, 33, 182
moral values, moral foundations, journalistic bias and priming of, 25–27
Morgan, Piers, 149
mosques, 33
MS-13, 94

MSM. *See* mainstream media
MSNBC, 92
Mueller, Robert, 108, 110
Mueller investigation, 7, 10, 110–12, 113, 116, 117, 150, 152

NAFTA. *See* North American Free Trade Agreement
national defense, national security and framing of, 43
national security: economic and, 57, 58, 61, 74; framing and, 40–44; moral foundations and, 44–47, 56–61; news media moral foundations and, 157–58; press response and, 48–55; press summary and, 61–62; with State of the Union address, framing, 95–96; strategy, framing of, 42–43; with Trump, speeches of, 39–40; Trump moral foundations and, 157; Trump summary and, 47
national security, framing and: of America First, 41–42, 47; American influence and, 44; with American leaders, past actions of, 41, 47; border security, 43; concluding thoughts, 150–52, *151*; in context, 40; economic security, 43; national defense, 43; strategy, 42–43
national security, moral foundations and: care/harm, 46–47, 56–59, 61; concluding thoughts, *156*; fairness/cheating, 45–46, 47, 59–60, 61; loyalty(ingroup)/betrayal, 44–45, 47, 60–61, 62
national security, press response and: America First, 55; cyber warfare/social media, 50–52, 61; framing of, 48; Putin/Trump/2016 election, 54–55, 61; with Russia and China as revisionist powers, 52–54, 61; speech versus report, 48–50, 61
National Security Innovation Base (NSIB), 58

National Security Strategy (NSS), 40–43, 45–47, 53
National Security Strategy (NSS) document, 39–42, 44, 46, 48–55, 57–58, 61
NATO. *See* North Atlantic Treaty Organization
Navy, U.S., 59
NBC News, 2, 92; with attack on press, 81; election (2020) and, 137; labeling and, 169, 170
NBCNews.go.com, 35
neutrality: with facts and frames, 1–2, 16; Lehrer on, 8; with news coverage, 5
news: bias with bad, 11–12; framing of, 15–20, *18*; neutrality with coverage of, 5; politics and, 32; sources, *172*, 172–73
news blogs, 18
*Newsbusters* (blog), 18
news media: coverage with moral foundations and framing, 1–3; fake, 81, 149, 183
news media bias: in context, 6–15; with framing of issues and events, 5–24; with Republic, future of, 181
news media moral foundations: economy and, 159–60; immigration and, 163–64; national security and, 157–58; State of the Union address and, 161–62
*The New York Times* (newspaper), 2, 13, 18, 37n38, 185; American First and, 77; with attack on press, 81; criticism of, 195n91; on cyber warfare/social media and, 51; election (2020) and, 138; family-based immigration and, 135, 136; journalistic ethics and, 179; labeling and, 169; "Liberal News Media Bias Has a Serious Effect," 14; politics section of, 32; speeches of Trump and, 35; with speeches of Trump and NSS document, 49; stem cells in, 34; with

subscription canceled, 149; women and, 104
New Zealand, 129
Nixon, Richard, 16, 111, 117
Northam, Ralph, 104, 105, 167
North American Free Trade Agreement (NAFTA), 94–95
North Atlantic Treaty Organization (NATO), 40, 42, 177
North Korea, 7, 9, 92, 95, 99, 112; human rights and, 114; NSS document and, 58; with nuclear program, 42, 47, 73, 85; as rogue state, 40, 49, 72
Norton, Quinn, 185
NSIB. *See* National Security Innovation Base
NSS. *See* National Security Strategy
nuclear programs: Iran, 42, 48; North Korea with, 42, 47, 73–74, 85; treaty, 49

Obama, Barack, 92, 127; with approval numbers, 103; climate change and, 39, 57, 59, 85; family separation and, 131, 173–74; with global cooperation, 55; immigration and, 7, 83; NATA and, 177; NSS document and, 39, 48, 53, 59; with presidency, first sixty days, 5; Putin and, 55; U.S. Supreme Court and, 143n3
objectivity, 25; confirmation bias and, 182; journalistic, 5; journalistic ethics and, 178; principles of, 7–8
obstruction of justice, 116
Ocasio-Cortez, Alexandria, 105–6
open for business, economy and press response with, 79–80, 85
oppositional information, omission of, 173–77
ownership/theft, 36n10

Pakistan, 46, 48
Paris Climate Accord, 46
Partial-Birth Abortion Ban Act, 11
Patterson, Thomas, 168, 186
PBS NewsHour, 8, 92
Pelosi, Nancy, 107, 113, 115, 117, 136, 138
perceptual bias, 8–9
The Pew Center, 5, 9, 183
Planned Parenthood, 104
pluralism, individual freedom and, 21n17
politics, 193n77; news and, 32; women in, 12, 13, 105–6, 107, 113, 115, 117, 136, 138–39, 167, 170
populations: Australia and Canada, 176–77; conservatives, 31; distribution, moral foundation, *31*; of immigrants, undocumented, 139; liberals, 31
populism/globalism, with economy and press response, 78–79, 85
prescription drugs, 96, 98, 99, 100, 108, 116
press: economy and attack on, 81–82, 85–86; social responsibility of, 8. *See also* national security, press response
*Press Bias and Politics* (Kuypers), 193n77
press response: economy and, 77–82; immigration reform and, 134; State of the Union address and, 102–3
press summary: economy and, 85–86; immigration reform, 142–43; national security and, 61–62; State of the Union address and, 117–18
principled realism, NSS and, 42–43
purity. *See* sanctity/degradation
purity language, 34
purity/taint, 34
Putin, Vladimir, 49; NSS document and, 53; Obama and, 55; Trump and, 51, 52, 54–55, 57, 61. *See also* Russia

race, 70, 93, 100, 140, 170
race relations, 12
racism, 83, 127
Rasmussen's Daily Presidential Tracking Poll, 103, 183

Reagan, Ronald, 12, 41
recency bias, 10–11
reciprocal altruism, 28
reform. *See* immigration reform
reform/results, with economy and framing of, 70–71, 75–76
religious freedom, 170
report, press response and national security with speech versus, 48–50, 61
Republic, news media bias and future of, 181
Reuters, 32, 173
*Roe v. Wade*, 104
Romania, 177
Roosevelt, Franklin, 91
Russia: care/harm and, 58–59; China and, 39, 40; with election (2016), 48, 49, 51, 61; investigation into, 7; Mueller investigation and, 152; NSS document and, 49, 50, 52, 53, 57–58, 61; as revisionist power, 52–54, 61; as threat, 60, 61; with trade, 59

salience, of facts, 19
Sanchez, Linda, 170
sanctity/degradation, 44; binding dimensions and, 27; MFT and, 26; moral foundations and immigration reform with, 133; moral foundations and journalistic bias with, 29; moral foundations and State of the Union address with, 100, 102, 117; trade and, 87
Sanders, Bernie, 12
sandwiching, 171–72
Scanlon, Mary Gay, 111
Schumer, Chuck, 139
Schwab, Klaus, 81
security: freedom and, 101; Homeland, 43; NSIB, 58; NSS, 40–43, 45–47, 53; NSS document, 39–42, 44, 46, 48–55, 57–58, 61; through technology, 130. *See also* border security; economic security; national security
selective bias, 8
sex scandal, 169
sex traffickers, 94
single payer healthcare, 16, 106
*Slate* magazine, 12, 13
slavery, modern-day, 94
smuggling: of children, 131, 176; of women, 131
socialism, 101, 103, 117, 118, 162; "gang of four" and, 117; rejection of, 95, 174; State of the Union address and, 105–6
social media, 43, 106; tweets, 50, 79, 107, 111, 149–50. *See also* cyber warfare/social media
social responsibility, 7–8, 184
Society of Professional Journalists, 178
sources: lopsided use of, 172–73; type of, *173*
Southern Poverty Law Center (SPLC), 136, 170
speeches. *See* Trump speeches
SPLC. *See* Southern Poverty Law Center
State of the Union address (2019): abortion and, 104–5, 174–75; framing, 92–97, 103–12; moral foundations and, 97–101, 112–17; news media moral foundations and, 161–62; press response and, 102–3; press summary and, 117–18; role of, 91; socialism in, 174; Trump moral foundations and, *160*, 160–61; Trump summary and, 101–2; word count and viewing audience, 92
State of the Union address (2019), framing: abortion and, 104–5; with call for collective action, 96–97; concluding thoughts, 152, *154*; with division, not unity, 106–8; economy and, 94–95; of facts, 92–93; healthcare and, 96; major themes, 106–12; minor themes, 103–6;

Mueller investigation and, 110–12; national security and, 95–96; socialism and, 105–6; with wall and illegal immigration, 108–10; women and, 103–4

State of the Union address (2019), moral foundations and: authority/subversion and, 100–101, 116–17; care/harm and, 98–99, 101–2, 112–14; fairness/cheating and, 99–100, 102, 115–16; loyalty(ingroup)/betrayal and, 97–98, 101, 102, 114–15; sanctity/degradation and, 100, 102, 117

status quo (conservative) bias, 8, 9, 11
stealth taxation, 72
stem cells, 29, 34, 165
Stoltenberg, Jens, 177
subversion. *See* authority/subversion
summaries: of findings, moral foundations, 3; framing, 156; moral foundations, 164–65. *See also* press summary; Trump summaries
Supreme Court, U.S., 143n3
Syria, 118

Taliban, 112
Tax Cuts and Jobs Act (2017), 70
taxes: cuts, 85, 93; stealth, 72
technology, security through, 130
TED Talks, 186
TELEMUNDO, 92
terrorism: CIA and, 55, 59; cyberterrorism, 43; financing, 45; Iran and, 73, 98; Islam and, 43, 48; jihadist, 40, 61
theoretical bias, 7–8
*Time* (magazine), 10
Tlaib, Rashida, 105–6
TPP. *See* Trans-Pacific Partnership
trade: anti-globalism and, 71; with economy and press response, 80–81; fairness/cheating and, 59–60, 61, 73–74, 76, 86; NAFTA, 94–95; sanctity/degradation and, 87; TPP and, 42, 46, 78, 81, 84, 85

Trans-Pacific Partnership (TPP), 42, 46, 78, 81, 84, 85
triggers, for liberty/oppression, 36n9
Truman, Harry S., 91
Trump, Donald: abortion and, 104–5, 112, 120n28; with approval numbers, 102–3; climate change and, 50, 55, 56–57, 59, 61, 82, 85, 158; DAVOS and, 69–70, 75, 76, 78, 173; descriptors for, 170; on election (2016), 45; impeachment and, 149–50, 184; Latinos and, 143n2; with presidency, first sixty days, 5; Putin and, 51, 52, 54–55, 57, 61; U.S. Supreme Court and, 143n3

Trump moral foundations: economy and, *158*, 158–59; immigration and, *162*, 162–63; national security and, 157; State of the Union address and, *160*, 160–61

Trump speeches: economy and, 69–70; immigration reform and, 128; MSM coverage of, 35; national security and, 39–40; press response and national security with report versus, 48–50, 61. *See also* State of the Union address (2019)

Trump summaries: economy and, 75–76; immigration reform, 133–34; national security and, 47; State of the Union address and, 101–2

tweets, 50, 79, 107, 111, 149–50

Ukraine, 49, 51, 52, 74
unemployment, 70, 93
United States (U.S.): criticism of, 61; Navy, 59; Russia and relations with, 7; Supreme Court, 143n3
the United States-Mexico-Canada Agreement (the USMCA), 95
UNIVISION, 92
U.S. *See* United States
*USA Today* (newspaper), 18

the USMCA. *See* the United States-Mexico-Canada Agreement

VA. *See* Veterans Association
Venezuela, 95
Veterans Association (VA), 93
Vidal, Gore, 169
viewing audience, State of the Union address (2019), 92
viewpoint diversity, 185–87
visual bias, 9–10, 11
Voto Latino, 136

wall. *See* border wall
War on Terror, 39
Washington, George, 91
*The Washington Post* (newspaper), 2, 13, 18; America First and, 55; American First and, 78; border wall and, 108, 110; care/harm and, 59; DACA and, 139; DAVOS and, 79, 173; on division, not unity, 107; election (2020) and, 138; family-based immigration and, 135; journalistic ethics and, 179; Mueller investigation and, 111; NSS document and, 53–54, 59; politics section of, 32; on Putin/Trump/2016 elections, 55; socialism and, 12; speeches of Trump and, 35; with subscription canceled, 149; women and, 104
watchdog, 8, 183
Watergate, 16, 111, 117
women: "gang of four," 117; in politics, 12, 13, 105–6, 107, 113, 115, 117, 136, 138–39, 167, 170; with slavery, modern-day, 94; smuggling of, 131; State of the Union address and, 103–4. *See also* abortion
word count, State of the Union address (2019), 92
World Economic Forum (DAVOS): America First and, 83; Global Risk Report and, 78; populism/globalism and, 79; Trump and, 69–70, 75, 76, 78, 173. *See also* economy

xenophobia, 127, 140, 170
Xi Jinping, 95

Yourmorals.com, 29

Zucker, Jeffrey, 149
Zuckerberg, Mark, 9

# About the Author

**Jim A. Kuypers** (Ph.D. Louisiana State University) is professor of communication at Virginia Tech. He is the author, editor, or co-author of 15 books, including *Purpose, Practice, and Pedagogy in Rhetorical Criticism* (winner of the Everett Lee Hunt Award for Outstanding Scholarship) and *Partisan Journalism: A History of Media Bias in the United States* (a Choice Outstanding Academic Title for 2014) and over 40 book chapters and journal articles. He is a former co-editor for the *American Communication Journal*. He is the recipient of the American Communication Association's Outstanding Contribution to Communication Scholarship Award, the Southern States Communication Association's Early Career Research award, and Dartmouth College's Distinguished Lecturer Award. His research interests include political communication, media bias, meta-criticism, and the moral/poetic use of language.

www.ingramcontent.com/pod-product-compliance
Lightning Source LLC
Chambersburg PA
CBHW070830300426
44111CB00014B/2506